Cowley Publications .. .. brothers
of the Society of Saint John the Evangelist, a monastic
order in the Episcopal Church. Our mission is to provide books and resources for those seeking spiritual
and theological formation. Cowley Publications is
committed to developing a new generation of writers
and teachers who will encourage people to think and
pray in new ways about spirituality, reconciliation,
and the future.

Humane Christianity

Arguing with the classic Christian spiritual disciplines in the light of Jesus of Nazareth

ALAN BARTLETT

COWLEY PUBLICATIONS
Cambridge, Massachusetts

Published in the United States of America by Cowley Publications, a division of the Society of Saint John the Evangelist. No portion of this book may be reproduced, stored in or introduced into a retrieval system, or transmitted, in any form or by any means—including photocopying—without the prior written permission of Cowley Publications, except in the case of brief quotations embedded in critical articles and reviews.

Published by Darton, Longman and Todd, London, UK, 2004
Copyright © Alan Bartlett

Library of Congress Cataloging-in-Publication Data:
Bartlett, Alan, 1958–
   Humane Christianity : arguing with the classic Christian spiritual disciplines in the light of Jesus of Nazareth / Alan Bartlett.
        p. cm.
   Includes bibliographical references and index.
   ISBN 1-56101-230-0 (pbk. : alk. paper)   1.   Spiritual life—Christianity. 2. Church of England—History—20th century.   I. Title.
   BV4501.3.B378 2005
   248.4'83—dc22

                                                                   2005008869

Cover design: Gary Ragaglia
Cover art: Rembrandt van Rijn (1606–1669) (attributed to). Head of Christ, Seventeenth Century. Oil on panel, enlarged on all sides; 9¾ x 7⅞ inches (24.8 x 20 cm). John G. Johnson collection, 1917.
Photo credit: The Philadelphia Museum of Art / Art Resource, NY
Philadelphia Museum of Art, Philadelphia, Pennsylvania, U.S.A.

This book was printed in the United States of America on acid-free paper.

COWLEY PUBLICATIONS
4 Brattle Street
Cambridge, Massachusetts 02138
800-225-1534 • www.cowley.org

CONTENTS

>←

PREFACE

>‹

I used to read prefaces and feel that the 'thank yous' were a little over the top. No longer. That I am sitting at this computer tapping out these words is the result of an immense amount of love and patience from family, friends and colleagues over many years. They know who they are – I hope – and I give them heartfelt thanks. This book, in particular, witnesses to the quality of the love that I have received from God, incarnated in so many people. Words are not adequate.

But there are specific thanks to be said. First, to the Revd Margaret Parker and the Chapter of Durham Cathedral for the generous invitation to give their Lent talks in 2002, which was the trigger for this book. Second, to my colleagues (staff and students) at St John's College, Durham, most especially, and also in the Department of Theology, and more widely here in the North-East of England, who make this such an immensely rich place to live and think and pray. The number of books in my footnotes that originate in the North-East is testimony not only to my limited reading but more to the quality and creative faith of my colleagues. Sincere thanks to those who have read parts of this book so carefully and have provided invaluable comments: the Reverends/Doctors Croft, Fyall, Hirst, Moberly, Morley, Rhodes and Wakefield. Thanks also to our former bishop the Right Revd Alex Graham who shared much wisdom in between (my) wheezing climbing of the fells. Thanks to our rector, David Glover, who provided key inspiration for Chapter 6 with a discussion on the atonement one Holy Week. Who says parish clergy don't talk deep theology? Thanks also to a diplomatic, patient and always encouraging editor, Virginia Hearn. I remain, in a more self-aware fashion now (I hope), entirely responsible for what remains. They are exonerated. A special thanks to Shirley for the generous use of her Franciscan cottage in the tranquillity of the Duddon Valley. Finally, to those who have walked the journey most closely with me over the last few years, who have borne the cost of my frailties and helped me to discover some humanity, Jill and Ruth. But above all thanks to 'H', for keeping it all together.

INTRODUCTION

There is no better way to encounter the inhumanity of the Church than to study church history. I would like to start this book with a little exercise we use at the beginning of our ordinands' church history course.

Eric Ives, a church historian and a Baptist, in reflecting on God's role in the Reformation quotes from two letters written in the sixteenth century. One was written by a Welsh evangelist (we might term him a separatist or congregationalist), trying to convert his people to committed Protestantism in the 1590s. The other, by a Jesuit, sent back to England to keep the Roman Catholic faith alive.

> My charge is, of free cost, to preach the Gospel, to minister the Sacraments, to instruct the simple, to reform sinners, to confute errors – in brief to cry alarm spiritual against foul vice and proud ignorance wherewith many [of] my dear countrymen are abused.

> I know not my danger in writing these things. I see you my dear and native country perish. It pitieth me. I come with the rope around my neck to save you, howsoever it goes with me, I labour that you may have the Gospel preached among you, though it cost me my life, I think it well-bestowed.[1]

The question is, who wrote which one? (The ordinands normally get it wrong too.) The grim reality was that both men were executed by the government of Elizabeth I, in effect for religious dissent, though technically they were executed for treason. Despite the myths 'we' tell each other as Anglicans about being a tolerant church, the Church of England does not have clean hands when it comes to religious persecution.

We may shiver now and feel superior to this sort of religious conflict. But translate this sort of hatred to the streets of Northern Ireland or 'Yugoslavia' and we have an up-to-date reminder of the inhumanity of the Church: its intolerance, its sponsorship of bigotry and its frequent role as a scandal to the name of the One who lived and preached radical love.

Eight years of teaching church history (and in a former life, three years doing an undergraduate history degree and six years doing a Ph.D. in church history), has taught me too much about the inhumanity of the Church. While I recognise the need not to make anachronistic judgements and to try to empathise with people living in different periods, every so often I sink into a state of despair as I contemplate the history of the Church.

Each year, for example, I try to teach about the Crusades with a sense of historical objectivity and distance as well as appropriate empathy, and there is good new writing around that enables this to be done.[2] But every year I am reduced to rage and despair when I get to the Fourth Crusade and the sacking of Constantinople by the crusading army. They never made it to the Holy Land, having been diverted by the Venetian shipping merchants to whom they were in debt – via a burning Byzantine town or two – to Constantinople, which was Venice's main trading rival. There were of course two sides to the conflict and, further, the crusaders had been drawn into the attack by one side in a Byzantine power struggle, but even so ... The attack culminated in the ransacking of Justinian's cathedral of the *Hagia Sophia* (Holy Wisdom). With a little exaggeration, in the words of Steven Runciman, the great historian of the Crusades: 'The sack of Constantinople is unparalleled in history.'[3]

The Greeks have not quite forgotten nor forgiven that yet, as we saw in 2001 when the Pope went to Greece. Nor has modern Western secular society. In 1995 no less a figure than Terry Jones, the ex-Python, fronted a TV series on the Crusades which more than amply confirmed Runciman's judgement that it was 'one long sin against the Holy Ghost'.[4] The most painful chapter title in Jones' book is 'Saladin – the Model Christian',[5] so called because he showed more mercy to his prisoners than his Christian opponents, including Richard the Lionheart.

These shameful events have regained literary prominence in the work of one of Europe's leading novelists and 'cultured despisers' (critics) of Christianity, Umberto Eco.[6] Listen to his imaginative account of the sack of the cathedral, the mother church of Eastern Orthodoxy:

> But just as he entered, he went white with horror. That vast space was sown with corpses, among which enemy horsemen, foul drunk, were wheeling their mounts. In the distance the rabble was shattering with clubs the silver, gold-edged gate of the tribune. The splendid gate had been bound with ropes to uproot it so it could be dragged off by a team of mules. One drunken band was cursing and prodding the animals, but their hoofs slipped on the polished floor. The soldiers, first with the flat of their swords, then with the tops, incited the poor animals, who in their fear loosed volleys of dung; some mules fell to the ground, breaking their legs, so that the whole area around the pulpit was a gruel of blood and faeces.
>
> Groups of the vanguard of the Antichrist were stubbornly attacking the altars. Niketas saw some of them rip open a tabernacle, seize the chalices, fling to the ground the sacred Hosts, using their daggers to prise loose the gems that adorned the cup, hiding them in their clothes, then throwing the chalice into a general pile, to be melted down. Snickering, some took their saddlebags flasks filled with wine, poured it into the sacred vessel and drank, mimicking the celebrant's actions. Worse still, on the main altar, now stripped, a half-naked prostitute, drunk on liquor, danced with bare feet on the table of the Eucharist, parodying the sacred rites, while the men laughed and urged her to remove the last of her clothing; she gradually undressed, dancing before the altar the ancient and lewd dance of the *cordax*, until she finally threw herself, with a weary belch, on the seat of the Patriarch.[7]

While these events were eventually condemned by Pope Innocent III, he did not prevent the imposition of a Latin Church on the Greek Orthodox Empire: church reunion at the point of a sword. There is a terrible sting in the tail of this story. The Greeks regained their independence after about fifty years but the Byzantine Empire never recovered its strength. Constantinople fell to the Turks in 1453.[8] Justinian's cathedral is now a bare if relatively well-cared for Islamic museum and tourist attraction. I still weep at the memory of the sight of this debased cathedral, with the irony and pathos of the huge mosaic of Christ, the ruler and creator of all, staring proudly but sadly down from the dome. What have we done? *Kyrie eleison.*

I want to start this book by reminding us of the guilt that the institutional churches, almost all of them, carry from the past, whatever it be: corruption, bitterness, deceit, suppression of the ideas of others, direct persecution of others (which began within only a few years of the ending of pagan persecution), racism, patriarchy, abuse, anti-Semitism. Scarcely a month passes without some scandal from the distant or recent past being aired in the media. It is thought-provoking to note what a huge surge of interest there has been (not entirely unrelated to modern Christian–Moslem tensions) in research into the Crusades. Alongside the expansion of academic studies in the persecution of witches, or the role of the churches under the Nazis, or the work of missionaries in the European colonies, this reminds us that not only *should* there be no hiding places for the Church's guilty secrets, there *will* be no hiding places.

We have begun to repent of our past, of our inhumane Christianity. Consider for example the apologies by Pope John Paul II for past sins of the Roman Catholic Church in respect of Galileo; or the 1995 walk of repentance following the route of the First Crusade; or the apologies by Anglican churches, with others, for the forcible removal, de-culturising and often abuse of the children of the indigenous inhabitants of Canada and Australia; or our shame here in the British Isles at the steady trickle of child sexual abuse cases at the hands of the clergy. But a deep part of the agenda of this book is to remind us that repentance requires a change of thinking and attitudes and behaviour, not just sorrow. Why did all this happen amongst the disciples of Jesus? Were there theological and spiritual reasons for these 'falls' from his values, as well as cultural and historical ones, for this inhumane Christianity? How can we try to ensure that it does not happen again? *Christe eleison*.

But I am running ahead of myself. Perhaps I should try to lay out some of the markers for this personal journey on which I am inviting you to accompany me over these next few chapters. When I was invited to give the Lent talks in Durham Cathedral in 2002, the invitation acted as a lightning conductor for a wide range of feelings and ideas and experiences which, for me, had been in the air for a long time, like a gathering thunderstorm, and the title and the overall shape of this series came very quickly: 'Humane Christianity'. Those talks, the interest which they aroused, and the passions which they stirred in me form the basis for this book.

The formal aim of this book is as follows: 'A reappraisal of elements of the classic Christian spiritual disciplines in the light of current theological insights, a theological reading of church history and contemporary missiological needs.' Put into English, what I am trying to do is to rethink some of the qualities that Christians have most valued in the past, in the light of some reflections about the sinful history of the Church, in dialogue with the beliefs and needs of modern Britain and above all driven by a theological and spiritual conviction that puts human flourishing in this life as well as the next, as nearer the heart of God's purposes than has often been the case in the Church's life and teaching. If there is a slogan for this book it is 'God is always the life-bringer'.[9] Specifically, if we allow our theology and spirituality to be more shaped by the human characteristics (underpinned by the divine nature) of Jesus of Nazareth, we will be more fully alive, more merciful, more humane. Most simply, if we reshape the question at the heart of Christianity from 'what are we saved from' to 'what are we saved for' then, I believe, we can articulate a more 'Humane Christianity'.

The overall scheme is to outline, first, what I see as the

current theological and missiological situation, particularly taking a hard look at the reputation of the Church in history and some of its classic teachings, as they are now perceived. This will include both snippets of history and also dipping into some modern novels. There is, of course, an important distinction to be drawn between what could be described as a reasonably fair-minded review of aspects of church history and the highly polemical account of the Church that is given by some sections of the media and 'liberal' intelligentsia. But our missiological reality lies in confronting common modern, secular perceptions of the Church. As John Drane remarked at a national conference on evangelism in 2001 at St John's College, Durham, there comes a time when we need to stop arguing about the details and simply face the big picture, because winning the battle on the details is no longer addressing the big picture.[10]

Each of the following chapters is structured around one of the great triad of much of historic Christian spirituality, and especially Christian monasticism – poverty, obedience and chastity – with further chapters reflecting on those two other elements of Benedict's original Rule, stability and conversion of life. My intention is to give a brief account of how this was taught and lived out in the Christian past, to make some critical reflections and then to try to offer a modern reworking of this classic discipline, in the light of our current situation. The word 'from' in the five chapter titles does not mean the complete rejection of the old virtue, as for example with 'chastity'. But it does indicate that I think there are real problems in imagining that we can or even should retain the totality of these old disciplines, because they were, in some respects, destructive of human flourishing. So, I hope this book will provide a positive vision of Christian life and faith which is marked by serious discipleship, without the in-humane fanaticism that so scars the life of the Church, but also without the impatience which ultimately rejects the essence of classic Christian orthodoxy and spirituality.

I am enough of an Evangelical to believe sometimes in giving the bad news first, so more of the first chapter is taken up with critical reflection and more of subsequent chapters with positive vision. I hope that in the course of this book we will have a chance to encounter some of the great models of the Christian life – Benedict, Cuthbert, Francis, Luther – as well as some lesser-known figures: Irenaeus of Lyons, the great orthodox bishop of the late second century; Richard Hooker, Elizabeth I's greatest theologian and arguably the 'founder of Anglicanism'; and Jeremy Taylor a chaplain to the Royalist armies of Charles I who was twice imprisoned by Parliament but ended his life as Bishop of Down and Connor after the Restoration.

Chapters 1 and 6 have a more theological flavour and the notes sometimes carry more of the detailed argument, especially with some aspects of modern Evangelicalism, which has both nurtured and frustrated me. The book is also written from the context of the North-East of England where it is not possible to withdraw into an ecclesiastical ghetto away from hard social realities but which is also an area strong in its sense of Christian history and community. Each chapter will finish with a biblical reflection (all taken from Luke's gospel), designed to be pondered over slowly and to take us deep into the life of Jesus, and a prayer.

Talking of the Bible, it is important to say that my main academic training is not in biblical scholarship and I am always reliant on others when handling Scripture in this book. But this is a good place to record simply my hermeneutical assumptions: which are that Christ is the pinnacle and plumb line of Scripture and that he continues to speak to us through Scripture, though not without the requirement that we, collectively, bring our reason to hearing and not presuming that we 'hear' infallibly. In John Drane's helpful phrase, 'the Bible is a compass not a map'.[11] Further, it is neither possible nor desirable to study the Bible without using the methods and insights of 'biblical criticism'. I am content to work in dialogue with a variety of forms of biblical criticism (discerning readers will spot versions of redaction criticism, etc.) but find myself drawn especially to 'canonical criticism', which respects the final literary form of the text and the sense of the canon as a whole. I bring to this book the explicit but not fundamentalist acceptance that the Bible is the Christian Scripture through which we believe we can hear God.

One last introductory point: this is very much a personal journey, gathering together fragments which have caught my eye over the last 25 years or so. I will do my best to use such meagre scholarship as I have as well as I can.[12] But even given a half competent deployment of this scholarship, I will also allow myself to say what I think and feel more straight-forwardly than I would do when writing a straight academic paper and, as well as ideas, to share with you thoughts and experiences gathered magpie-like from a broad range of encounters. Because of the wide range of material that this book covers, in places there are careful arguments. In other places I have to leave it at simple assertions. I draw on both Scripture and tradition, but will try to be honest where I am shaping them according to my own insights rather than received opinion. You may or may not agree with my interpretation of our current context, of the life of the Church, of what it is to live the Christian life, but I hope that you will find this material provocative, challenging and stimulating.

But first a prayer. Each chapter of this book will finish with a prayer to help us to 'pray in' our reflections. The first is the 'Collect for Purity', placed by Thomas Cranmer at the beginning of the service of Holy Communion in 1549 as a prayer of pre-paration for the whole People of God not just the priest. We can make it a prayer for honesty and change as we begin this journey together:

> Almighty God,
> to whom all hearts are open,
> all desires known,
> and from whom no secrets are hidden,
> cleanse the thoughts of our hearts
> by the inspiration of your Holy Spirit,
> that we may perfectly love you
> and worthily magnify your holy name:
> through Jesus Christ our Lord.
> Amen.

CHAPTER ONE

Inhumane Christianity

How does the Church look to 'modern outsiders'?

I start with the big picture, with some modern secular perceptions of the Church, but not from the trendy post-modern
commentators of the *Guardian* and the *Observer*. I start rather
with my own first research area, modern British religious history
and the most significant book to be published recently on that
topic: Callum Brown's *The Death of Christian Britain*. He argues
that, contrary to much received opinion, the churches were
central to British society until as late as the 1950s and that the
key period of their 'failure' is not in the nineteenth century – with
the problems of the mission to the new urban working class or
the intellectual crisis of Darwinism et al. – nor even the post-
World War I period, but rather the 1960s. So he stresses that 'All
of the indicators show that the period between 1956 and 1973
witnessed unprecedented rapidity in the fall of Christian
religiosity amongst the British people. In most cases, at least
half of the overall decline in each indicator recorded during the
century was concentrated into those years.'[1]

Amusingly, Brown makes 1963 and the arrival of the Beatles
and the miniskirt the apogee of this collapse.[2] Whatever fine
tuning his argument might need, these figures are reinforced by
some of the churches' own statistics.[3] The churches have
suffered a catastrophic crisis of credibility in the last two
generations. And this is not just a British phenomenon. All

across Western Europe (and in parts of the East) the churches have been 'in retreat' for the last 40 years.[4] In the memorable phrase of John Arnold, former Dean of Durham and one of the foremost European church leaders of our generation: 'the age of Christendom is over'.

But it is not just in its statistics that Brown's book is thought-provoking. Two quotations will have to suffice. The first is the last two sentences of the book: 'But the culture of Christianity has gone in the Britain of the new millennium. Britain is show-ing the world how religion as we have known it can die.'[5] The serious point of the book is that the Christian ethos and life-cycle no longer make any sense to – in particular – modern British women. While I question some of Brown's material,[6] now is not the time to evaluate it, but it is highly significant as a barometer for how some parts of contemporary academia see the Church – archaic and doomed. Brown would claim to be writing in a neutral, scholarly fashion about this process, but there is passion behind his account of the gains for modern British society from the decline of the Church:

> Many people will be able to identify gains from the decentring of rigid moral codes – such as increased sexual freedom and freedom for diverse sexualities, greater gen-der equality, and a new tolerance of religious and ethnic difference. One could say, not altogether flippantly, that the decline of Christian certainty in British society since the 1950s has meant that respectability has been supplanted by respect – in which moral criticism of difference has been replaced by toleration and greater freedom to live our lives in the way we choose.[7]

Again, I do not want to evaluate this statement here (though the accusation that the Church valued 'respectability' over 'respect' is stingingly close to the mark), but simply to note its message: the Church is doomed and deserves to be doomed.

On the other hand, we might consider the portrayal of Christianity in some modern fiction – typical summer-holiday reading perhaps. First, from the popular and definitely not liberal end of the market, Bernard Cornwell's novels: either the Grail Quest series set during the Hundred Years' War, for example *Harlequin*[8] or his chronicles of Arthur.[9] There are some good Christian characters. In *Harlequin* there is a Father Hobbe: a socially humble travelling priest and chaplain who can swear, sink a pint, fire a longbow, is a dab hand with a quarter staff and will say absolution without taking the sins of the flesh too seriously. This is one more than in the chronicles of Arthur, where the Christians are uniformly corrupt, cowardly and less spiritual than the Celtic druids whom they are gradually suppressing. And one of the most obviously pious Christians in *Harlequin* – a French duke – is cold, psychologically disturbed, anti-Semitic and a rapist. These are clichés, of course, but with a huge circulation and just perfect for TV. I could point you to a number of similar authors who may now be outselling the famous Ellis Peters. The message? The institutional Church has always been corrupt.

At the more high-brow end of the market there is Louis de Bernière's satirical novel *The Troublesome Offspring of Cardinal Guzman*.[10] Don't read it if you will be offended by either brutality or bawdiness, because it is by turns a shocking and hilarious account of life in a chaotic South American dictatorship. One of the key characters is the deeply corrupt but guilt-ridden cardinal who persecutes the liberationist priests, fosters old-time religion and is only humanised by his love for his native Indian mistress and illegitimate son. He is personally redeemed by the tragic death of his son, in which he is implicated, and goes off to run an orphanage in the mountains for the children of the poor, but not before he has launched a new inquisition led by a mad Dominican supported by brutal thugs. The Dominican – Fr Anquilar – is visited by the spirit of Thomas Aquinas (an early Dominican) on the eve of the crusade. Aquinas tries to persuade Anquilar to give up the crusade: 'It won't work. I have come on your crusade to see for myself the results of my work. I have come to see you forcing Jews and Muslims to eat pork in public, to see you extinguishing enquiry and burning innocents who have more enthusiasm than intellect. I am watching you confiscate the goods of the poor and torturing women for fear of your own lusts.'[11]

It may just be worth reminding ourselves of one of Thomas Aquinas' teachings that profoundly shaped the life of the Western Church thereafter: 'To corrupt the faith, whereby the soul lives, is much graver than to counterfeit money, which supports temporal life. Since forgers and other malefactors are summarily condemned to death by the civil authorities, with much more reason may heretics as soon as they are convicted of heresy be not only excommunicated, but also justly be put to death.'[12] When confronted by Anquilar with his own writing, Thomas says sadly: 'It's not worth it. I have completely re-written it. When I was alive I had a revelation, and from that point I wrote nothing more on earth because all my words turned to straw, even the words I had already written.'[13] This is a direct account, in part, of Thomas' own words after a mental and spiritual crisis and vision towards the end of his life.

Thomas fails to persuade Anquilar to change his plans and so the spirit of Thomas accompanies the crusade as penance for the consequences of his own writing. At the end of the book when the crusade has been defeated by the unorthodox and even pagan free-living villagers, Thomas returns to take the defeated friar with him because 'this man is, so to speak, a child of mine and I would like to take him'.[14] Thus the mad friar is doomed to wander eternally with the melancholy but now gentle saint.

In the two novels that make up the *Cochadebajo de los Gatos* set,[15] Christianity is portrayed as, at worst, corrupt, abusive and oppressive; philosophically and theologically absurd; and, at best, as being lived by marginalised priests and religious who preach and live liberation among the poor. In essence Christianity is a deathly religion. Of the inhuman friar it is said: 'This was a madness that seems to have been attained by fol-lowing a line of perfect reason from a dubious premise, which makes him responsible for what he did, don't you think? Also, he was in love with death.'[16]

Satire about religious folly and hypocrisy is, thankfully, not a new thing. Jesus of Nazareth was no mean satirist. He called the

Pharisees and scribes 'white-washed tombs' – clean on the out-side but inside full of stinking decomposition or dry bones – and used as proof the tithing of herb gardens whilst justice and mercy were neglected.[17] I wonder if this is one of the parts of the teaching of Jesus of Nazareth where we are supposed to laugh out loud? Humour can be a spiritual weapon.

To help us in our journey into inhumane religion, we can swiftly compile a list of odious Christians portrayed by writers as varied as Chaucer, Erasmus, Trollope, Tressell, Winterson and others. The friars under Francis and Dominic had been the inspiration of the Church, but by Chaucer's time (just over one hundred and fifty years later), they were often mistrusted and despised for their hypocrisy. Almost at random from Chaucer, the Prologue to the 'Somnour's Tale', where the friars are described as living in hell, in 'Satan's ers' ['arse'] because they are so corrupt:

> 'Hold up thy tayl, thou Sathanas!' quod he;
> 'Shewe forth thyn ers, and lat the frere se
> Wher is the nest of freres in this place!'
> And, er that half a furlong-wey of space,
> Right so as bees out swarmen from an hyve,
> Out of the develes ers ther gonne dryve
> Twenty thousand freres on a route,
> And thurgh-out helle swarmeden aboute,
> And comen agayn, as faste as they may gon,
> And in his ers they crepten everichon.[18]

So soon had the idealists fallen!

By the sixteenth century the satire was fiercer. Erasmus, the great scholar, mocked the Renaissance papacy mercilessly. Again almost at random, from *In Praise of Folly* (1509), dedicated to Thomas More: 'Under the present system what work needs to be done is handed over to Peter or Paul to do at their leisure, while pomp and pleasure are personally taken care of by the popes … Miracles are considered to be antiquated and old-fashioned; to educate people is irritating; to pray is a waste of time; to interpret Sacred Scripture is a mere formality.' [19] No wonder he was regarded as the forerunner of the Reformation.

By the nineteenth century the new Evangelicals provided a juicy target. We have to include Trollope's hilarious description of the Evangelical clergyman, Mr Slope:

> His looks and tone are extremely severe, so much so that one cannot but fancy that he regards the greater part of the world as being infinitely too bad for his care. As he walks through the streets, his very face denotes his horror of the world's wickedness; and there is always an anathema lurking in the corner of his eye ... I could never endure to shake hands with Mr Slope. A cold clammy perspiration always exudes from him, the small drops are ever to be seen standing on his brow, and his friendly grasp is unpleasant. [20]

It sounds funny but there was real anger behind Trollope's portrayal of Evangelical hypocritical self-righteousness.

An even angrier and more savage satire can be found in Tressell's *The Ragged Trousered Philanthropists*, where the corruption and dishonesty of the churches, from the perspective of nineteenth-century working-class men, was vividly portrayed, and to an increasing audience. Here is his account of the conditions of employment of a widow as the caretaker to a Free Church chapel:

> An evil-minded, worldly or unconverted person might possibly sum up the matter thus: these people required this work to be done: they employed this woman to do it, taking advantage of her poverty to impose upon her conditions of practice and labour that they would not have liked to endure themselves. Although she worked very hard, early and late, the money they paid her as wages was insufficient to enable her to provide herself with the bare necessaries of life. Then her employers, being good, kind, generous, Christian people, came to the rescue and bestowed charity, in the form of cast-off clothing and broken victuals. [21]

This is just the tip of the iceberg of working-class fury at the immorality, oppression and hypocrisy of the churches.

From the perspective of a modern feminist, the satire continues. First, a simply funny account of a Pentecostal exorcist in 1950s Lancashire, taken from Jeanette Winterson's, *Oranges Are Not the Only Fruit*:

> I'd forgotten that Pastor Finch was visiting on his regional tour. He arrived in an old Bedford van with the terrified damned painted on one side and the heavenly host painted on the other. On the back doors and the front bonnet he'd inscribed in green lettering, HEAVEN OR HELL? IT'S YOUR CHOICE. He was very proud of the bus, and told of the many miracles worked inside and out. Inside he had six seats, so that the choir could travel with him, leaving enough room for musical instruments and a large first-aid kit in case the demon combusted somebody. 'What do you do about the flames?' we asked. 'I use an extinguisher', he explained. We were very impressed.

But the book is less funny when Jeanette is ferociously disciplined for a teenage lesbian relationship. The explanation for Jeanette's fall is that she had been allowed to preach, which is contrary to God's will for women, so she had been attacked by a demon: 'So there I was, my success in the pulpit being the reason for my downfall. The devil had attacked me at my weakest point: my inability to realize the limitations of my sex.'[22] Both as a novel and as a television programme, this semi-autobiographical story had a significant impact in portraying the Church as corrupt and oppressive.

But in our era, this satire has become more than another biting exposure of religious hypocrisy. The point is bigger. There is now a broad and substantial consensus that organised religion is a bad thing in itself: 'spirituality good, religion bad.' Private, individual, non-dogmatic, experiential spirituality is life-enhancing. Organised, institutional, dogmatic, and so by definition lifeless, implicitly false religion is inevitably corrupting. Many Christian commentators are noting this cultural phenomenon.[23] We might be tempted to agree! But those of us committed to belief in the value of a visible Church now have a huge problem. In Western Europe the Church is perceived as a conservative, even reactionary force in human life. It is now doomed and deserves to be so – the Church and Christianity with it?

Of course, this is only part of the story and I am sure that we would want to point to people and moments when the Christian faith and Church are still wonderfully, publicly and sharply relevant – the Jubilee campaign for international debt relief or the extraordinary crowd outside St Paul's cathedral for the memorial service for 9/11. But, as a spiritual exercise, read for a little while a liberal broadsheet (or even a conservative one for that matter) and discern how our churches and our Faith are perceived amongst the opinion-makers of our day. There was a classic example in the newspapers just as I was writing this chapter. Sam Fox 'came out' as a lesbian. She reflected on her own spiritual journey, including time at Holy Trinity, Brompton, doing the Alpha course, as follows: 'I think we've come a long way since the Bible was written. No, Alpha never made me feel bad about my sexuality, because I believe all God wants for us is to be happy and love each other.' [24] Note in passing Fox's self-confidence in her personal (individual?) spiritual life, her view of the Church as profoundly out of date, the presenting issue of sexuality and the fact that she was in touch with a section of the Church, arguably at the cutting edge of mission. She speaks both to and for the readers of the *Observer* and the *Sun*. The Church as seen in modern Britain is archaic, by turns irrelevant or oppressive, especially of human freedom, and carrying such a load of guilt that we are doomed, and deservedly so. As for the tabloids, at least the clergy can still be guaranteed a full spread when they run off with the organist. The only puzzle is that Christianity persists at all.

We need to hear our missionary context. If we are living, at least in the West, in a new age where deference and hierarchy are despised (except for pop idols and footballers); where at least the rhetoric of social justice is a high priority; where women are arguably freer than they have ever been in human history; where the environment is a big concern for primary school children (I speak as a parent); where sexual orientation is a matter of justice not morality: then how are we to commend Christ? And if we are perceived as being too often reactionary, are there things we can do and say that will subvert that prejudice? Conversely, are there positive, healthy trends in our society to which we may need to listen? If we have become in fact and not just in perception rather reactionary, even deathly, is it possible that the Spirit is active outside the Church? In which case, are we listening?

How to create an inhumane Christianity

Turning more specifically to inhumane Christianity, I will begin with a series of stark assertions, which try to expose the theologies and ideologies that have bred this inhumanity. I think inhumane Christianity has five main component elements that often operate exponentially.

First, there is a denial of the proper goodness of creation, of human createdness, of all that is good about natural human living as made by God. This has been justified by an interrelated understanding of sin and of perfection. So when the Church has taught about sin, it has done so in such a way that much of human life, and especially human desire, has been understood as essentially concupiscence, or sinfully driven desire, and often located in the 'flesh' and even more specifically in sexuality (see Chapter 4).[25] The translation of the Greek word *sarx* into the English word 'flesh', is a topic in itself,[26] but its negative use has filtered through even into modern charismatic choruses. Many of us will have sung the chorus with the line, 'Make my flesh life melt away'. As Nigel Forde comments on this song: 'God gave me my flesh, and I love it. When I no longer want to hear Bach or birdsong, no longer want to smell wallflowers or bonfires, no longer want to trudge through snow or sit by a blazing fire, drink wine, eat food, soak in a bath, read poetry or write it, then I'll promise I'll sing it. But I don't expect to in this life or expect I'll need to in the next.'[27] Alongside this correlation of sin and embodiment, perfection is often defined as freedom from this world in such a way that it becomes an other-worldly, incorporeal and arguably unnatural account of human living.

This is linked intimately to the second element: the belief that the essential flaw in humanity is pride and that therefore the key spiritual work is to break the human will (see Chapter 3).[28] Thus both human desire and human will are portrayed in a largely negative light.

The third element is the Church's frequent inability to live in a counter-cultural way, in particular when related to the social, economic and political hierarchies of human societies (see Chapter 2). So the Church colludes with the preservation of unjust social orders and justifies this, explicitly or unconsciously, on the basis of the assault on human desire and human pride among the disadvantaged.

The fourth element enters the picture when the Church – the visible institutional Church – takes to itself inappropriate and unwarranted authority and becomes a master rather than a servant, pretending to be infallible rather than honestly fallible and structurally designed to manage the consequences of fallibility. For someone nurtured in the Evangelical tradition, I have to note that this also applies just as much to our handling of the Bible.

The fifth element is an inappropriate, unrealistic and even illusory supernaturalism that fosters belief in systematic miraculous interventions at the cost not only of truthfulness but also of a commitment to enabling people to develop towards mature human responsibility (see Chapters 5 and 6).

So we create a Church that is hostile to human desires and careless about human dignity, indifferent to a full life in this world but also too closely allied to existing unequal human power structures and authoritarian in its attitudes and practices. We see churches that in theory teach Christian poverty and obedience but in practice enforce submission to unjust structures and promise relief only in the next life or perhaps through a miracle in this life, thereby playing on people's deepest desires and longings but without enabling them to strive positively for change. A caricature? Perhaps, but I fear that we could find much hard historical evidence to back up this gloomy view.

Many of these problems flow from a distorted theological understanding of the significance of Jesus of Nazareth as God incarnate, not least, ironically, a devaluing of his real humanity. A firm hold on this conviction that Jesus is God's Son in human form, and what that implies for humankind, is the theological engine that is driving this book. It has an important correlate: that the consequences of faith in the role of the Son in the work of creation are also crucial for 'Humane Christianity'. It is these two convictions that I will explore in the rest of this chapter.

First steps to Humane Christianity

I am reluctant to be too neat and tidy and offer a definition of what I mean by 'Humane Christianity' too early in the book. But if I have a hope, it is to articulate a way of being Christian that is marked by a fundamental shift from a primarily negative to a primarily positive conception of life in this world and from a primarily negative to a primarily positive motivation for the Christian life. It is celebrating the best of what it is to be human at the heart of our faith and life – not because we are subverting the place of God but because he has placed such value on human life, in creation and redemption. God is always the life-bringer. Therefore the heart of the Christian faith is not threat but invitation. Not, 'you are bad and I will punish you, unless ...' but, 'I am offering you goodness, beauty and life: respond to me.' Jesus preached repentance and new life, but the only people he got really angry with – apart from snatches of impatience with his disciples – were those who were keeping God's forgiveness and new life locked away.

All this leads us inexorably to ask questions – biblical, theological and spiritual – about our faith and our traditions. How are we to find the resources to live and speak a different sort of

Christianity? A humbler, less judgemental, more passionately just, more resolutely focused on 'love', form of Christianity? Then, how do the classic Christian spiritual and moral values look when they are read through this set of repentant and longing spectacles?

Underlying all this analysis are four interrelated theological questions which, in the course of this book, will pop up from time to time, even though it is not my intention to try to answer them systematically and explicitly. I do think, however, that wise answers to these questions will provide the basis for a more affirming and positive theology of life in this world, but one that does not finally undermine the perspectives of eternity to which Easter points us.

1. What is the proper theological relationship between doctrines of creation and redemption? (In part, how 'bad' are we? And who and what and how does Christ redeem?)
2. What does it mean to be saved? (How distinctive and set apart are Christians from the rest of humanity?)
3. What is the proper balance between a this-worldly and a next-worldly focus on salvation? ('Jam today' or 'jam tomorrow'?)
4. How do we understand God's interaction with humanity and the created order in the context of all the above? (What does God actually do?)

I am not a systematic theologian and I well remember the pain of trying to get my 'systematic' foundations right during my ordination training. But being forced to examine our fundamentals and to check that what we say in one area coheres with what we say in another is a good spiritual discipline. So it is time for a little systematic theology.

Matter matters, to God and to us

To begin with, how might we articulate a way of being Christian that takes our createdness and our natural humanity seriously as good gifts of God's creation and as the place where God encounters us?[29]

I must start by stressing that God intentionally created matter, things, physicality. It was not a mistake on his part or a temporary whim. This seems to have been a very Hebrew insight, whereas Classical Greek culture was much more cautious about matter and tended to want to keep a distance between 'God' and the business of creation itself. This reached extreme expression in one of the first and most serious 'heresies' to challenge the Church, namely Gnosticism. The Gnostics had developed an elaborate scheme of creation by intermediate semi-divine beings, precisely to keep the supreme God far beyond messy creation.[30] The great hero of orthodox Christianity who won the argument against Gnosticism was Irenaeus, Bishop of Lyons in the last quarter of the second century. In contrast with the negative view of matter portrayed by Gnosticism, Irenaeus was emphatic in his assertion that God created matter: 'They [the Gnostics] do not believe that God (being powerful and rich in resources) created matter itself, inasmuch as they do not know how much a spiritual and divine essence can accomplish.'[31] This is God's world. He could, did and is making it. It gives him pleasure and he is to be seen in it clearly: 'For even creation reveals him who formed it, and the very work suggests him who made it, and the world manifests him who formed it.'[32]

We must be careful not to be naïve here. As I was writing this paragraph, I saw a hunt go up the hillside here in the Lake District (a working hunt to clear the foxes from the fells before lambing season, not a fancy-dress one), and it reminds me that nature is 'red in tooth and claw' and even these fell-sides are brutal as well as beautiful. But this is fundamentally God's world.

This conviction that matter is of God's making but that creation is not perfect brings us to a huge point about 'creation'. Even in this section I am conscious that I have strayed into using the word in the past sense, as if God 'created' the world as a one-off act and is only subsequently involved in rescuing it. But there is another, better, way of conceiving of creation: that it is an ongoing project. The universe is still expanding. The animal world and humankind are both still developing. The mechanisms of growth and development that God implanted into the universe are still running. It is easy to understand why Christians have traditionally thought in terms of a strict chronology of creation and then redemption. Surely that is the chronology of the early chapters of Genesis. But if Genesis was written as explanation of the human condition – aetiology and myth in a strong and positive sense – rather than as some sort of cosmic history book, then we are not tied to a strict chronology. Genesis tells us a story to help us to understand what it is to be human, and not, for example, when and how a 'Fall' occurred.

Genesis itself points us in the direction of God's continuing involvement in the work of creation. So we note that in Genesis 1 there are three modes of creation described: direct creation *ex nihilo* (out of nothing) (v. 3 where light is created by God's word); fabrication, where something is created out of something already in existence (v. 9 where the waters and the land are gathered together); and mediation where the work of creation is done via the fecundity of another part of creation (v. 20 'let the earth bring forth').[33] It is also worth asking ourselves a simple question after reading Genesis 1: is the writer imagining a previously wonderful perfect world 'before the Fall' or is he (sic) describing the good world as he sees it before him now?[34] When we blend all these ideas together, this is a much more dynamic, interconnected and, frankly, real account of creation.

Another crucial element that convinces us of the importance of matter to God is emphasised in the work of a distinguished modern Reformed theologian, the late Professor Colin Gunton, who approached this from the perspective of systematic theology as well as biblical exegesis. He asked a question about chronology, God and creation. If God is 'outside time', but has created a universe that is time-constrained, how are we to understand God's relationship to the timefulness of the created order? His answer is that God constrains himself to work within the timefulness of the created order. In Gunton's own words: 'It is therefore a function of the wisdom of God that he allows the world time to become that which it is called and created to be. That is the reason why the past tense for creation cannot be readily distinguished from the present, creation from providence, even though some distinction remains necessary.'[35] He believes that God is patient enough to allow the world the time it needs to grow and develop.

So far, I have argued that God's creative work is ongoing and that we must not let our language of creation and redemption separate what God inextricably holds together. Gunton moves this argument to a much higher plane when he reinforces these points by stressing the role of Christ as the instrument of creation. He laments the classic Western theological textbook account: 'It is the *one* God who creates, the *triune* who redeems, and while to put it in this way is something of a caricature, there is a failure of Christology to be discerned in this area. Christology is simply not determinative enough of the doctrine of creation in the West, and that is why we need the uniquely integrating focus provided by the notion of Christ as the Wisdom of God.'[36] In other words, because we don't talk enough about the work of Christ, the Son, in creation we contribute to the separation of God's work in creation and redemption. This is such a crucial point that I encourage readers to tackle Gunton's work for themselves, but as I understand him, he would say that the value of the New Testament description of Christ as creator (read the prologue to John's gospel, the hymn to Christ in Colossians 1:15–20 or Hebrews 1:2–3)[37] is that all this has the effect of holding together doctrines of creation and redemption very tightly. The world God is creating he is also redeeming, and he has shaped himself to meet the needs of an imperfect, vulnerable, but rescuable world. The Son is both a divine agent of creation and God incarnate. This is running ahead to a later section in this chapter, but Gunton makes the profound point that the doctrines of the Trinity and the incarnation tell us something about God 'in himself' as well as in relationship to us: 'To say that Jesus Christ is the mediator of creation is to say, among other things, that God's being is in some way orientated to the world of time and space that he takes to himself in the Incarnation.'[38]

15

It would be difficult to find a theology that gives more weight to the value God has put on his creation. In the words of *The Mystery of Salvation*: 'The distinction between creation and salvation should not be absolutised. It makes a distinction within a continuity.'[39] God's work is indivisible, even when working in different situations with different problems. 'Creation' and 'redemption' are in one way simply descriptions of God's different modes of working. This is why I have been using a simple slogan that holds together creation and redemption: God is always the life-bringer.

Humanity is matter – and this matters to God and us

Within this understanding of God's creation of and valuing of matter is humanity, the 'crown of creation'.[40] We will note in Chapter 2 how this idea has been abused by Christians, to the damage of creation and to our own scandal. But we can stress simply and clearly at this point in the argument that human beings are the most wonderful part of God's creation. This is evident in the structure of the first two chapters of Genesis, where both creation narratives differently highlight humanity.

So in Genesis 1 humankind is uniquely made in the very image of God[41] as the pinnacle of creation.[42] The word translated 'image' – *selem* – is strong. It is the word for statue, duplicate, even idol. Remembering the Old Testament ferocity about idols, it is extraordinary that humanity is described as being the 'idol', the representation of God.[43] Brueggemann stresses the dramatic significance of this point: 'There is one way in which God is imaged in the world and only one: humanness!'[44] We note in passing that the phrase 'the image of God' has been the source of much later reflection and is often taken to apply to humanity's spirit, conscience or ability to reason – all incorporeal aspects of humanity. But Gerhard von Rad, another very significant OT scholar, argues strongly that it is in human totality that the image of God is seen: 'Therefore one will do well to split the physical from the spiritual as little as possible: the *whole man* is created in God's image.'[45] Wilkinson helpfully goes further in making two more crucial points. First, that the

16

essence of this 'image' is that humankind is to be in relationship, especially to God: 'The image should not be imagined to be a 'part' of us, whether our body, our reason or our moral sense. It is not about something we have or something we do; it is about relationship.'[46] Second, that the 'image' of God is to be seen most clearly in Jesus of Nazareth.[47] Irenaeus strengthens this point by arguing that when the Word became flesh he confirmed that humanity was originally and truly made in the image of God, and note again that Irenaeus stresses the physicality of this likeness.[48] We will return to this point later but it is good to get it fixed in our thinking now. We might also note one little subversive element here. Normally an 'image' was of a great person and was itself great and grand, but Wenham points out: 'Whereas Egyptian writers often spoke of kings as being in God's image, they never referred to other people in this way. It appears that the OT has democratised this old idea. It affirms that not just a king, but every man and woman, bears God's image and is his representative on earth.'[49]

In Genesis 2, where the account of the creation of heaven and earth is compressed to half a verse with the focus being entirely on the creation of humanity, God breathes his own breath into Adam, a unique mode of creation.[50] In one of the most celebrated of the psalms, there is a profound affirmation of the status of humanity within the wonder of creation and this inspires praise for the majesty of God in his work as creator. God and humanity are exalted together:

> O Lord, our Sovereign, how majestic is your name in
>   all the earth …
> When I look at your heavens, the work of your fingers,
> What are human beings that you are mindful of them,
> Mortals that you care for them?
> Yet, you have made them a little lower than God,
> And crowned them with glory and honour.[51]

So humanity is not to be denigrated. We are the jewel in God's crown of creation and the part of creation that is most like him, but we are also clearly and rightly and inseparably part of that physical creation. Again Irenaeus is wonderfully physical about this. He describes Adam as God's *plasma* or handiwork, literally made by the hands of God. As Behr, an insightful Orthodox scholar of Irenaeus, vividly writes: 'Human beings are, for Irenaeus, essentially and profoundly fleshy or earthy: they are skilfully fashioned mud.'[52] There are very serious consequences for us if we lose sight both of the essential goodness and materiality of creation and of our inextricable place within it.

A recent lament for the weakness of sacramental spirituality among Evangelicals stresses precisely this point, that it is the loss of a vibrant doctrine of creation that has allowed Evangelicals to fall into a foolishly cerebral, falsely 'spiritual' and narrowly 'human' perspective on God's concerns: 'From Israel's biblical theology we learn, firstly, that *creation is fundamental*: Genesis 1 is the starting point. "Embodiment is the end of all God's works." Creation is basic and blessed, however warped and under judgement.'[53] The sacraments of course keep us earthed in physical water and bread and wine.

I will return to this question of a 'warped' creation often in this book, but here I re-emphasise that whenever Christians are tempted to become too spiritual to take their bodiliness seriously as a God-given reality about who they are and how they know him, then it ought to set off alarm bells immediately. Indeed Irenaeus argued passionately that we will stay as material beings for eternity. Interpreting Paul in 1 Corinthians, he writes: 'How then is it not the utmost blasphemy to allege, that the temple of God, in which the Spirit of the Father dwells, and the members [i.e. parts of the body] of Christ, do not partake of salvation, but are reduced to perdition?'[54] If Irenaeus (and Paul) are right, we will be bodies for eternity,[55] so we had better get used to it! But it matters to God too. I have already argued that by incarnating himself into the world, he is treating his creation with immense seriousness. But he shows that he takes humankind with especial seriousness by embodying himself in the world as a human being.

There are two further clusters of consequences that derive from giving creation and humankind this sort of priority. The first is to do with how we meet God and the second with how God is saving his world; and the two are inextricable.

The wisdom of God in creation – how we meet God

A systematic theologian colleague, Dr Georgina Morley, gives us a lead into a way to see how creation, revelation, incarnation and redemption are all to be held together. She has been revisiting 'natural theology' and has found resources for this in the writing of John Macquarrie, the Oxford theologian. I quote her words rather than Macquarrie's: 'God redeems, not redeeming human being *from* the material cosmos, but redeeming the cosmos *through* human being. Human self-transcendence and capacity for God is not a sign of ontological difference between human being and the non-human creation, but of ontological affinity …' [56] The language is complex but it leads us to two very significant insights. First, the world God is saving is the world God is making. He makes it to be in relationship with himself,[57] and humanity above all is the part of creation most able to do this, again as part of God's ongoing work of creation. But this is emphatically not to set humanity apart from the rest of creation. We are inextricably part and parcel of the created universe, of nature, and we are saved as part of that, through our place in that, and as its representatives (with Jesus as our perfect representative). In Screwtape's wonderful phrase, we are incurably 'hybrid' creatures.[58]

Given that God has made us to be 'hybrid' beings immersed in a physical as well as a spiritual world, it would be bizarre if God did not intend to communicate with us within his world. We can amplify this point but from a different direction. Building on New Testament language (John 1:1–4, 9–10, 14; cf. 1 Cor. 8:6; Col. 1:15–17; Heb. 1:1–3), the early Church developed a profound and evangelistically effective *Logos* (Word) theology.[59] *Logos* was a word rich in meaning. It meant both the spoken word but also the action and principle of reason. As such it was not a free-standing principle, but was an aspect of the very character of God himself. Indeed elements in both Hebrew theology and Classical Greek philosophy had personified the *Logos* so that it was more than an attribute of God, but almost a separate expressed entity. All this was very important for the developing Christology of the Early Church. But it is significant for my argument that the *Logos* or indeed the Wisdom (*Sophia*) of God was what gave life and reason and wisdom to the world and to humankind. We might talk of the *Logos* permeating the created order, giving it wisdom and a rational shape. In other words – to compress a lengthy argument – as John discerned the continuity between the Logos of God and the person of Jesus of Nazareth he was teaching Christians that the values and the wisdom of this Jesus will cohere with and express the wisdom embedded in humankind by the Creator *Logos*, who are one and the same Person. Theologically this is of immense importance, because even if the 'world' is sometimes blind to this linkage – as the prologue to John's gospel states and as Paul argues in his Corinthian letters – the linkage is still there and still open to the eyes of reasonable faith. *Logos* theology cautions us against making sharp divisions between Christ, the eternal creative Wisdom of God, and the incarnate Christ.

All this has implications for how we know anything of God and how we express our relationship with God. For example, one consequence is precisely that we ought to be able to discern and encounter God in his world.[60] One way to talk about this is to use precisely the language of 'wisdom'. Professor D. Hardy, another systematic theologian, when reflecting on the nature of wisdom, starts with the doctrine of creation:

> A distinctive feature of wisdom is that particular promi-
> nence is accorded to non-human nature, and the need for
> intimacy with it, which are unfamiliar to us who are
> trained to be 'above' non-human nature, and who have
> learned to see the world as largely determinate and
> mechanical. And this nature is directly affected by the
> presence and 'holding' of God, who is not seen as 'above'
> it, as if in a supernatural realm as we tend to think. The
> coherence and permanence of the cosmos are attributed to
> wisdom as present in them.[61]

20

So, we become foolish when we cease to be aware that we are part of the created order. This may sound a little like 'New Age' thinking and, ironically, Hardy goes on to reinforce his point by quoting a saying from a Native North American, but he could equally have chosen quotations from a number of world religions: 'But the old Lakota was wise. He knew that man's heart, away from nature, becomes hard; he knew that lack of respect for growing, living things soon led to lack of respect for humans too. So he kept his children close to nature's softening influence.'[62]

It may be that it is precisely this sort of wisdom that has helped to make 'New Age' ideas so attractive, but this way of thinking has deep roots in the Judaeo-Christian tradition. To take one simple example, so many of Jesus' parables are 'nature' parables. They only work if there are real continuities and parallels between the natural and the human/spiritual world. Jesus often made use of this sort of wisdom: 'Look at the birds of the air; they neither sow nor reap nor gather into barns, and yet your heavenly Father feeds them. Are you not of more value than they?'[63] Perhaps we need to help Christians get outdoors a bit more! In this, of course, we will yet again find ourselves following in the footsteps of the wise of this world.

In all this we find strong echoes of Richard Hooker, whom we will encounter frequently in subsequent chapters. Hooker was a passionate defender of the *via media* of the Church of England between Swiss Reformed Protestantism and Roman Catholicism. So he was clear that the world is flawed and fallen, but embedded in it are still God's laws – or perhaps we would say principles – and one of these is the human capacity to discern the will of God by humbly using our God-given reason (another way of describing wisdom).[64] And God would have us use that reason. We are not brute beasts. 'There was no need for men to be tied and led by authority, as it were with a kind of captivity of judgement, and though there be reason to the contrary not to listen to it, but to follow like beasts the first in the herd they know not nor care not whither, this were brutish.'[65] It is the same God who speaks to us through natural wisdom as through revelation therefore the two messages will cohere (except where human reason is blinded by sin – Hooker was not a man of the Enlightenment or naïve). David Neelands, a recent historian of Hooker's attitude to Scripture puts this very well: 'God is the source of nature and of grace; God's wisdom is the source of Scripture as much as it is the source of human wisdom.'[66] God's revelation of himself to us in this world is all of a piece.

Behind this lies a piece of fundamental theology, which is clearly to be found in Hooker and is a key part of my argument. Grace perfects nature, it does not 'scrap' it.[67] In other words there is not an absolute discontinuity between the 'before' and 'after' of salvation. We bring our natural human gifts – including for example, reason, but also the need to live in community, to generate political systems, to learn by seeing and doing as well as by hearing – into the life of faith. Neelands goes further in pointing out how for both Aquinas and Hooker, 'grace presupposed nature'.[68] So, for example, if we do not bring our reason and experience to the reading of Scripture, we will not understand it. I will explore this at more length in Chapter 3, but for the moment as we reflect on this insight, it ought to restrain our claims to be so 'redeemed' that we have been or even need to be set free from the human nature, which God gave us in creation. (I will have to return to the whole question of spiritual 're-birth' in the final chapter on conversion.)

God's work in this world is all of a piece. We must not rip asunder what God has joined together. Hooker is often described as eirenic, and so it is of note when he loses his temper. His rage at the 'Puritan' attempt to separate natural wisdom, revelation and the work of the Church, and at its consequences for church life, was severe: 'You have already done your best to make a jarre between nature and Scripture. Your next endeavour is to do the like between Scripture and Church. Your delight in conflicts doth make you dream of them where they are not…'[69] Hooker saw the consequence of this separating as excluding most people from the life of the Church and producing unrealistic, unstable, conflict-ridden and hyper-spiritual churches. It sounds familiar.

The conclusion from all of this is that human beings are creatures of dignity and responsibility as well as need. That means that Christians can listen with open ears to the wisdom of non-Christians and expect to encounter God's truth in them. Discerning what it is to be human, how to be alive, is not a task for Christians to undertake on their own, however much Christians have unique insights and experiences to contribute to this reflection. But the tragedy, to my mind, is that in its diagnosis of the human condition and attempted remedy, the Church has too often come to despise humanity rather than honour it as made in the image of God and so has become an instrument of death. So, we start from the opposite place. The honour and dignity of humanity, as we are being made by God, is fundamental to this book.

The humility of God and the humanity of Jesus – how God is saving the world

But we need to go much further. Even given this good creation and God's wisdom accessible in it, we still find it difficult to see what is good and life-giving and even more to do it. Worse, humankind seems prone to destruction. Put us on an island paradise and we will spoil it. We need help.

I do not intend to offer a systematic account of human 'sin', but want to note here the following. First, any language we use about human sinfulness must be descriptive of human behaviour, analytical even, but it must remain dynamic. I am deeply cautious about language that describes sinfulness as a permanent account of our status before God. I am convinced that all human beings will 'fall', that we are flawed (and somehow inherit our flawedness) and so are prone to 'fall', but when we move from that (biblical) conviction to abstract statements that declare, for example, God's condemnation of all humanity because of its 'totally depraved' status, we have turned into a rigid straitjacket what is, properly speaking, heuristic language. Second, and ironically, part of our sinfulness is precisely an unwillingness to accept our identity as material creatures, whether that is seen in the modern quest for endless youth or our arrogance towards the dignity of the rest of the created world, and towards God. Third, the journey of salvation is ultimately into God's eternity, and this does involve movement from mortality to immortality, which is primarily a gift of God. If I have a preference it is for conceiving of the human problem being more like a disease than just an issue of moral and spiritual failure. Yes, we are 'to blame', and we will have to return to the issue of blame in Chapter 6. But we are also trapped, not least by our frailty and mortality, as well as by our selfishness. So we need help.

But when God saves this – his – world he does so by becoming part of it, including its limitations, and in doing this he maintains respect for the dignity of humanity, not least by what we might call self-limitation. God does not overpower us into loving him and his world. He is our helper more than our master.

There are two elements to this. First there is the point, so obvious when we look honestly at the world (and normally included in arguments of theodicy), that God often appears at worst absent and at best hidden. Hooker expressed this elegantly:

> If therefore it be demanded, why God having power and ability infinite, the effects notwithstanding of that power are all so limited as we see they are: the reason hereof is the end which he hath proposed, and the law whereby his wisdom hath stinted the effects of his power in such sort, that it doth not work infinitely, but correspondingly unto the end for which it worketh, even 'all things chrestos [well] in most decent and comely sort'.[70]

Here Hooker is attempting to relate God's purposes and his means. God desires that all shall be well. But one of the conditions of the world 'being well' is that human beings grow into the sorts of persons God hopes we will be. That requires God to step back from constant visible direct intervention. All will be well, but by growth not by divine dictat. All the time God is encouraging us into life.

But what, then, secondly, is the significance of Jesus Christ? Is he an optional extra or a sort of top-up for the rest of life, which we have got almost sorted for ourselves? No. Put simply, I believe that we can see God most clearly in Jesus of Nazareth but that in the incarnation – within which I include Jesus' life, teaching, cross and resurrection – God is decisively and unique-ly saving the world. By which I mean that, through Jesus of Nazareth, God is not just communicating with the world but is also liberating and renewing it. (I will engage more fully with the whole issue of dealing with the negative consequences of sin in Chapter 6.) And so I believe that Jesus shows us God's character embodied in a real human being more clearly than anyone else. But the apparent clarity of these convictions requires careful unpacking.

Jesus has to be fully human to communicate God authentically

It is here that not simply the doctrine of the incarnation but more specifically modern *kenotic* (self-emptying) Christology is so important.[71] Some versions of modern Christology – at a congregational rather than at an academic level, where the problems are often the opposite – have so stressed the divinity of Jesus of Nazareth, that his humanity is all but forgotten, except as a sort of sentimental veneer. But as the early Church discerned, it was only if he was truly human that Christ could really save humanity. If he was incompletely human then he was not really one with us. Indeed, according to the famous patristic slogan, whatever is left outside Christ's 'assumption', or incorporation, of humanity will not be saved.[72] But this is more than a description of the mechanisms of salvation: it takes us deep into the manner in which God relates to his world.

I believe that Jesus of Nazareth performed miracles, though our records of them benefit from careful and honest reflection, and I have a straightforward faith in a bodily resurrection (for theological reasons, to do with the value of embodiment, as well as for historical reasons). But it was also clearly possible not to be 'persuaded' by Jesus Christ, not to see the meaning of his miracles, and even to regard him as a blasphemer. There is a variety of ways of understanding the rejection of Christ. It is possible to refer in some global sense to human sinfulness. Other reasons remain dangerously near to anti-Semitism. But to put it crudely: people had choices. They were not overwhelmed into faith. In part this was because if we had been standing alongside them, we too would have seen a wandering, often tired, sometimes angry and emotional, and eventually deserted and destroyed, radical Jewish rabbi.

Trying to penetrate the self-consciousness of Jesus of Nazareth is a perilous task, for a whole variety of reasons.[73] But if we ask ourselves a ludicrous question – did Jesus walk around knowing consciously that he was the eternal Second Person of the Trinity? – then for historical and exegetical reasons the simple answer has to be 'no'. In other words, I would argue (putting it rather crudely again) that when he took human form, the 'Son of God' became truly the 'Son of Man' and gave up – emptied himself – of much of his divinity. If we are accustomed to describe divinity with a series of 'omnis' – omnipresence, omniscience, omnipotence – then it is evident from the gospel record that Jesus was not like this. This is where the combination of modern biblical criticism of the gospels and some modern Christology have crucial things to say, which go further than the patristic formulations. They give us a more realistic account of Jesus' humanity than much earlier exegesis. Serious biblical study does not have to lead to a loss of faith in Christ but often leads to new, deeper and sharply relevant insights. For example, a recent account of how Jesus interpreted his sonship, which takes both Jesus' humanity and the authority of Scripture with full seriousness, makes very positive use of both Matthew's and Paul's account of Jesus' renunciation of power for himself:

> What is the nature of the power that God gives to Jesus? *It is not the power of coercing but the power to renounce coercion,*

26

the power of channelling God's power to others for their well-being (which may of course regularly take challenging and even abrasive form) while refusing to take advantage of it for oneself, the power of living human life in unqualified trust and obedience which will do anything rather than deny that trust.[74]

Jesus as God Incarnate was authoritative, not authoritarian. He embodied the humility of God.

But why did God come to us in this self-limited form? Because it is God's characteristic way of not overwhelming humanity into belief or love. (In this respect the transfiguration stands out as a moment of divine disclosure and the result is awe among the inner circle of disciples.[75]) Normally God 'woos us into love'. I write this sentence dimly conscious of the experiences of those who have felt overwhelmed by the love of God, even driven into submission. But it seems to me that in the spiritual life such moments of overwhelming experience are followed by, or balanced with, periods of space and even distance from God. John of the Cross remains a mysterious example here. As so often C. S. Lewis was here first: 'But you see now that the Irresistible and the Indisputable are the two weapons which the very nature of his scheme forbids him to use. Merely to over-ride a human will (as his felt presence in any but the faintest and most mitigated degree would certainly do) would be for him useless. He cannot ravish. He can only woo.'[76]

If God is like this, then how can the Church have been so different? Moberly spells this out sharply: 'the Church cannot be permitted to try to sustain itself by those very means which Jesus renounced and upon whose renunciation the value of the Church's life is predicated.'[77] As believers, we must learn an appropriate humility to set alongside passionate faith.

Jesus shows us what it is to be fully human

There is one further fundamental point to make, which will be amplified in the chapters to come. We can argue our case that creation is fundamentally good, and human life within it –

including key human goods such as love, friendship, pleasure, creativity, beauty – not just from Genesis but with even more conviction based on the significance of the incarnation. Irenaeus captured something of this vision when he expressed what is perhaps the pinnacle of his theology: 'For the glory of God is a living man, and the life of man consists in beholding God: for if the manifestation of God through the creation affords life to all living on earth, much more does that revelation of the Father which comes through the Word give life to those who see God.'[78] Here Irenaeus may be giving a double sense to his words, referring both to living human beings and to Jesus. Behr writes on this: 'This is perhaps the most profound and beautiful reflection of Irenaeus: the vibrant unity between the glory of God and the living man, the life-giving manifestation of God and the vision of God by his creatures.'[79]

For Irenaeus, Jesus of Nazareth was the model of an ideal human life. In a theme to which I shall return in Chapter 6, Irenaeus writes beautifully about the example of Jesus on the cross:

> And from this fact, that he exclaimed upon the cross, 'Father, forgive them, for they know not what they do,' the long-suffering, patience, compassion, and goodness of Christ are exhibited, since he both suffered and did himself exculpate those who had maltreated him. For the Word of God, who said to us, 'Love your enemies, and pray for those who hate you,' himself did this very thing upon the cross; loving the human race to such a degree, that he even prayed for those putting him to death.[80]

Hence the glory of God is (this) living man. But is even this enough really to liberate us?

Jesus is God's 'kick-start' for humankind

As we will see throughout this book, 'sin' is very serious; more serious than the neurotic focus on bad language and teenage sexuality that was common when I was a young Christian. We are capable of appalling cruelty to other human beings, directly or through indifference, and our collective life can be, apparently effortlessly, destructive of our well-being and of the planet. There is something wrong with humankind and we have a range of language to describe this, some of it helpful, some unhelpful: 'fallen', 'lost the image of God', 'original sin', 'totally depraved'.

Irenaeus saw Christ as the 'recapitulation' of humanity. To try to express this in our terms: in Christ, God did not just provide us with the best example of being human, he dealt with the consequences of human sinfulness (see Chapter 6) and gave the whole project of creating human beings a huge surge of re-creative energy. 'When he became Incarnate, and was made man,' writes Irenaeus, 'he commenced afresh the long line of human beings, and furnished us, in a brief and comprehensive manner, with salvation; so that what we had lost in Adam – namely to be according to the image and likeness of God – that we might recover in Christ Jesus.'[81] It is not accurate to describe this as a beginning all over again. Elsewhere Irenaeus writes in a way that strongly reinforces the sense of a renewing rather than a replacing: 'Why then did God not once again take mud, rather than work this fashioning from Mary? So that there should not be another fashioning, *nor that it should be another fashioning which would be saved, but that the same thing should be recapitulated, preserving the similitude.*'[82]

Irenaeus, while he took human sinfulness seriously and read the story of the Fall in what is to our eyes a naively straightforward way, also conveys the sense that this was, almost, all part of the journey. Humankind in the Garden of Eden was not at the peak of its powers. If you like, it was in its infancy. To grow to maturity it had to be stretched. This is not to say that God intended the Fall to happen, but Irenaeus weaves it into a less perpendicular account of human history, in which it was always God's purpose that humankind should grow into his eternal life. In his own words: 'Now it was necessary that man should in the first instance be created: and having been created should receive growth; and having received growth, should be strengthened; and having been given strength, should abound;

and having abounded, should recover [from his disease of sin]; and having recovered, should be glorified; and having been glorified, should see his Lord.'[83] We should note that this could take us into a huge discussion about the 'necessity' of the incarnation. Was it fore-ordained by God or was it a response to the catastrophe of the Fall? Behr, expounding Irenaeus on this, is helpful:

> The Incarnation of the Word is thus central to the accomplishment of the divine economy, and although perhaps conditioned by human apostasy, the Incarnation was certainly not occasioned by it. The goal of the economy is the manifestation of the glory of God in a fully living man, partaking of the life, incorruptibility and glory of God ... On the one hand, God himself needed to be incarnate, to become man, so that man, joined to or bearing the Word, might be adopted as a son of God; whilst on the other hand, man needed to be trained in preparation for this 'ascent to God'.[84]

So Irenaeus saw humanity, as renewed in Christ, as being the pinnacle of God's creation destined for a life in glory with God. A fully alive human being is also the place where God's glory can be seen most clearly. In a beautiful phrase, Irenaeus said that 'Just as the physician is proved by his patients, so is God also revealed through humanity.'[85]

Hooker, writing in the knowledge of Irenaeus, whom he cites frequently and respectfully, put this with classic English understatement: 'The honour which our flesh hath by being the flesh of the Son of God is in many respects great.'[86] How often do we look around us and wonder at the glory of God in our fellow human beings? If not, why not?

Is Jesus of Nazareth the final and complete model for humanity?

To go back to Jesus, we can see something of this sense of him as the 'model' person in the gospel accounts of his life. He is, for example, the model martyr, the model teacher, the model believer. But again all this needs surprisingly careful reflection as we express it. Part of the theology of the incarnation is that the Son of God took human form in a particular time and place: a rabbi in first-century Palestine, not some mythically universal person. It is tempting to look to the life of Jesus of Nazareth to provide absolutist examples of how we ought to live. Indeed one of the key arguments of this book is that when the Church stops trying to model its life on Jesus of Nazareth, then it begins to slide to corruption. But Jesus models humanity for us not as a timeless, permanent, unchanging role model, but as a dynamic, specific, thought-provoking, real life. It is striking how hard it is to live the Sermon on the Mount, not just because it is hard – which it is – but because we have to translate this into, for example in my case, the life of a husband and father in early twenty-first-century Britain.[87] Do I simply give my shirt to the next *Big Issue* seller? One of the terrifying things for me is that the example of Jesus can be so elusive. So I moderate away the parts I find difficult – giving away all my money, or pacifism – but retain the bits that are easier because they affect 'other' people: divorcees, adulterers, religious hypocrites. There is no easy answer to the question of how we are to apply Jesus' teaching and lifestyle. Perhaps that in itself ought to teach us something.

Indeed, it is surprisingly complex to ask ourselves the question: 'In what sense is Jesus of Nazareth the model of a full human life and how then are we to live?' Jesus was a man (not a woman).[88] He never married. In some ways he had many fewer opportunities than many of us do now: travel, education, modern technology. Part of the work of the New Testament was precisely about working out how to live 'the Christlike life' in different circumstances, even in the generation after Jesus. 'Should Christians marry?' was a real issue then.[89] The questions are as sharp for us and perhaps more complex. Not just 'How should I try to be like Jesus now?' but also 'What can we expect from Jesus now as "God for us"?' In John's gospel, when Jesus is recorded as saying, 'I came that they may have life and have it abundantly',[90] what did he mean? Part of my own 'conversion' experience in the 1970s was the promise that Jesus would 'make life better and happier'. In its extreme form this is of course the 'Prosperity Gospel'.[91] In a more moderated form, the promise that life in Christ is tantamount to a 'happy and successful' life is still too widespread. It produces foolish, anxious or complacent Christians.

Nonetheless, without wishing to deny the sacrificial side to the life of Jesus of Nazareth, he was also a man who liked to party, a friend of sinners and was accused of being a drunkard and a glutton (Luke 7:31–5). On that occasion Jesus explicitly contrasted himself with the ascetic John the Baptist. Note especially Jesus' self-description as someone who invited people to dance with him. He strikes us as a man with whom life was fun as well as challenging beyond imagination. It seems as if children were drawn to him. He did set people free. He did make the powerful uncomfortable. He did show us how to live a life of love for God and for others. Millions of people – Christian and 'non-Christian' – are still drawn to him. In all of this he is a model of how to be humane.

How then can the community of those who follow Jesus have become so often dull, lifeless, excluding and even deathly? 'Jesus good, Church bad.' If we are such a stumbling block to faith in him, then perhaps we ought to change, and if not simply close down? Strikingly, the research for 'Mission England' in 1989 showed that 'the Church' was one of the six most frequently cited reasons why people did not believe.

To sum up: God in Christ is graciously and gracefully, even humbly, creating and renewing the world. The world is also responding to him through the very character that he has given it. God in Christ has come into our world in its weakness to help us to regain what it is to be truly and joyfully and faithfully and eternally human. God is always the life-bringer. If this is all true, then perhaps the Church needs to focus more energetically on the flourishing of human being through Christ and put that nearer the centre of our faith, life and teaching and not focus quite as much on a negative critique of human living.[92] Celebration before condemnation.

Gospel Reflection: Jesus the Liberator

I would like to finish this chapter with a brief biblical reflection on Luke 13:10–17, which may open up to us new insights into both inhumane religion and 'Humane Christianity'.

> Now he was teaching in one of the synagogues on the sabbath. And just then there appeared a woman with a spirit that had crippled her for eighteen years. She was bent over and was quite unable to stand up straight. When Jesus saw her, he called her over and said, 'Woman, you are set free from your ailment.' When he laid his hands on her, immediately she stood up straight and began praising God. But the leader of the synagogue, indignant because Jesus had cured on the sabbath, kept saying to the crowd, 'There are six days on which work ought to be done; come on those days and be cured, and not on the sabbath day.' But the Lord answered him and said, 'You hypocrites! Does not each of you on the sabbath untie his ox or his donkey from the manger, and lead it away to give it water? And ought not this woman, a daughter of Abraham whom Satan bound for eighteen long years, be set free from this bondage on the sabbath day?' When he said this, all his opponents were put to shame; and the entire crowd was rejoicing at all the wonderful things that he was doing.

You are probably not surprised that we are working from Luke. It is the gospel that shows Jesus at his most compassionate, that shows him most warmly in relationships with women and most careful about the poor. This story is in fact unique to Luke, though it has similarities to other healing stories.

Points to ponder
- It is the last time Jesus teaches in a synagogue in Luke's gospel.
- Notice just how damaged this woman is – 18 years of physical and therefore emotional and psychological pain. Notice too that she cannot stand upright, she is bent and oppressed.

And where did she come into the synagogue? She arrives 'just then' but was she coming to hear Jesus or trying to creep into the women's seats? Jesus calls her to the front.

- A touch of modernity now – in the New Revised Standard Version, Jesus of Nazareth describes her as being 'set free from your ailment'. Other translations are more literal, reminding us that Luke wrote that she had 'a spirit (*pneuma*) of infirmity' and later as being 'bound by Satan'. It is too easy to slip over this. Would we use the same words to describe her? One of the Evangelical commentaries speculates about a medical diagnosis – *spondylitis ankylopoietica* or *skoliasis hysterica*.[93] If we would not use the language of demonic oppression, how do we stand in relation to Jesus? Surely we cannot simply take his words straight? Do we not need to acknowledge the difference between then and now? But perhaps I am being too strident. Jesus heals her.[94] He does not exorcise her. And he heals her by touching her; in a synagogue, in public, on the sabbath. He is breaking both religious and respectability taboos. He is breaking the rules especially about sexuality and gender. This is dangerous.

- We sit light to the sabbath now, but it was part of the revealed word of God. No work on the sabbath.[95] And as is the way of the world, human beings want to be precise. Exactly how much 'no work'? The *Mishnah*, showing due concern for animal welfare, laid down rules for watering animals, un-tying or tying knots, etc.[96] I suppose the woman could have waited another day but Jesus seems to be contrasting her lack of freedom with the freedom even of animals on the sabbath. It is a painful contrast. A number of the stories we will look at will see Jesus straining at sabbath observance. But the sabbath had become a blood-soaked mark of Jewish faithfulness to God.[97] We can hear the poor synagogue leader repeating ('kept saying') the mantra, 'But the Bible says …' This was sacred territory Jesus of Nazareth was disturbing. Why?

- Perhaps the point Jesus wanted to make, or that Luke wants us to remember, is that her welfare as a 'daughter of Abraham' mattered more to Jesus than the community's sacred religious rules. Her dignity mattered. It mattered that she could stand straight and free. It mattered enough for Jesus to get angry. I cannot imagine him accusing his opponents of 'hypocrisy' in a quiet tone of voice. Certainly the synagogue leader was 'indignant'. This is a situation of open conflict.

- Why 'hypocrites'? Perhaps because they were claiming to speak for God but they had got the whole thing wrong? Why not then simply correct them? Perhaps Jesus thought they could, ought to, perhaps even did within themselves, know God better? Perhaps putting human religious rules, even ones issued in the name of God, above human welfare is hypocrisy because the image of God it presents is a lie, which people know to be a lie, but which is used by the powerful to control other, 'weaker', people?

- So what might we learn from the story? That Jesus cared passionately about the welfare of an ill woman? Yes. That he had the power to change this situation? Yes. Was she saved? She certainly responded by glorifying God, which is Lucan evidence of a faithful response to God. And does our doctrine teach us that these might still be God in Christ's priorities? Yes. So, the welfare of women ought to be priority for the disciples of Jesus? Yes. So, those who don't put the welfare of women above sacred rules are hypocrites and the adversaries of Jesus? Yes.

- What would the Church do, look like and say if these were to be our real priorities now? How might this communicate in modern Britain? Would it be attractive? What do we need to do differently to make it real in our Church and why don't we do it?

Lots of questions I'm afraid, but one of the things that reading Jeremy Taylor has taught me is that repentance is not repentance without change:

> But because I have observed, that there are some principles entertained into the persuasions of men, which are the

seeds of an evil life, such as are – the doctrine of late repentance … the sufficiency of contrition in order to pardon, the
efficacy of the rites of Christianity without the necessity of
moral adherancies … My great purpose is to advance the
necessity, and to declare the manner and parts, *of a good
life*.[98]

So perhaps these questions may function as 'Lenten' questions
for us to bring about real *metanoia*, change of direction as well as
change of feelings, so we can live, and live 'a good life'.[99]

Prayer

To help us to 'pray this home', I end this chapter with one of
Cranmer's most personal and most beautiful collects. Note how,
despite Cranmer's sense of the severity of God's judgement, it
is God's love for all creation and his desire to save which most
come through:

> Almighty and everlasting God,
> Who hatest nothing that thou hast made
> And dost forgive the sins of all them that are penitent:
> Create and make in us new and contrite hearts,
> That we worthily lamenting our sins and acknowledging
>   our wretchedness,
> May obtain of thee, the God of all mercy,
> Perfect remission and forgiveness,
> Through Jesus Christ our Lord.
> Amen.
>
> (Ash Wednesday Collect from the Book of Common
> Prayer)

CHAPTER TWO

From Poverty to Simplicity

The reality of poverty

I would like to start this chapter with two personal anecdotes. When I was an ordinand in Cranmer Hall, the most powerful pieces of training I experienced happened away from the building and not during any lectures. (It sometimes makes me wonder about what I do with my time.) Before ordination training, I had spent seven years as a youth worker and housing worker in Bermondsey in South-East London – it is where the Millwall fans come from – and in the East End. I prided myself, with that sort of inverse snobbery common among such workers, that I really knew something about urban poverty. Then I came to theological college in Durham. In my third year I was required to go to Gateshead for two days a week, to our Urban Mission Centre, and attached to a school on the Old Fold Estate. It was a typical 'sink' estate, cut off from the rest of Gateshead by roads and railway lines, isolated, dilapidated and neglected. I was shaken, not so much by the poverty, because I had seen that before, but because I had forgotten what poverty looks and smells like. I had forgotten that some people did not have carpets, not because they had nicely stripped pine floors but because they had so little money. I wondered at myself that two years in Durham should have helped me forget so much.

This was all the more surprising because also during my training we had spent six weeks in Nigeria. It was a wonderful experience and we will never forget Nigerian hospitality – or

Nigerian roads! At the end of our trip we stayed for a little while with my wife's uncle and aunt who had been missionaries there, teachers, for 30 years. I mentioned to them how well fed we had been by all the Nigerians with whom we had stayed and how the little children in the village we had visited had large tummies. That was a real African village: straw huts; a witch doctor; a church with a thatched roof, no walls and tree trunks for pews; and one well. The only incongruous sight was the sofa and armchairs in the main hut of the local evangelist – who had a degree from a polytechnic in fact. (Quite a sacrifice to give all that up for a straw hut.) Anyway, the moral of the story is that Helen's family gently pointed out that the Nigerians had gone without so that we could be well fed and that the children with big tummies were in fact malnourished because of a diet lacking in protein.

This chapter is about poverty. I will start by taking note of our setting, the context of British and global poverty, so that I sustain the method I have used already, of looking at the needs of our world and how the Church is perceived and should be perceived in this context. The commitment to voluntary radical poverty, as we shall see, has its roots deep in the New Testament, and soon became a dominant feature of the monastic strand of Christianity. So I will touch briefly on the Rule of Benedict, the lives of Aidan and Cuthbert and in particular on Francis. I have one underlying question: what is the appropriate Christian response to real, unchosen poverty, in the light of the positive emphasis I want to put on the goodness of creation and a natural human life within that?

Let me fill that out a bit. What, in the past, was the spiritual purpose of the vow of poverty? A few Christians still take vows of poverty, but do you think a vow of poverty should be required of all Christians? If not, why not? Is it wrong to enjoy the good things of life? And what is the right way to approach poverty in the light of the global crisis? Do we need a different agenda now compared to that of Benedict or Cuthbert or Francis?

Another impact of our own trip to Nigeria was that I stopped believing, in my guts, that life is inevitably getting better. I think, despite my reaction as a historian/theologian and as a Christian to the horrors of the twentieth century, that I still instinctively believed life, for most people, was getting better. Surely, the benefits of increased prosperity and better health care were gradually spreading around the world? Nigeria convinced me then that this was not so. Certainly at the end of the 1980s it was deteriorating, and for much of sub-Saharan Africa, that decline has continued. During the 1990s, 54 countries became poorer, that is, suffered average income declines, and most are in sub-Saharan Africa.[1] Using a different set of indices, while four countries suffered a reduction in their Human Development Index in the 1980s, the comparable figure for the 1990s was 21.[2] This is an issue that is focused in real people. It is simply and shockingly the case that the rich are getting immensely richer while the poor are getting poorer. In 1997 the richest 348 people were worth more than the total income of the poorest 45 per cent of the earth's people, some 2,300 million people.[3] In 2001, despite the turmoil in the global stockmarkets, the richest people (those with more than 1 million dollars to invest) increased the amount of their wealth by 6 per cent.[4] The impact of global monopolist capitalism may bring benefits for some factory workers in China, but for, say, African farmers, or the people of Argentina, the impact is mostly harmful. To change our focus slightly, all this is hugely exacerbated by the climate problems that seem to be so deeply related to our patterns of manufacture and consumption.

The Church's response

There is, of course, no neutral position on this. I may rigidly believe that salvation means the salvation of individual souls to eternal life, but if I continue to consume and pollute in the same old way, then it is my own environment and that of other more vulnerable people, and of my own children and grandchildren that I am destroying. Concern for the environment is not a theological option only for those Christians committed to social justice. It is a priority for all of us. I note – and note how few English Anglicans are aware of this – that it has been made one of the 'Five Marks of Mission of the Anglican Communion': 'To strive to safeguard the integrity of creation and sustain and renew the earth.'[5] Along with marks 3 and 4, which read as follows: 'To respond to human need by loving service' and 'To seek to transform unjust structures of society.' Even if we might be ignorant of these Anglican aspirations, the work of the Jubilee campaign has made easily available the hard information about life in parts of the developing world. We have no excuses.

There is good news. I noted in Chapter 1 the significant impact that the Jubilee campaign has had on the public profile of the churches. Locally, individual churches can now do a 'green audit' to check that they are using their resources in an environmentally friendly way.[6] I think it is the case that almost all the churches have made significant shifts since World War II in terms of their public commitment to social justice. I still read with profit and wonder William Temple's little book *Christianity and Social Order*. He and others were so influential in the founding of the British welfare state, but hear him on land, something about which he was unfashionably very radical (he called for its nationalization):

> The fundamental source of all wealth is Land. All wealth is a product of human labour expended upon God's gifts; and those gifts are bestowed in the land, what it contains and what it nourishes. Most truly the 'Malvern Conference' declared that 'we must recover reverence for the earth and its resources, treating it no longer as a reservoir of potential wealth to be exploited, but as a storehouse of divine bounty on which we utterly depend.'[7]

We are far from the language of 'dominion' here. Not that we can simply ape his ideas now. The issues are both different and if anything more complex. We need to speak with renewed and theologically informed spirituality in the debate about globalisation, as well as with up-to-date economic and political wisdom.

But I have a regret and a concern in this area. First, the regret that the Church was so slow off the mark about environmental issues. It would have been good had the Church listened to the voice of the prophets 20, 30, 60 years ago and made the environment a central part of our public proclamation instead of the rather bland and negative condemnations of 'materialism' which abound in Church teaching from the late nineteenth century onwards. Why was the Church not a founder of Greenpeace or Friends of the Earth? Why is environmentalism associated in popular culture with 'New Age-ism' rather than Christ the Creator? Indeed, I have to note how often the Church is associated with the destructive forces because of crude readings – by Christians – of Genesis 1:28: 'Be fruitful and multiply, and fill the earth and *subdue* it; and have *dominion* over the fish of the sea and over the birds of the air and over every living thing that moves upon the earth.' Who almost wiped out the buffalo from the American plains? Pagan Native Americans or revivalist white Christians? In his wild, hilarious and enraged book, *Stupid White Men*, Michael Moore casually asks: 'Of the 816 species that have gone extinct since Columbus got lost and landed here (another man who wouldn't ask for directions) – most of which are necessary links in our fragile ecosystem – how many do you think were eradicated by women? Once again, I think we all know the answer.'[8] I am tempted to gloss this as 'stupid white *Christian* men'.

Now the concern: whatever our public rhetoric – and as someone whose life was made practically better and whose heart was lifted by the *Faith in the City* report,[9] this public rhetoric matters – I am worried that we will have no credibility if we do not live our words, and with all the risks which it entails, live them more publicly. Does the Church of England invest its money ethically? It is coming slowly.[10] Does the Church model just employment practices? Not always.[11] Does the Church of England as a public institution model simplicity as a Christlike way of life? You can answer that for yourselves. (I was impressed by the recent decision to sell the Zubaran paintings of the Patriarchs kept in Auckland Castle – the home of the

Bishop of Durham – and with the caveat that they stay in the North East to be enjoyed by local people. 'Prince bishops' are a modern-day scandal to Christ.) But whenever I think of the Church of England now, I am reminded of Professor Euan Cameron's judgement on the late medieval Church: 'In spite of gifts prodigally given to some sections of the Church, the institution as a whole managed to appear simultaneously impoverished, grasping and extravagant.'[12]

It is so easy to be judgemental, and yet, I used to drive an old diesel car and shudder at the exhaust fumes it pumped out. I have an eye for buying goods as cheaply as possible. I even enjoy McDonalds! In a more positive light, I am content to spend money on, for example, going with my wife to see *Cats*, as we did recently; and I felt much better after I had done so. How am I to understand and change my own sinfulness with regard to my own wealth and patterns of life? Should I give all my money to the poor and not go to musicals?

Benedict, Bede and Francis on poverty

It is time to turn to dialogue with a Christian classic: the *Rule of St Benedict*.[13] This was written by Benedict in the early sixth century, probably during his time as abbot of Monte Casino. He had himself come from quite a privileged background. When he first gave up his life as a student in Rome to join a semi-monastic community, he took his nanny with him! It is also the case that, despite what look like the rigours of his Rule, it was in fact quite a moderation of the extreme rigour of the Desert Fathers of the Egyptian and Syrian deserts (see Chaper 5). But partly because of its clarity and partly because it was adopted and recommended by a series of influential people – Pope Gregory the Great, Augustine of Canterbury, Bede, Charlemagne – it became the dominant monastic rule in the West.

This is what Benedict teaches about poverty. In chapter 58 Benedict gives instructions for receiving new novices. He writes: 'If he has any possessions, he should either give them to the poor beforehand, or make a formal donation of them to the monastery, without keeping back a single thing for himself; well aware that from that day he will not have even his own body at his disposal.'[14] There is evidence of a double motivation. Poverty is in part a concern for the welfare of the poor. Elsewhere in his Rule, Benedict lays down rules for the care of the poor and at its best the Benedictine ideal has fostered a genuine spirit of hospitality. (But note the sharply down-to-earth comment of a modern Benedictine: 'Sometimes "Benedictine values" such as hospitality and community are abstracted and made so generic that they become a kind of spiritual etiquette attractive to all, offensive to none, and meaning little in concrete terms.'[15])

However, the core of the motivation is about obedience and commitment. It is about the monk surrendering himself in obedience to the community and through that to God. I will come back to obedience in Chapter 3, but here let me just note that this was not a cruel or mindless poverty. While all the property was held in common, justified by Benedict's reading of the Acts of the Apostles, brothers were to get clothes that fitted and that were appropriate for the climate. But, even given this common sense, the monks' beds were to be inspected regularly and in chapter 55 we read: 'A monk discovered with anything not given him by the abbot must be subject to very severe punishment. In order that this vice of private ownership may be completely rooted out …'[16] Here the emphasis is on rooting out the sins of greed and envy. I think this is the fundamental driving force in Benedict's Rule. Human inability to handle possessions without falling into greed – even the modest possessions of a sixth-century monk: cowl, tunic, sandals, shoes, belt, knife, stylus, needle, handkerchief, writing tablets – required ferocious discipline. There is generosity for the needs of others here, but I think it is secondary. The greater point is learning to let go of the 'world' (another word whose translation is the cause of much controversy and confusion, see Chapter 3).

We catch echoes of this range of motives in Bede's accounts of the lives of Aidan and Cuthbert, who were arguably more important than Augustine of Canterbury in the conversion of England. As monks in the Irish Celtic tradition, they were by their way of life committed to a disciplined, even ascetic lifestyle. Bede praises Aidan for the strength of the example of fasting he provided[17]and Cuthbert's life as a hermit was simple in the extreme. Indeed the account of Cuthbert's life on the Inner Farne, where, reputedly, all he could see from his walled enclosure was the sky – the heavens – is a stark reminder of the world-rejecting part of what we now meet in its more cuddly form of 'Celtic Christianity'.[18] But with Aidan and Cuthbert there is a stronger sense of an outward-looking purpose for poverty. Both men were remembered for their concern for the poor and their courage in shaming monarchs and rulers into giving away their own possessions to the poor. There is something deeply counter-cultural in the story of Aidan giving away the horse, which King Oswin had given him, because he thought it more appropriate for a Christian bishop to walk:

> When this action came to the king's ears, he asked the bishop as they were going in to dine: 'My lord bishop, why did you give away the royal horse which was necessary for your own use? Have we not many more valuable horses or other belongings which would have been good enough for beggars, without giving away a horse that I had specially selected for your own use?' The bishop at once answered, 'What are you saying, Your Majesty? Is this child of a mare more valuable to you than this child of God?'[19]

All this is in sharp contrast to Augustine of Canterbury, whose refusal to stand on meeting the British bishops confirmed to them a prophecy that he was not to be trusted.[20] Perhaps that is why the memory of Aidan and Cuthbert was preserved with such care and affection by their successors, not least by Bede, whose own views were in fact more deeply shaped by Rome than by Iona or Lindisfarne. This is simply what saints were supposed to do. Their memory continues to refresh and challenge the Church here in the North East today and could do elsewhere if more widely known.

Of course, the ultimate Christian example of poverty, and in his own way as un-followable in this as was Jesus himself, was Francis. Again we have a range of motives. Francis' love affair with Lady Poverty seems to have been profoundly shaped by his revolt against his upbringing in a prosperous bourgeois home.[21] Indeed his revolt had more than a flavour of a modern-day 'bourgeois revolutionary'. Selling or giving away his father's cloth to raise money for the poor – without of course getting his father's permission – was quite an act of rebellion. The aggression and the symbolism of stripping naked in public as a proof of his rejection of his parental home would be envied by many of our modern rebellious youth icons.

What lay behind Francis' choice of poverty? I think there was a combination of this rejection of his past, positive action to help the poor and identification with Christ. At times, Francis' rejection of money seems almost pathological. A recent biographer writes that: 'He used to say that money is simply dirt to be crushed underfoot; that it must be treated like excrement and shunned like the devil in person.'[22] He so loathed possessions that he would not even allow his friars to own a breviary. All this was in part because he had become so sensitised to the suffering of the poor by living among them. As he wrote in his Second Rule, 'Alms is the legacy and due right owed to the poor.'[23] For the friars to receive such money was theft. So Francis, despite his profound obedience to the authority of the Church, made it clear where he felt the institutional Church was compromising. According to his 'Admonitions', the brothers were to 'honour clergy who live according to the laws of the holy Roman Church' but themselves were to observe 'the gospel of our Lord Jesus Christ, living in obedience, with chastity and with no possessions'.[24] In other words, the friars were to follow exactly the lifestyle of Jesus of Nazareth whereas the Church ... Remember the text that Francis is reputed to have heard at mass in Portiuncula. De Celano tells us in his biography:

Hearing that the disciples of Christ should not possess

gold, or silver or any money at all, nor to have any baggage, nor carry any staff as they went about, nor to wear shoes, nor have more than a single tunic; but that they were to preach the Kingdom of God and repentance, Francis at once cried out in exultation: 'This is what I want. This is my goal. This is what I long to do with all my heart'.[25]

Which takes us back to Jesus himself. What of his teaching about possessions and his own example of an apparently homeless, impecunious Jewish prophet, especially as portrayed by Luke?[26] It was an example that haunted the mind of much of the Church till the sixteenth century. It is not, interestingly, an idea that features much in modern preaching. Francis took the ideal with immense seriousness, fundamentalist seriousness, in a way most of his friars could not follow. Do we even take note of it at all? Why does this verse not feature among the station Bible texts that are still so popular with a certain kind of Evangelical?

A brief theological note: much of the modern writing about the Celtic or Northumbrian saints or Francis stresses their closeness to the world of nature, a sort of early ecological spirituality.[27] I hope I have already indicated that some of this is anachronistic, and yet ... In the depth of their experience of God in nature and in their sense of God's pleasure in nature, they do model something immensely precious for us.[28] It is in part a reminder of our solidarity with nature, our common created-ness. So the otters warm Cuthbert's feet after he has been praying penitentially in the bitterly cold North Sea.[29] We need Nature.

They also had a sense of the proper and distinct authority of Nature. Remember the story of Columba's death, and how it is to the milk-delivery horse that God reveals Columba's imminent death and so it is the horse that grieves first, not the holy monks.

> It [the milk horse] approached the saint and – strange to tell – put its head against his bosom, inspired I believe by

God for whom every living thing shows such understanding as the Creator bids; it knew that it would see him
no more, and it began to mourn like a person, pouring out
its tears in the saint's bosom and weeping with foaming
lips ... When the servant tried to shoo it away, Columba
intervened: 'Let him be ... Look how you, though you have
a man's rational soul, could not know of my going if I had
not myself just told you. But according to his will the
Creator has clearly revealed to this brute and reasonless
animal that his master is going away'.[30]

Or think of that wonderful story of Francis preaching to the
birds, and telling them to love God and to go and do what God
wanted them to do, which was to praise him by being birds,
because that was their special and particular responsibility to
God, as birds.[31]

The same theme is found in their evangelism. Which modern
evangelist would follow Patrick in pointing to the hugeness of
creation and God's intimate involvement in it, as the first proof
of the character of God? A legendary account of Patrick converting the daughters of the High King of Tara has Patrick
describing God: 'He has his dwelling around Heaven and Earth
and sea and all that is in them. He inspires all, he quickens all,
he dominates all, he sustains all. He lights the light of the Sun;
he furnishes the light of the light; he puts springs in the dry land
and has set stars to minister to the greater lights ...'[32] They were
converted! This theological insight grew out of Patrick's experiences and spirituality. As a slave Patrick prayed out doors: 'so
that in one day I said about a hundred prayers, and in the night
nearly the same; so that I used to remain in the woods and in the
mountains; before daylight I used to rise to prayer, through
snow, through frost, through rain, and felt no hardship; nor was
there any slothfulness in me, as I now perceive, because the
Spirit was then fervent within me.' Living simply within the
reality of Nature had profoundly shaped his faith.

I mentioned in Chapter 1 that one of the underlying questions for this book is how to hold together doctrines of creation

and redemption, the sense of the presence and action of God being present and connected in both. These Christians, in some ways, have much to teach us and the wholeness and depth of their lives witness to the soundness of their theology. And yet probably Cuthbert,[33] and certainly Francis, fasted to the point of damaging their health. Francis was not careful of Brother Ass, his own body. There was something destructive even in the spirituality of this most Christlike of human beings, something inhumane.

Our response

As we begin to sum up this chapter, I would like to quote some words written by Michael Ramsey well over a quarter of a century ago which still give us the best overall perspective on how to balance concern for people in this world with an eye for heaven:

> In bearing its witness in this manner in the political and social realms the Church will see every part of its mission in the total perspective of the reconciliation of mankind to God and of heaven as the goal for every man and woman made in the divine image. This grasp of total perspective will prevent us from substituting the denunciation of the misdeeds of other communities for our own repentance and our own response to the way of holiness. It will no less prevent us giving absolute and final significance to causes or policies which may be only small fragments within the ultimate range of the Kingdom of God. It will prevent us also from allowing our concern for physical suffering and material welfare to diminish our concern for the eternal life in another world which is the destiny of every man or woman who does not forfeit it.[34]

This from a man who wanted the government of the day to fight against the white regime in post-UDI Rhodesia. Christians can never forget the perspective of eternity but should never lose the imperative it brings to love now.

However much joy Francis experienced in his life, and it is clear that there was much that he enjoyed when he would allow himself – good wine, the music of the lute, crayfish, the love of his friends – I would not want to live his life. There is an extremism that I find disturbing, an asceticism which may have damaged his own health, an attitude to his own sinfulness too firmly bound into the twelfth century for me to swallow undiluted.[35] But it is not for nothing that he is known as the most Christlike Christian. For the rest of us, is it simply a matter of living with a bad conscience or as a second-class Christian, if we do not vow poverty?

Two thoughts: first, if it is right to say that the good things in life are given by God to be enjoyed – whether it is the taste of good wine or singing and dancing – then these take time and money. Jesus himself was a party-goer and parties are not free. I want to say that it is alright to party. More seriously, the ministry of Jesus and the ministry of Francis depended on the wealth and productivity of others. I am minded to suggest that part of the vocation of the Christians who vow poverty is to remind us of the uncomfortable radicalism, the absolutism of Jesus, in the same way as those who vow pacifism, but that this cannot be the rule for all. I sense in myself at this stage a deep sigh of relief.

Second, if I want to suggest on the one hand a moderating of this world-rejecting radicalism, on the other I want to increase the emphasis we put on our response to global injustice. Compared to Jesus of Nazareth and Francis of Assisi, we have so many more resources of knowledge and of wealth. Even given our sense of powerlessness in the face of global capitalism, we can give and we can speak and pray, and we can live simply. I do not want to be drawn into giving precise prescriptions. It is not a matter for rules. I still find myself drawn back to Richard Foster's little book, *Celebration of Discipline*, and squirm at his detailed suggestions, though it took an Englishman to suggest sharing lawnmowers.[36] (All this marked, in my youth, a flourishing of 'radical Evangelicalism', which took a just lifestyle very seriously. It seems to have lost out, in the inter-Evangelical battle, to voices whose 'radicalism' is focused in controlling how other people behave. Has it lost out because it was found to be 'ineffective' or has it been lost sight of because it is too demanding? Clearly the poverty has not gone away.)

But when I want to keep the requirements vague and under my personal control, I have to note that Richard Foster, and William Law and Jeremy Taylor before him, ask impossibly precise questions of how people spend their money. We might laugh now at Law's persistent nagging about how much money women ought to spend on their dresses[37] (dangerous territory), but I also remember that when I came back from Nigeria I vowed to live more simply and I failed abysmally to keep to that. This is where the uncomfortable radicalism of Jesus and Francis and the stern scepticism of Benedict combine. I may be wanting in this book to question our traditional categories of sins and sinfulness, but I am being forced to be increasingly aware that my attitude to my money reveals my possessive selfishness far more than I would like it too. That is why we prayed the Ash Wednesday Collect at the end of Chapter 1. Perhaps I am at my most sinful when it comes to love for others. Perhaps I need a little of the rigour of Benedict or the extremism of Francis or the precision of Law when it comes to a personal audit of my money. And if I am wavering, rather than focus on the negation of this world perhaps I need to reflect on the fact that God's image is to be seen in the faces of all his children and keep a photograph of a hungry child always before me; and so be motivated to live more simply, give more and speak more passionately. If more of us did that, how might that redeem the image of our Church?

Gospel Reflection: Jesus the holistic revolutionary

This gospel reflection takes us to the heart of the holistic and socially revolutionary vision of Jesus of Nazareth. He did not make our neat and safe distinctions between our bodies and our spirits. We are looking at Luke 4:14–21:

Then Jesus, filled with the power of the Spirit, returned to Galilee, and a report about him spread through all the surrounding country. He began to teach in their synagogues and was praised by everyone.

When he came to Nazareth, where he had been brought up, he went to the synagogue on the sabbath day, as was his custom. He stood up to read, and the scroll of the prophet Isaiah was given to him. He unrolled the scroll and found the place where it was written:

> 'The Spirit of the Lord is upon me,
> because he has anointed me to bring good news to
>   the poor.
> He has sent me to proclaim release to the captives
> and recovery of sight to the blind,
> to let the oppressed go free,
> To proclaim the year of the Lord's favour.'

And he rolled up the scroll, gave it back to the attendant, and sat down. The eyes of all in the synagogue were fixed on him. Then he began to say to them: 'Today, this scripture has been fulfilled in your hearing.'

Points to ponder
- As with chapter 1, this is material unique to Luke. Mark records a visit of Jesus to the synagogue in Nazareth, but not his words, only the words of rejection from the people. I don't want to become embroiled in the questions of whether this is material that is from one of Luke's personal and unique sources, or that Luke alone has kept it from Q, or that it is Luke's creation based on his own understanding of Jesus.[38] Canonical scripture is canonical scripture. The story is of course absolutely consistent with Luke's understanding of Jesus and his mission and is located at the beginning of the gospel, along with the Magnificat, to make sure that we read the gospel with the right sense of priorities. One commentator suggests that it may comprise part of Jesus' typical synagogue sermon and I would love to think that is the

case.[39] We must note that it gives us an authentic – the earliest – account of synagogue worship, including the fact that Jesus sits to preach.

- But what did Jesus mean by it? The commentators tell us that Jesus quotes mostly from Isaiah 61 though the phrase about 'setting at liberty the oppressed' is added from Isaiah 58:6. Luke cites almost the whole text from the Septuagint (the first Greek translation of the Old Testament, begun probably some 250 years before Christ). By the first century AD, the passage had come to be seen as a Messianic text and was also used as such by the Qumran community. (Naively, I think that the debate as to whether this is a 'prophetic' or a 'messianic' event is rather redundant. The declaration by Jesus that this is fulfilled – he is fulfilling – the prophecy 'today' seems to me to bypass the debate.) In other words, these hopes for liberation and renewal had an eschatological future flavour for these people, whereas Jesus says they are coming true now. He emphasises the word 'today': 'Today this has come true in your own hearing.' A more dramatic moment it is hard to imagine. But, again, what did Jesus of Nazareth mean? What did he imagine he was doing and introducing? It is possible to overlook obvious questions of this kind – as, for example, when we sing the Magnificat regularly and religiously but miss its revolutionary content.
- Old Testament messianic texts seem to operate at a range of levels. There is what we might call a 'spiritual' reading, whereby a phrase like 'release to the captives' is taken to mean release from the control of sin. I do not want to jump on the bandwagon of those who reject such a reading as 'spiritualising'. One of the things that Jesus did not do, for example, was to release prisoners of war, which is apparently a good translation of 'captives'.[40] There is a metaphorical, theological, imaginative meaning to these words.
- But Jesus did, I believe, give sight back to the blind. He did set at liberty those who are 'bruised', that is, he healed the damaged. He did preach good news, especially to the poor. The Lucan beatitudes are especially sharp because they come

with the 'woes'. 'Woe to you who are rich, for you have received your consolation.' 'Woe to you that are full now, for you shall hunger.' The words, the context and the rest of Luke's gospel, not least the parable of Dives and Lazarus, show what Luke believed about Jesus' understanding of the fate of the rich. In Howard Marshall's crisp sentence: 'The rich have already received all they are ever going to get.'[41] The rich who have not shown love to the poor by feeding them, or who have basked in the enjoyment of their wealth without regard for eternity, will be punished. This is revolutionary stuff. It is not surprising perhaps that it is the apparently milder Matthean beatitudes that we teach children in our catechisms.

- Responsible exegesis requires that we state this carefully. One commentator gets it right when he says: 'The Lukan Jesus is no social reformer and does not address himself in any fundamental way to the political structure of his world, but he is as deeply concerned with the literal physical needs of men (Acts 10:38), as with their directly spiritual needs.'[42] But we can note that these words do have revolutionary significance when heard by those who really are physically oppressed. There is a powerful conclusion to a recent book, *Jesus the Liberator*, which is a sustained study of this passage. The author explains first something of the process: 'These [oppressed] communities engage the biblical text, in such a way that it becomes a basis for a programme of liberation. The text itself of course does not provide the strategies required.'[43] But he goes on more uncomfortably:

> Whether or not a Christian, or group of Christians, lives frugally is not a phenomenon of absolute significance, and is probably a matter of marginal interest to the poor. The poor do not require Christians to adopt the destitution of their lifestyle. In any case, because biblical scholars and all church officials are secure members of the empowered class, their 'practice of poverty' can never be more than a gesture. In our western society, at

least, Christian leaders and exegetes can never share the degradation of the poor. In antiquity, as also today, professional religious people, including those vowed to a 'life of poverty', by designating themselves as 'living in poverty', distort the meaning of the word 'poverty', and misrepresent and probably insult those who are really poor. What the poor can with justification require is that Christians use their power in their favour.[44]

- The Old Testament – and so Jesus – did not operate with our division of life into spiritual and physical. The reign of the Messiah was believed to bring real liberation to those oppressed by foreign rulers, or unjust landlords, or corrupt courts. There is more than a faint echo in these verses of the Year of Jubilee, when there was, as we have all discovered in recent years, a cancellation of debts and the release of slaves. (Funny how this one neglected bit of Leviticus has suddenly become so popular when the Church has lived for generations emphasising other bits of Leviticus, such as hostility to homosexuals. That in itself is a proof of the benefits of a proper modern contextual reading of Scripture.) 'Political' action is not a luxury just for the zealous.
- But the liberation of the Messiah in the Old Testament also, inevitably and essentially included the knowledge and love of God. Have we only got half the message if we only cancel the debt? Is it not absolutely important that we keep both together – physical and spiritual liberation? How are we to do this unless our care for human beings is rooted in a sense of the importance God gives to them, now, as well as in the eternal future? If we struggle to hold this together, as Christians have so often done, then perhaps we need to go back to Jesus of Nazareth and his indivisible sense of what it was to care for another human being? When God comes – as he does in Jesus – people are set free.

The story of Jesus preaching in Nazareth is very near the heart of 'Humane Christianity'. It teaches us to neglect no part of a human being. All of us and every part of us are precious to God. God is always the life-bringer. These values are articulated and lived out in a real human life, even one specially anointed with the Spirit and with ultimate theological significance. Tragically, if perhaps not surprisingly, this story continues with the rejection of Jesus by his home town. We too may still find this message of holistic love too uncomfortable to hear.

Prayer
This is from a litany written by the base liberation-theology group at Cranmer Hall.

> If the hunger of others is not my own,
> If the anguish of my neighbour in all its forms touches
>   me not,
> If the nakedness of my brother or sister does not
>   torment me,
> Then I have no reason to go to church and live.
> Life is this: to love one's neighbour as oneself;
> This is the commandment of God.
> Love means deeds, not good wishes.
>
> Let the Spirit of the Lord be upon us,
> Anoint us to bring good news to the poor,
> Send us to proclaim release to the captives,
> Recover our sight when injustice and hate blind us,
> Help us struggle for the freedom of the oppressed,
> And to proclaim the year of the Lord's favour.
> Amen.[45]

CHAPTER THREE

From Obedience to Responsibility

Inhumane obedience?

I saw recently a TV documentary about Adolf Eichmann. It had that doubly chilling feel that is so typical of any investigation of human evil. On the one hand he was a married man with four sons. The villagers from the farming community in Germany where he hid after the war remembered him as a quiet but friendly man who played the violin at one of their weddings. And there in the group wedding photo was Adolf Eichmann. Alongside this we had to hold the memory of the man who, both as a bureaucrat and in person, organised much of the concentration camp system and in particular the murder of hundreds of thousands of Jews. At his trial in Israel people could point to him as the man who had supervised the rounding up of their family or their ghetto but, when pressed, he replied that he was only obeying orders, that he had to obey orders, that it was against the law to disobey orders.

The example of the last century has taught us in a way that we should never forget that 'obedience' is a word to be treated with great caution. Whom are we being asked to obey? Why? And to do what? It is easy for me to write this; but it was not, and never can be, right to answer, 'I was just obeying orders', whether that is said by an SS camp guard, or a servant of the Inquisition, or a New England witch-finder.

In some ways, I think, this chapter is the heart of the book in that it explores the relationship between human beings and

God, and between human beings and each other. In the last chapter I argued that one of the fundamental flaws in the ancient Christian approach to poverty was its negation of the goodness of God's creation: that conversely it is right to enjoy the good things that God has given us. But I also wanted to argue that while one of the key motivations of Christian poverty in its classic form was the rejection of the world, a modern commitment to simplicity of living must be driven primarily by a love for this world and especially for our fellow human beings. As I have said before, the fundamental shift is from a negative to a positive conception of this world and from a negative to a positive motivation for Christian living. It is placing the best of what it is to be human at the heart of our faith and life, not because we are subverting the place of God but because in creation and redemption he has placed such value on human life. God is always the life-bringer. The tragedy is that so often the Church has had to learn the value of humanity from those who have rejected God and the Church, because of the Church's inhumanity. In terms of our mission, we need to recognise that we now live in a 'humanist' world and so we must be focused on addressing that agenda.

As I hope I made clear in the last chapter, this does not mean a lessening of our sense of the seriousness of sin. Indeed, as I reflect on my own words, I feel deeply uncomfortable at my own hypocrisy in daring to write them, because I find it so difficult to 'live simply – so that others may live', as the classic Christian Aid slogan puts it. The love of self and indifference to others goes very deep in me.

How we understand and describe what it is to be sinful determines how we understand the relationship of human beings to God: and how God, and each of us, needs to deal with human sinfulness. Let me explain a little more what I mean. Much of my understanding as a Christian in my teens and early twenties was shaped by the conviction that my primary sin was pride and rebellion against God. If I struggled to pray, read the Bible, or feel faithful, it was because in some sense I was rejecting God. While I recognise, perhaps more clearly now than before, the depth of my ingratitude to God, I can no longer affirm quite this view of the world. I remember being profoundly influenced by C. S. Lewis and his account of the incarnation as the landing on a disobedient planet of God's Son to begin to reclaim parts of this rebellious world for his Father's kingdom. I quote from *Mere Christianity*: 'Enemy-occupied territory – that is what this world is. Christianity is the story of how the rightful king has landed, you might say in disguise, and is calling us all to take part in a great campaign of sabotage.'[1] Even allowing for the shadow of wartime metaphors – and more seriously for the echo of the prologue from John's gospel (1:10) – I worry that this image denigrates the continuing goodness of God's world.[2] 'World' (*kosmos*) is almost a technical term in John's gospel. It is essentially the world of human beings (not normally the whole of creation). Like 'flesh' for Paul, its meaning ranges from the neutral to the negative. So God loves the world (John 3:16) and Jesus did not come to condemn it (John 3:17) but it is often 'the world' that rejects Jesus and so is condemned (John 3:18–19 or 7:7). At times, John almost slips towards a dualistic sense of this world over against a 'heavenly world', whence the Word came (John 8:23). Notice how, in contrast to this complexity and subtlety, some Christians unthinkingly use the phrase 'the world' in an entirely negative sense forgetting that this is still the 'world' God is making, loves, fights for, dies for. Looking back, I was hugely happy that I was now in this new kingdom and, perhaps less graciously, I was also fairly clear who was outside it.

If the core of my sinfulness, of human sinfulness, is pride and rebellion, then the primary spiritual task is to break our pride. I think both I and the church to which I then belonged devoted a good deal of attention to that. I remember a particularly fierce talk at the youth group on idolatry, after which I went home and broke my favourite tank model! But if the core of my and human sinfulness is selfishness, self-centredness, a sort of egotistical self-preoccupation, which encompasses indifference to God and to others, then the core spiritual task may be to soften and open up my heart to the love of God and of others.

Love must be received by me so that it can be given by me. In the next chapter I will return to the issue of love as the key to what it means to be saved. In this chapter I want to focus more on this issue of human pride and how it has shaped so much of the understanding and spirituality of the Church for hundreds of years, especially in the West.

Let me put this as starkly as I can, at the risk of some simplification: the more sinfulness is conceived as being pride, the more the relationship with God, and subsequently with the Church, will be conceived as a conflict which one side has to win. The result can be an oppressive sense of conflict between God and the human being. This is greatly compounded by the extent to which the human being is seen as having been contaminated by sinfulness. If we follow the strict Calvinist line and believe in the 'total depravity' of humankind and of individual human beings, then how can we not want to increase the severity with which human beings should be disciplined for their apparent 'pride'? What, then, if my understanding of 'pride' lacks self-awareness, and being in authority over others I do not like what they are doing or saying in criticising me? Here I am on dangerous ground. One man's pride may be another woman's dignity. For if we were to replace the word 'pride' by 'dignity' or 'responsibility' then the problem looks very different. This is even more the case if instead of 'total depravity' we use the language of being 'flawed' or 'falling short' or 'lacking', which imply partial, but not complete failure.

We must first remind ourselves of the ferocity with which humankind was denounced by the Church for its sinfulness. We can too easily try to forget or soften the completeness of the condemnation that was proclaimed. The Synod of Dort, held in 1618–19 in the Netherlands, was the most decisive gathering of Reformed theologians in the seventeenth century, including senior representatives from the Church of England, and it ensured the 'orthodoxy' of Calvinism over against the new 'heresy' of Arminianism, which believed that all could be saved (an idea which came to be central to the Wesleys and so to Methodism), not only the elect. The Synod is famous for coining the acronym TULIP: the Total depravity/inability of humankind (we deserve God's eternal punishment); Unconditional election (God simply chooses); Limited atonement (Christ dies only for the elect); Irresistible grace (you can't resist God); Perseverance of the saints (once God chooses you, you are in for ever).[3] Its Canons state of us:

> However, through rebellion against God at the devil's instigation and by his own free will, he deprived himself of these outstanding gifts. Rather, in their place he brought upon himself blindness, terrible darkness, futility, and distortion of judgement in his mind; perversity, defiance, and hardness in his heart and will; and finally impurity in all his emotions.[4]

And:

> Therefore, all people are conceived in sin and are born children of wrath, unfit for any saving good, inclined to evil, dead in their sins, and slaves to sin; without the grace of the regenerating Holy Spirit they are neither willing nor able to return to God, to reform their distorted nature, or even to dispose themselves to such reform.[5]

This was the mainstream view across almost all of Protestant Europe at this time and for many, many years afterwards. Lest we think this to be a Continental aberration, listen to the thoroughness with which 'total depravity' was defined in the famous Westminster Confession, the key formulary for English Reformed faith: 'By this sin they fell from their original righteousness and communion with God and so became dead in sin, and *wholly* defiled in all the parts and faculties of soul and body.'[6] This is all set in the cheery context of double predestination, which Calvin clearly taught:

> By predestination we mean the eternal decree of God, by which he determined with himself whatever he wished to happen with regard to every man. *All are not created on equal terms, but some are preordained to eternal life, others to*

eternal damnation; and accordingly, as each has been created for one or other of these ends, we say that he has been predestined to life or death.[7]

I can barely express the revulsion that this portrayal of God arouses in me.

It is not that I believe that humankind is not in need of the decisive divine initiative for salvation. The argument is really about just how helpless and damaged is humanity. A key verse in helping us to get the sense of this is Romans 3:23, and the key word is *hustereo* which means, in the sense used here, to 'fall short of' and so to lack. I have in mind the image of an arrow falling short of its target. This 'lacking' has a wide range of meanings. As Professor Dunn writes: 'So Paul probably here refers *both* to the glory lost in man's fall *and* to the glory that fallen man is failing to reach in consequence.'[8] This 'lacking' still applies to Christians. As Professor Cranfield writes: 'Here both the tense of the verb and the fact that its subject is *pantes* (all) should be noted. They clearly imply that not only all other men but also all believers still lack this "glory of God". Attempts to soften this or to explain it away have the disastrous effect of obscuring the transcendent majesty of the glory which is yet to be ours.'[9] We are damaged goods and without God's intervention we unravel completely. But, we are not without a key role in the journey of salvation. God requires of us a real contribution. And if we use this more open theological frame-work, then there may be more space for life-giving and digni-fied co-operation between God and human beings.

All this is part of the complex debate about what part God plays in our relationship with him, our salvation so to speak, and what part we play. Here is another issue where I will have to make some rather simplistic remarks. If the point of speaking about the dominant role of God in salvation is to undermine our ever-present temptation to try to justify ourselves – the classic English sin of self-righteousness perhaps – then it has value. If the point of speaking about the dominant role of God in salva-tion is to stress the essential part God's grace plays in our salvation, then again that has merit. It reminds us of God's over-whelming love for us. (So far Luther would be walking with me.) But if the point of speaking about God being the one who saves is that human beings have nothing to contribute – crudely speaking, if they can contribute nothing of worth to the process – then I want to object. Here I imagine Luther would part company with me.

Again it is worth pausing to remind ourselves of the thoroughness with which, for example, Luther erased human involvement: 'If we believe it to be true that God foreknows and predestines all things, that he can neither be mistaken in his foreknowledge nor hindered in his predestination, and that nothing takes place but as he wills it (as reason itself is forced to admit), then on the testimony of reason itself there cannot be any free choice in man or angel or any creature.'[10] This is the first of Luther's five conclusions in his treatise *The Bondage of the Will*, published in 1525 to contradict Erasmus' *Diatribe on Free Will*, published in 1524 (and which had simply stressed, arguing from Scripture, that human will is a secondary factor in salva-tion after the primary role taken by God's grace). It is striking that it was this issue that finally broke Luther's relationship with Erasmus – the extent and nature of human free will. This was not a new debate, was indeed highly technical theologically (for example, Luther allowed that humanity has the passive capacity of being capable of being taken hold of by God), and Luther was apparently not entirely consistent in his rejection of human choice. But he saw himself following clearly in the footsteps of Paul and Augustine in stressing that the human will was now so corrupted that human beings could not help themselves. Total depravity ...

Let me try to put this as crisply as possible. I believe passion-ately that if we are to get our church life right, we have to get our theology right, and that means saying that God works in co-operation with human beings, not by dominating them. I will try to fill out this vision a little more by drawing on some more ideas from Richard Hooker. Then, with a critical eye, I will look again at the Rule of Benedict because I think that, as well as containing much wisdom, it models inappropriate patterns of authority. Here especially I will remember the cautions with which I started this chapter about 'obedience'. Then I will try to give, briefly, a couple of more positive models before finishing as usual with a reflection on Luke's Gospel.

Richard Hooker – theologian of human dignity

To try to introduce the complex ideas of Richard Hooker, even in a few more paragraphs, is foolish beyond belief, but here goes ...[11] Hooker was a minor Oxford academic plucked by his political sponsors from academic life and dropped into national public controversy. He was in 1585 appointed Master of the Temple in London, the lawyers' church, where he had to confront one of the leading 'Puritans' of his day, Sunday by Sunday, as he and his opponent traded sermons like heavy-weight boxers trade blows. In the end Hooker won both politi-cally and theologically and his ideas are foundational for Anglican theology.

As we saw in Chapter 1, Richard Hooker started with the deep conviction that this was God's world, carefully ordered by a series of laws – we might say principles – which started within God himself and extended to every part of his creation. It is striking that Hooker stressed that God is a law for himself, in other words, not even God can act with total freedom.[12] Something is good because it is good, not just because God says it is good. God then laid down laws for the angels, for nature, and for human beings. If, then, human beings humbly applied their God-given reason to the world and their own behaviour, they could learn much about God and about how they ought to behave: this is the law of reason. So far, Hooker is very close to Aquinas. But he is also convinced, as a good Protestant, of the radical fallen-ness of this world and therefore of the crucial significance of Christ in redeeming it.[13] Hooker has a rich Patristic soteriology. Through Christ we are given his Spirit, set free from the consequences of our sinfulness, united with him and his life in the Church, his body, and ultimately in the

Godhead and 'deified': 'Finally, sith God hath deified our nature, though not by turning it into himself, yet by making it his own inseparable habitation, we cannot now conceive how God should without man either exercise divine power, or receive the glory of divine praise. For man is in both an associate of deity.'[14] As I argued in Chapter.1, God and humankind are now inseparable.

Hooker retains a strong doctrine of revelation. For example, he goes on to argue that Christ also reveals to us things that even our God-given reason could not discern, such as the resurrection of the body[15] and he has a classically Protestant doctrine of the perspicuity of Scripture: 'The main drift of the whole New Testament is that which St. John setteth down as the purpose of his own history; "These things are written, that ye might believe that Jesus is Christ the Son of God, and that in believing ye might have life through his name".'[16] But the overall effect is to reinforce, not denigrate, the sense of the value of humanity.

It is this significance that Hooker gives to humble human reason that makes him, for me, a theologian of human dignity. Rather than lots of quotations, let me give you one of my favourites. Hooker is discussing the authority of Scripture, which he regarded as infallible, but he comments: 'For our belief in the Trinity, the co-eternity of the Son of God with his Father, the proceeding of the Spirit from the Father and the Son, the duty of baptising infants: these with such other principal points, the necessity whereof is by none denied, are notwithstanding in Scripture no where to be found by express literal mention, only deduced they are out of Scripture by collection.'[17] Note here that Hooker is not wanting to undermine the authority of the Bible but he is pointing out how many crucial beliefs of the Church have to be derived from the Bible by a process of reasoned thought and argument, not simply read off the page. If we study the life of the early Church we see what a complex process this reasoned argument was.[18] But is this an accident, or is it sinful? No. Hooker responds to precisely this point:

So I trust that to mention what the Scripture of God leaveth unto the Church's discretion in some things, is not in any thing to impair the honour which the Church of God yieldeth to the sacred Scripture's perfection ... it is no more disgrace for Scripture to have left a number of other things free to be ordered at the discretion of the Church, than for nature to have left it unto the wit of man to devise his own attire.[19]

Here is a marvellous vision of the integrated world that God has created and which is part of his way of redemption. Just as God has left it to human beings to work out how to clothe themselves – a metaphor for growing into proper responsibility for our welfare – so even in areas of the truth about God himself and about the Christlike life and – for Hooker in particular – about how the Church is to be run, God requires us to work at it for ourselves. He does not always give us the answers on a plate. God's own truth is revealed by the process of reasoned human reflection on God's revelation, which itself comes to us in a range of ways. God has made us so that we can, need and ought to discern his purposes: by prayer; study of Scripture; reasoned discussion; listening to the wisdom and traditions of the past, Christian and non-Christian; all working together. This is giving a high value to human responsibility, maturity and dignity.[20]

We have seen in Chapter 1 how angry Hooker became when he sensed that this integrated and dignified world that God had created was being undermined. Why was he so angry? In part because of the dishonesty of his 'Puritan' opponents who, of course, used their own reason while claiming to despise reason. In part also because they used Scripture, as Hooker saw it, to oppress and devalue others. But at heart, he was, I think, angry because their theology devalued the world that God had made and the human beings whom God had placed at its pinnacle, however flawed they might be. Hooker fought what he saw as contempt for humankind because he was convinced of the gifts that God had given human beings, including crucially, reason and responsibility.

Benedict on humility and obedience

I turn again now to the Rule of Benedict.[21] I am going to ask some critical questions of the Rule, but I want to start by stressing again some of its profound treasures, so that we can find some good old-fashioned 'Anglican' balance on this. First, while I will be critical of the role of obedience in the Rule, Benedict's monastery was not a crude dictatorship. A recent study reflects insightfully about the nature of authority in the Rule of Benedict:

> People in the sixth century were not constitutionalists, and Benedict's constitutional restraints on the abbot were nugatory. I am speaking of restraint by Benedict's assumption of shared moral and spiritual objectives; by the erection of a yardstick external to his will against which the abbot's actions could be measured; and by the development of a notion of stewardship which made the abbot accountable to God for his flock.[22]

The abbot was initially elected by his fellow monks. He then had considerable authority but he was to model his life on Christ. Some of Benedict's most lyrical writing is about the abbot. In Chapter 27 he reminds the abbot: 'Let him know that what he has undertaken is the charge of weakly souls, and not a tyranny over the strong ...'[23] The point of the severe communal discipline under which a Benedictine monk lived was to help genuine and deep spiritual growth. In a moment we will look at Chapter 7 of the Rule in some detail, but it finishes with a wonderful vision of a liberated Christian life:

> Then when all degrees of humility have been climbed, the monk will presently come to that perfect love of God, which casts out all fear; whereby he will begin to observe without labour, as though naturally and by habit, all those precepts which formerly he did not observe without fear: no longer for fear of hell, but for love of Christ and through good habit and delight in virtue. And this will the Lord

deign to show by the power of his Spirit in his workman now cleansed from vice and sin.[24]

The purpose of the Rule was to bring the monk to the place where he followed Christ out of sheer love, not from fear or to gain a reward.

In reflecting on the Rule of Benedict it has come home to me that in two fundamental ways my vision of the Christian life is very different from Benedict's. First, in that he thinks that the work of driving sin out of a human being is a long, difficult and demanding task, and second, that he thinks it can be done. In comparison, I am less committed to perfection in this life but also less optimistic about it. I want to stress again that the purpose of Benedict's tough discipline was to change lives. A new novice coming into a Benedictine community vowed 'stability, conversion of his life, and obedience'.[25] (Chastity was, of course, taken for granted.) But note here that the purpose is 'conversion of his life'. It does not mean a series of 'Billy Graham' type experiences but rather sanctification. If we can say it simply, holistic conversion (see Chapter 6).

One of the key ways in which the monk was to be converted was by obedience. This is in part spelt out in the disciplinary elements of the Rule. The monk was to obey orders from a superior without delay or question or resentment, as if it were a word from the Lord.[26] While he could question the order if he felt it was impossible, in the end he was required 'to obey out of love, trusting in the assistance of God'.[27] (One of my favourite bits of the Rule is the instruction that when a monk sins, if he is too young or stupid to understand why he has transgressed, he is to be beaten. Only the mature and intelligent were internally excommunicated.[28])

This conviction that we will hear from God and become Christlike by obedience to another human authority is deeply alien to an Anglican frame of mind. (For that reason I am wary of criticising it too much. Coming from the Anglican tradition, I more than most may have something to learn here.) But for reasons I laid out at the beginning of this chapter, unquestioning obedience to another human authority leaves me feeling very uneasy. Anglicans are profoundly convinced of the fallibility of human authority structures, in the world and in the Church, and we are rightly hesitant of anything which smacks of absolutism.[29] While the abbot who issues the orders may be under the ultimate authority of God, we know in the meantime how much harm can be done.

But there is a deeper reason why I am cautious about this pattern of Christian life. The longest chapter in the Rule is Chapter 7, 'Of Humility'. That in itself is very significant. Benedict clearly believed that pride was of the essence of human sinfulness. Self-exaltation was the road to destruction: 'Brothers, divine Scripture calls to us saying: "Whoever exalts himself shall be humbled and whoever humbles himself shall be exalted." In saying this, therefore, it shows us that every exaltation is a kind of pride ...'[30] To combat this, Benedict described twelve 'degrees' of humility through which a monk had to pass before reaching the state of liberation we described a bit earlier. These start with the essential fear of God and God's punishment: 'The first degree of humility then is that a man keep the fear of God before his eyes ...' and 'how hell will burn for their sins those that despise Him ...'[31] Progress requires, of course, the rejection of our own will and of our 'evil desires': 'We are indeed forbidden to do our own will by Scripture ... We must be on guard, then, against evil desires, for death lies close by the gate of delight ...'[32] Degrees 3 and 4 are about obedience within the community: '... a man for the love of God subjects himself to his superior in all obedience ...' and '... that meeting in this obedience with difficulties and contradictions and even injustice, he should with a quiet mind hold fast to patience, and, enduring, neither tire nor run away ...'[33] Benedict justifies much of this section directly from the example of Jesus.

Degree 5 is confession to the abbot of sinfulness, especially 'secret sins': '... he humbly confess and conceal not from the abbot any evil thoughts that enter his heart, and any secret sins that he has committed ...'[34] Degree 6 is particularly humiliating and feels, frankly, dishonest and unhelpful: 'The sixth step of humility is that a monk is content with the lowest and most menial treatment, and regards himself as a poor and worthless workman in whatever task he is given …'[35] Degree 7 requires the monk not just to say that he is the most sinful, but even more to believe it inwardly: '… he should not only in his speech declare himself lower and of less account than all others, but should in his own inmost heart believe it …'[36]

Degree 8 is about obedience to the Rule and to superiors again. Degree 9 is about silence and degree 10 is about restricting laughter: '… a monk should do nothing except what is commended …'; 'a monk should restrain his tongue and keep silence, not speaking until he is questioned …'; '… that he be not ready and prompt to laughter …'[37] Benedict seems to have seen laughter as an activity of the fool – citing Ecclesiasticus 21:20. Those of us who have read Umberto Eco's *The Name of the Rose* will see here how well informed Eco is about medieval spirituality and theology and how acutely he depicts inhumane Christianity. Note these two little bits of dialogue which illuminate bigger themes in this book. Jorge, the fierce old Benedictine argues with William the Franciscan:

> 'John Chrysostom said that Christ never laughed.'
> 'Nothing in his human nature forbade it,' William remarked, 'because laughter, as the theologians teach, is proper to man'.[38]

Earlier Jorge has expressed the Benedictine suspicion of the new Franciscans: 'I heard persons laughing at laughable things and I reminded them of one of the principles of our Rule … But you come from another order, where I am told that merriment, even the most inopportune, is viewed with indulgence.'[39] Why is it that laughter, one of the psychological, physiological and spiritual sources of relief for humankind should be forbidden? Why is it that in classic Christian art, of East or West, depictions of the adult Christ smiling are so rare?[40]

Degree 11 draws 9 and 10 together to produce quietly, seriously and briefly spoken monks: '… a monk, when he speaks, do so gently and without laughter, humbly and seriously, in few and sensible words and without clamour ...'[41] And degree 12 is what I understand to be called 'the courtesy of the eyes': the monk is required to go about when working or in the monastery or out in the world, with 'his head bowed and his eyes downcast, pondering always the guilt of his sins and considering that he is about to be brought before the dread judgement seat of God'.[42] It is difficult to read – especially this last instruction – without getting the sense that these disciplines run the risk, in all but the wisest and most psychologically and spiritually balanced of hands, of distorting or even crushing the human spirit. Is there a confusion here between 'self-exaltation' or pride and proper human dignity, responsibility and maturity? Few modern religious orders would follow this teaching today literally and we need to be honest about the fact that we have changed and why.

Our response

If we read historical accounts of monastic life, or even some quite modern ones, we will find examples of this sort of discipline and of its destructive consequences. You may have seen Karen Armstrong on the TV on one of those late-night religious chat-shows. She has become a prolific if rather angry writer on religion. But her views make much more sense when you read her account of her time as a young nun. She is very clear that she is describing a pre-Vatican II experience and she writes of the remarkable changes in her convent after the Council. But the deep structures of obedience remained embedded in the Order. One of her fellow sisters, suffering from chronic *anorexia nervosa* quotes the Rule of Ignatius, the founder of the Jesuits: '"Everyone should give himself up into the hands of his superiors", Rebecca quoted St Ignatius' Rule of Obedience, her eyes steadily boring into mine, "as a dead body allows itself to be treated in any manner whatever".'[43] In reflection Armstrong writes: 'Huddled in her mackintosh she was shivering violently, freezing cold on a mild, even warm summer day. Of course she would stay where she was, even if it killed her. A nun was meant to die to herself. Rebecca was just taking the idea to its logical conclusion.'[44]

It is difficult to get the balance right in evaluating this way of life. I personally appreciate very much going to stay with, for example, the Anglican Franciscan friars at Alnmouth and, as a college tutor, one of my jobs used to be finding spiritual directors for our ordinands. They would often ask for a monk or a nun, someone whose life had been shaped by discipline and prayer. The Church has benefited hugely from the service that monks and nuns have brought to it and for many people it has been a life-giving way. But it seems to me there are elements of the theology that lie behind obedience, as well as elements of this actual way of life (which for so long provided the highest ideals for the Church), which can be deathly. An authoritarian God leading to an authoritarian Church, leading to inappropriate and excessive religious obedience, is one of them. It can crush the human spirit and warp the Church. It can be inhumane.

Many of our churches in the West carry a legacy of this culture of obedience, however ameliorated or attenuated. The churches remain one of the most visibly hierarchical institutions in a profoundly non-deferential society. Remember that modern Anglican clergy, for example, still promise obedience to their bishop (even if it is only in 'all things lawful and honest'[45]) and kneel before him in a gesture of feudal obedience. (My Methodist and Roman Catholic ordained colleagues can, in theory, still simply be 'sent' by their church authorities, though both denominations have 'humanised' their appointment systems in our generation.)

I am not wanting to argue against obedience *per se*. Any institution, indeed any community, needs clear authority structures to function. The lack of deference in modern British society can be highly problematic as well as being a sign of liberation from previous oppressive social structures. Ask any teacher. It is striking how the Armed Forces, the most 'obedient' section of our society, remain the institution of last resort when our country faces a serious crisis, whether it is 'foot and mouth', a firefighters' strike, or war. The Church, too, needs to be able as an institution and as a community, to 'get things done'. As a priest, one of my convictions is that I am a person in orders and so 'under orders', having taken, indeed, vows of obedience and commitment. But if as a Church we are serious about modelling mature adult relationships of co-operation and responsibility, real collegiality, 'every member ministry', or 'the priesthood of all believers', then do we not need to revisit some of our deepest assumptions about obedience and how that is exemplified in the patterns of life and public worship and liturgy of our churches? If we want to be counter-cultural, not just by retaining appropriate obedience, but more strikingly by modelling a different pattern of authority and leadership in ways that follow Jesus' radical standards – 'it shall not be so among you'[46] – then this too may be a powerful witness.

To take one example: I am always struck by the liturgy at the Maundy Thursday service in Durham Cathedral for the renewal of vows, where the bishops are asked by a *lay* person to confirm their consecration vows.[47] Or we might reflect on how Robin Greenwood suggests new liturgies to make it clear that, for example at parochial level, we mean what we say about 'working collaboratively', whereas in fact we often remain stuck with services which focus mostly on the priest:

> Priest: 'Although I believe I have been called simultan-
> eously by you, the bishop and God, to be your parish
> priest, please never forget that I am like you, a baptized
> member of this congregation.'
> People: 'Yes, we are glad to hear you acknowledge that at
> heart you are one of us by baptism, but we also ask you, for
> as long as it seems right from both sides, to be president of
> this local community in a spirit of persuasive and
> courteous leadership.'[48]

(This might need polishing if it was to work as real liturgy ...)
To say it again, we firstly and fundamentally need to renew our understanding of how God relates to human beings, if we are to renew our understanding of how we relate to each other.

Does God respect human beings? That is the question that has lurked behind much of this chapter. Much classic Christian theology would lead us to believe that he does not. To return to some reflections on the doctrines of 'original sin' or 'total depravity', arguably doctrines that lie behind much of the pastoral practice of respectively Catholicism and Protestantism; bluntly speaking I think both doctrines have been used to abuse people. If someone is unavoidably sinful in their very self or, worse, sinful in every area of their life, how can God treat them with dignity or respect? In both theological systems, a human being in those circumstances is, classically, under God's judgement. (Hence Augustine's conviction that unbaptised babies go to Limbo, a doctrine which is still wreaking pastoral havoc 1600 years later.[49]) This contributes directly to an authoritarian pattern of church life.

Therefore, for example, we need to be careful in how we handle, especially, scriptural material on sin and on obedience. Thus I have already reviewed Romans 3:23 as a centrepiece of classic Protestant theology. The bulk of Romans 3 is a catena of quotations from the Psalms to prove that all humanity is fallen. It is a piece of typically Pauline exegesis of the Old Testament, subverting the other tradition in the Psalms where the writer asserts his/her righteousness over against the sinners and uses it as a basis to appeal to God. For Paul the crucial point here is that Jews are as fallen as Gentiles, but his rhetorical theological point has been systematised into meaning that all humanity is wholly sinful and that the key human sin is self-righteousness and self-justification before God. This is such a crucial text and a crucial point in the overall argument of this book, that I will quote at some length the – to my mind – key modern interpretation of it. Professor Dunn carefully unpicks the Reformation understanding of 'works of the law' as being equivalent to 'self-righteousness' or 'earned salvation':

> There is, we might say, therefore, a hidden middle term in 3:20 between 'works of the law' and 'shall be justified' – a middle term which Reformation exegesis largely missed,

> as indeed also most exegesis deriving from the controversies of the Reformation period in general. The connection of thought in 3:20 does not run directly from 'works of the law' to 'shall be justified' and is not aimed directly at works of the law *as a means to achieving* righteousness and acquittal. The connection of thought is more indirect, of works of the law *as a way of identifying the individual with* the people whom God has chosen and will vindicate and of *maintaining his status within* that people. In a word the hidden middle term is the function of the law as an identity factor, the social function of the law as marking out the people of the law in their distinctiveness (circumcision, food laws, etc.).[50]

In other words, Jews knew themselves to be 'saved by grace' too and we cannot use this passage to argue against human endeavour *per se*.

There may be moments when we feel, or think of ourselves as helpless and utterly sinful and dependent, for good or ill, but it is never the whole story. So these verses from Romans must be held in tension with other verses that show Paul's clear stress on human responsibility and capability alongside God's action – classically Philippians 2:12–13: 'work out your own salvation with fear and trembling; for it is God who is at work in you, enabling you both to will and to work for his good pleasure.'[51] Again, this is a complex case to make. It is back to my argument with Luther. Are we utterly hopeless and helpless, or is there work for us to do, even if God's love and action is primary? Further, any use of the language of sin that smacks of contempt for human beings must set off alarm bells immediately.

I would like to suggest that there is another important strand to the biblical story. One of the pieces of study that has most impact on our ordinands is to reflect on the lament tradition in the Old Testament. They realise that not only do large sections of the Wisdom literature reflect a debate with God about how he deals with people and even his created world, but the Psalms – the public songs of worship of Israel – are full of lament, complaint, grief, anger. My personal favourite is Psalm 44, which begins with the classic recounting of the triumphs of God but then suddenly asks God why he has stopped blessing Israel, and why his people are suffering terribly, because they have done nothing wrong:

> All this has come upon us, yet we have not forgotten you,
> Or been false to your covenant.
> Our heart has not turned back,
> Nor have our steps departed from your way,
> Yet you have broken us in the haunt of jackals,
> And covered us with deep darkness.[52]

Unlike some of the lament psalms that finish on a note of resolution, this one finishes with a plaintive bargaining note – familiar to many of us – reminding God of his qualities and almost trying to embarrass him into helping. Indeed the psalmist is trying to wake God up:

> Rouse yourself! Why do you sleep, O Lord?
> Awake, do not cast us off for ever!
> Why do you hide your face?
> Why do you forget our affliction and oppression?
> For we sink down to the dust;
> Our bodies cling to the ground.
> Rise up, come to our help.
> Redeem us for the sake of your steadfast love.

We often feel profoundly uncomfortable with this self-justifying and sometimes apparently self-righteous element in the Psalms and try to spiritualise it away, but there is a simple human reality behind them: the cry, 'Lord, I don't deserve this treatment'. In my experience of watching other people suffer, I think this is often simply true. But instead of being crushed or excluded, the angry psalmist is held within the people of faith. Indeed these psalms of lament were given formal approval by being used in public worship. If we take the doctrine of the canon of Scripture seriously, we can hear these psalms of lament as part of the Word of God. Crudely speaking, we could see them as having God's seal of approval. In the Old Testament, God is not frightened of dialogue, of conflict even. As Walter Brueggemann, the greatest living scholar on the lament tradition writes, in respect of individual psychological, emotional and spiritual well-being: 'The absence of lament makes a religion of coercive obedience the only possibility.'[53] He goes further with respect to society: 'When the lament form is censured, justice questions cannot be asked and eventually become invisible and illegitimate.'[54] In other words, there is a direct link between a theology of God that does not allow human beings the right to answer him back and a social and economic and political and ecclesiastical system that will not allow one human being to answer back to another. Theological totalitarianism leads all too swiftly to human totalitarianism.

Finally, we have seen how, for example, Benedict appealed to the example of Jesus to justify severe obedience. The strand of the New Testament that highlights that it is Jesus' obedience, above all, which demonstrates his sonship is strong. Hebrews expresses this particularly sharply and reinforces my earlier argument for taking the combined humanity and the divinity of Jesus with real seriousness: 'Although he was a Son, he learned obedience through what he suffered; and having been made perfect, he became the source of eternal salvation for all who obey him …' (Heb. 5:8–9). In other words, Jesus needed to develop spiritually during his life. This is why the Christology of Hebrews is so striking: 'This theme [Jesus' learning] is understandably rare elsewhere in the NT, since in the Gospels Jesus is presented as the teacher and his followers as *mathetai* [disciples], while outside the Gospel and Acts *mathetes* is hardly used at all. What is most distinctive in this verse is the clear statement that the sufferings of Jesus had effects on Jesus himself.'[55] Nevertheless, I must make the simple point that this was an obedience rooted in love and intimacy and for the good of others. Could these be tests of our use of 'obedience' but strengthened by an awareness of our own greater fallibility?

All this is not an argument for easy, cosy chumminess with God. Intimacy yes, chumminess no. We are creatures of a different order of existence to God. So much of his very essence is beyond our grasp that silent reverence is often the only right way to be before him. There is an obedience that properly flows from that. But the incarnation both shows us how God wished to reveal himself when he came as a human being – humble and accessible – and shows us how the Son relates to the Father, a relationship of intimate love. Here is the paradox of Christian faith: the unimaginable becomes, incomprehensibly, touchable. In other words, how humble is God? Anglicans constantly pray to an 'Almighty God', rightly remembering his indescribable immensity, but do we pray enough to a gentle God who came to us as a human being, born naked and dying naked? If God can be that humble to win us, how ought his people, his Church, to treat each other and those for whom he died? Can we conceive of a Church where people are treated consistently with honour and respect as partners with God in creation and redemption? I am not asking for a soft Church where anything goes, quite the reverse. But I am dreaming of a Church where all are treated with dignity leading to flourishing and freedom.

Gospel reflection: Jesus against legalistic authoritarianism

All this leads us to our Gospel reflection where Jesus confronts authoritarian legalism. The passage is Luke 6:1–5.

> One sabbath while Jesus was going through the cornfields, his disciples plucked some heads of grain, rubbed them in their hands, and ate them. But some of the Pharisees said, 'Why are you doing what is not lawful on the sabbath?' Jesus answered, 'Have you not read what David did when he and his companions were hungry? He entered the house of God and took and ate the bread of the Presence, which it is not lawful for any but the priests to eat, and gave some to his companions?' Then he said to them, 'The Son of Man is lord of the sabbath.'

Points to ponder

- This is a story that Luke has probably taken from Mark (2:23–8) and adapted slightly. Indeed Luke makes one important omission that we will note in a moment.

- The outline of the story is clear. The Pharisees – and commentators wonder if there is a memory here of them spying on Jesus and his disciples – challenge the disciples for 'harvesting' on the sabbath. Luke fills out what the disciples did, compared with Mark. They pluck the grain, rub it in their hands to get at the edible part and then eat it. Now it was permissible to pluck grains of cereal like this. Provided that those passing through a field did not use a sickle, they were allowed to glean in this way. But not on the sabbath. By their simple action the disciples had reaped, threshed and winnowed on the sabbath, all of which were forbidden. It was also permissible to eat on the sabbath. What was not permissible was to prepare a meal on the sabbath. That had to be done before the sabbath commenced. So the disciples had broken this law too.

- The Christian commentators are agreed in their condemnation of the Pharisees' question.[56] They are described as 'legalistic', 'obsessive', living in a relationship with an 'aloof God' with whom they have no sense of 'grace' or 'trust' or 'confidence'. Their behaviour appears 'fantastic', out of proportion, the resort to fierce rule-keeping in the absence of love. I could go on. Yet the Pharisees were lay people trying to live holy lives in keeping with the Old Testament and the rabbis' teaching. The point was to take holiness out of the Temple and away from just the priests and encourage everyone to live holy lives so that Israel would be a holy people. That seems entirely commendable and in keeping with some strands of Protestantism. They wanted the best – God's rule on earth – but it appears that they actually encouraged the worst: inhumane religion. We can only touch on it here, but one of the most valuable books on religious self-deception is *Suspicion and Faith: The Religious Uses of Atheism'* by Merrold Westphal. He studies Marx, Freud and Nietzsche and argues that instead of merely refuting them, Christians need to hear their criticisms and allow them to provoke us to self-examination. We need to do this he says, 'because their critique of religion seems to be (1) all too true all too much of the time and (2) a modern echo of an ancient assault on the devotion of the devout, the one developed by Jesus and the prophets of Israel.'[57] Very briefly, Westphal shows us for example, how often religious persons, Jew or Christian, deceive themselves about the real nature of their faith. Marx's little phrase, 'religion is the opium of the people', was meant to describe both how the poor were kept in obedience by being taught that this was how God wanted the world to be, but also how the consciences of the rich were quietened by the same beliefs. Bad religion and self-deceived believers – this nightmare lies behind much of this book. What is striking is how often it comes as a shock to our students that Christians could be self-deceived about themselves. Here, in this story, we see the Pharisees, the supposed model of holiness for their contemporaries, using their rules to oppress others, being self-deceived.

• The story itself is interesting because Jesus refutes the Pharisees by pointing to the Scriptures, to their own tradition, which they have not read with open eyes. He reminds them how David had taken and eaten the holy bread from the 'house of God', bread which, in the Torah, was explicitly reserved for the priests (Lev. 24:5–9), thereby breaking Old Testament law on the basis of the need of his soldiers for food. The principle of need before law had already been established in Judaism but the Pharisees had forgotten that. They were blind to the meaning of their own Scriptures. They are not alone in that. When the Church of England researched our lectionary back in the 1980s, we discovered how often stories of women had been omitted from the lectionary.[58] Because of the male prejudice of the Church and of its liturgists, the role of women in the story of faith had in fact been substantially down-played. But my guess is that if you had asked the lectionary compilers, they would not have noticed

79

that they were operating according to skewed criteria. This is where the much despised 'political correctness' comes into its own, revealing the structures of prejudice so deeply embedded that they shape how we see things and what language we use to describe what we think we see. For me, one of the exciting things about this story in Luke is well put by John Drury: 'The past is not the preserve of the conservatives'.[59]

- There is a little controversy in the commentators about the point of the story. Some want to stress that when Jesus uses the example of David, he is making an implicit messianic point. He is the new David and therefore has authority over the laws of the people of God, even laws in the Torah. So the climax of the story for Luke is: 'Hence the Son of Man is lord of the sabbath'. But Mark has two sayings by Jesus, one of which Luke omits: 'The sabbath was made for humankind not humankind for the sabbath.' This was in fact a version of a rabbinic saying. It seems to me that here Jesus is laying down a wider principle about the relationship between law and human flourishing. As Barclay notes, if the rabbis could reshape the law on the basis of human need, how much more will Jesus with his Gospel of love do that.[60]

- Again we must remind ourselves that while we might regard rethinking the law of the sabbath as a minor amendment, for the Jews this was a fundamental test of their obedience to God. It was one of the Ten Commandments personally delivered by God on the tablets of stone. It was an obedience that had marked the Jews off from their neighbours for centuries, at some risk to their own well-being. But Jesus makes the holy sabbath not primarily a test of obedience to God, but something that is under the authority of the principle of love. If the law is not life-giving, then change it. Do not simply obey.

Prayer

For our closing prayer, I have chosen some words from Jim Cotter, a radical Anglican priest, now living on the coast of

Wales caring for a tiny hillside church. He wrote 'A Litany of Repentance for Misuse of Authority in the Church.'[61] It is immensely powerful and uncomfortable. I quote only part of it.

We have been deceived by the lust for power and have not embodied the power of love ...

We have followed too much worldly ways and lorded it over your followers ...

We have hardened our hearts for fear of losing control ...

We have colluded with thrones and carved chairs and not been content with stools and benches ...

We have used the excuse that people love to have it so, and we have not gently but firmly insisted on the Gospel way ...

We have not been seen to enjoy the company of the stigmatized lest our reputation should suffer ...

We have dismissed years of service with a curt wave of the hand ...

We have cloaked our iron fists in velvet gloves and believed God to be like that too ...

We have not had the courage to use our authority to restrain the bullies and protect the pioneers: we have not passed on the uncomfortable messages of the prophets ...

We have abused those in our care, children, women, men – spiritually, emotionally, sexually, our guilt and their shame colluding in a hidden silence ...

We have cut off the divorced and the laicised as though they had never been ...

We have refused to recognize love in unexpected places ...

We have colluded with those who would project sanctity on to us and place us on pedestals ...

We have pretended that evil is no longer mixed with good in our hearts and deeds ...

We have used paper and computers, colleagues and diaries, to protect us from the awkward and the needy ...

81

We have subtly and smilingly assumed that we know best, treating congregations as if they knew nothing …

We have delegated tasks and taken them back when they have been done more slowly than we would like …

We have put our personal relationships and friendships under strain by allowing our role to take over our lives …

None of us has done all of these things, all of us have done some of them.

Sincerity of motive has sometimes blinded us to institutional evil, with which we have colluded and in which we have blindly played our part.

For we belong to one another, we inherit the thistles of our ancestors' sins,

We have contributed, culpably or not, by our own misdeeds,

And we are called to bear one another's burdens …

And a prayer for our future ministry:

Living God, Communion of Eternal Love,
whose Word insists even while it whispers,
whose Touch is adamant, however gentle it may be,
requiring of us that we respond in faith:
>   in drawing nearer to your Church's heart,
>   may we draw even closer to your world,
>   in our families and among our friends,
>   in our communities and the places of our work;
encourage us to follow the example of the One,
who took the Towel and gave us of the Body,
who went the Way of the Cross and gave us of the Blood,
without whose friendship we shall misuse the power you
>   place,
as with the shepherd's Staff, into our hands.
Amen.

CHAPTER FOUR

From Chastity to the Joy of Sexuality

Inhuman sexuality

I would like to begin with a personal story. In former times, when a person went on a Church of England conference for ordination selection, one of the exercises that we were required to undertake was the small group exercise. We were given a topic – a question or a quotation – which we had to introduce in a minute, then chair a discussion for eight minutes and then sum up the discussion. It could be about any current issue in the life of the Church or the country. I got a classic: '"Page 3 girls are wholesome and fun" says Peter Bruinvels, MP and member of General Synod.' I am afraid I just burst out laughing, which may not have been the right response. But I soon found myself in a heated debate with a rather more conservative group member. He maintained that 'Page 3 girls' were wrong because they offended against God's holiness. I was arguing that they were wrong because they demeaned women, and therefore offended God's holiness. It may seem like arguing about angels on pinheads, but I still think I was arguing for an important principle: that we cannot separate God's holiness, his moral character, from his love for people. His holiness, defining it here as a moral rather than a numinous quality, is always a relational holiness. The senior selector later asked me why none of us had had the honesty to say what some of us (it was an all-male selection conference) might have been feeling; that 'Page 3 girls' might also be 'fun'!

More seriously, it is too easy to find horrifying material in church history when it comes to the Church's attitudes towards and teaching on human relationships and sexuality. One of my 'favourites' is the story of Thomas Aquinas, who had decided to become a Dominican. At the time they were a new, rather extreme and disreputable order. His family wanted him to become a Benedictine, because that was a highly respected order, suitable for the minor aristocracy. So his family kidnapped him and locked him in one of their castles. Then, the *coup de grace*, they hired a prostitute and sent her into the room. Thomas, however, was not so easily seduced, and drove her from the room with a brand plucked from the fire. His first biographer tells us that ever thereafter he avoided women as a man might avoid a snake.[1]

There are several interesting things to notice here. First, that his family obviously assumed that if Thomas had sex with a prostitute he would no longer feel fit to join a holy order like the Dominicans. But second, presumably he would not now be so unholy that he couldn't join the Benedictines! I think in our age we would say that he needed post-trauma counselling or family therapy. I don't think he got it.

As I said, it is too easy to duplicate stories like this. Several books have chronicled patriarchy – that is, the male oppression of women and its grim consequences – which is a great cloud hanging over the reputation of the Church.[2] As we turn specifically to the issue of human sexuality, I want to remind us of the overall point that we noted at the beginning of this book; the Church being portrayed in modern culture is doomed and deservedly so.

I think the contrast with much of the past is striking. If I was going to treat myself to one more huge generalisation, I would say that whereas for most of its history the Church has been a progressive institution – there is some argument about the transition from the Anglo-Saxon to the Norman Church in England – I would argue that until the mid-seventeenth century, the Church is on the side of the angels when it comes to issues of human liberation. But that increasingly thereafter, and especially in the last century, the Church has come to be seen as an oppressive force.

Even in the nineteenth century, while we all like to mock the Victorians for covering up piano legs so that young ladies did not get improper thoughts (and I am really not convinced that is true[3]), many Victorian Christians were campaigning for the safety and freedom of women and children. It was not universal, of course, and there is a strong feminist case that Victorian Britain saw the role of women being compressed back into the home, but there are also shining counter-examples, like Josephine Butler from Northumberland. She is one of my personal heroines. Butler came from a liberal Christian home and was set for life as the wife of a minor academic, when she tragically lost a daughter. To console herself in her grief, she befriended a Liverpool prostitute and ended by bringing her back to her own home to nurse her as she died from a sexually transmitted disease. Not content with a growing ministry to these outcasts of Victorian society, an extraordinary ministry for a woman of her class, she then became involved in the campaign against the Contagious Diseases Acts. This may have passed you by, but in 1864 the British Government passed an Act requiring the inspection of prostitutes in military towns for sexually transmitted diseases, with imprisonment and compulsory treatment for the infected. Apart from the indignity of such a law, and its injustice in that there were no similar penalties for men, there was also the not inconsiderable risk that ordinary working-class women living in these same areas would find themselves arrested, forcibly inspected and humiliated. And Butler – despite much ridicule and personal abuse – led the hugely unrespectable public campaign for the repeal of the Act. It was a campaign that spread internationally as she discovered similar attitudes and legislation in other parts of the world. It is a remarkable story, not celebrated often enough.[4]

But that is not the reputation of the Church now. Now in the West we are seen as restrictive, as enemies of human and especially women's liberation. We are the reactionaries. One key point to stress again is that human relationships and sexuality are now seen as issues of justice, not of personal morality. Hence, the Church is seen as repressive and our traditional arguments sound more than irrelevant, they sound abusive and prejudiced. It does not matter how often we put a clergyman up on the TV to say how much the Church approves of sex within marriage (and there are few more embarrassing sights), all across the board – whether it is contraception, pre-marital sex, divorce, homosexuality – we are portrayed as guardians of an archaic and prejudiced era.[5] I wonder if our churches have quite appreciated the huge damage being done to them by the scandal of child sexual abuse and if we have realised that this ought to provoke as profound a reformation as in the sixteenth century. Anyone familiar with the history of Ireland in the last generation cannot fail to see how the once dominant moral, spiritual and practical authority of the Roman Catholic Church has been broken by the seemingly endless stream of abuse scandals. To the extent that, as a recent article put it: 'Clerical collars are now a rare sight in Dublin. The scandal of sexual abuse by priests and members of religious orders has made their wearers reluctant to don them in public.'[6] This in Ireland! (I write as an Irishman.)

To put this with brutal simplicity, we must recognise that the level of abuse that has happened, and the institutional secrecy that has surrounded it, flow directly from the distorted understandings of authority that we explored in the last chapter, especially as they have been focused on profound inequality between men and women in the Church's teaching and life, as well as from wilful blindness about human sexuality. Structural abuse requires structural as well as theological change, real repentance and changes of thinking and behaviour as we face up to the twisted values of the Church, concerned to protect its public reputation rather than the vulnerable. Further, in this context, where we have such gruesome skeletons in our cupboards and where we have had to learn from 'the world' about orthopraxis (right behaviour), we may reflect that Christians might need to speak about issues of human sexuality with a measure of humility and teachability.

For Christianity is now being portrayed as the implacable enemy of any sensual pleasure. Have you read the novel *Chocolat*?[7] The story is of Vianne, a travelling women and her child – she is portrayed as in some sense descended from an ancient line of witches or wise women – who arrive in a very sleepy little French country town, where she sets up a *chocolaterie*, that is a shop where you can buy the most exquisite chocolates as well as drink a wider variety of what the English would call 'hot chocolate' than we could ever imagine. The chocolate is of course an instrument and a symbol of sensual pleasure, all the more threatening because the shop opens during Lent and she is working towards a great celebration of chocolate at Easter. Note some of the little features of this novel: the mentally unstable, repressed and ultimately psychotic *curé*; one of his protégés is a wife-beater and in the course of the novel his wife finds the courage to leave home and finds a refuge with Vianne; Vianne's lover is a gypsy whose people are of course attacked by the hate-filled *curé*. I could go on. Simply put, read this book if you want to get a vivid portrayal of the Church in a negative light. It sums up so much of what I have been trying to explore. The *curé* becomes increasingly disturbed:

> I know my duty. I sleep very little now, having extended my penance to include those stray moments of abandon. My joints ache but I welcome the distraction. Physical pleasure is the crack into which the devil sends his roots. I avoid sweet scents. I eat a single meal a day, and then only the plainest and most flavourless of foods. When I am not going about my duties in the parish I work in the churchyard, digging the beds and weeding around the graves. There has been neglect there for the past two years, and I am conscious of a feeling of unease when I see what riot there is now in that hitherto orderly garden. Lavender, marjoram, goldenrod and purple sage have shot up in lavish abandon amongst the grasses and blue thistles. So many scents disturb me. I would like orderly rows of shrubs and flowers, perhaps with a box hedge around the whole.[8]

In the end the poor *curé* does go mad, breaks into the shop with the intent of smashing the chocolates but succumbs to temptation and instead of smashing them stuffs them into his mouth. All this on the morning of Easter Sunday:

> 6am. *He is risen!* The sound of the bells jangles me out of my enchantment. I find myself sitting on the floor, spilled chocolates around me, as if I have indeed, as I imagined, rolled in them ... *He is risen!* Drunkenly I stagger to my feet. In five minutes the early worshippers will begin to arrive for Mass. Already I must have been missed ... *He is risen!* And that was how they saw me, père, crouching in the ruins of her window, face smeared with chocolate, eyes haggard. From nowhere people seemed to come running to her aid ... And the laughter. God! The laughter. And all the time the bells are ringing *He is risen* across St Jerôme's square.[9]

Here is an author writing who has seen something of the inhuman, festering and destroying side of Christianity and described it unforgettably. Here the Church is portrayed as a defeated enemy of human pleasure, even of human life.

Now I want to make a very important point. Much of the Church's caution about human sexuality is very well justified, given the way Western society seems to have descended into a sex-obsessed state. The sheer size of the sex 'industry' is terrifying. We could take pornography as an example, especially as it is becoming increasingly 'cool' to commend it and anti-libertarian to criticise it, as it seeks respectability. A 2003 BBC Radio Four programme estimated that in the USA the porn 'industry' is worth $5 billion a year, at least a quarter of the size of Hollywood.[10] Later the same year the *Guardian* estimated it at $15 billion.[11] It is of course far from the happy free idyll that its wealthy propagandists make out. In the same BBC programme a leading pornographer stated that the majority of recent USA pornography features anal sex between men and women, which strikingly *The Joy of Sex*, the modern groundbreaking work on sexual practices, refused to describe on the grounds of the health risks and lack of pleasure for most women.[12] What is most chilling is the reluctance of many of the producers and directors to participate themselves and above all to allow their wives/girlfriends or daughters to participate.

Pornography is a world built on injustice and deceit. Margaret Atwood in her 2003 Booker-nominated novel *Oryx and Crake* depicts a nightmarish future of climate collapse, violent unjust social segregation and scientific manipulation of humans and animals. One of the few ways to cope is through being distracted by 'porn'. The two leading male characters in the novel pass their adolescence:

> So they'd roll a few joints and smoke them while watching the executions and the porn – the body parts moving around on the screen in slow motion, an underwater ballet of flesh and blood under stress, hard and soft joining and separating, groans and screams, close-ups of clenched eyes and clenched teeth, spurts of this or that. If you switched back and forth fast, it all came to look like the same event.[13]

Lest this be thought to be scare-mongering, it is widely known that the huge majority of internet usage now is for pornography and much of it for 'extreme' pornography.[14] And once we stray beyond the fantasy confines of sanitised mass consumption Anglo-Saxon porn, disease and abuse are of course rife in the global sex 'industry', as are forms of virtual slavery. I have never seen anything that turned my stomach as much as the sight of middle-aged, overweight, white men buying young Thai girls in Bangkok. But the sheer horror of all this makes the Church's loss of credibility more, not less of a cause for shame.

We ought to be able to say two simple things. First, that real, as opposed to fantasy, women do not like being abused. (It is difficult for a Church which has been careless of abuse of women to say this simply.) Second, as the *Guardian* journalist honestly wrote: 'Relationships are difficult. Intimacy, having a good relationship, loving your children, involves work. Pornography is fantasy in the place of reality. But it is just that:

fantasy. Pornography is not real, and the only thing human beings get nourishment from is reality: real relationships.'[15] To which a character – a Far Eastern ex-child prostitute and 'porn star' in Atwood's novel – adds a crisp commentary: 'But Jimmy, you should know. All sex is real.'[16] (It is difficult for a Church which has been frightened of human sexuality to say this simply.)

What is the point of this lengthy introduction? Chastity, the choice of a celibate way of life, was the third of the great Christian monastic virtues: the giving up of the possibility of human romantic and sexual love and marriage in favour of a life of dedication only to God. Now it is often seen as a distortion or a cause of distortion. It is the final proof of the Church's hostility to human bodiliness, sexuality, and too often, women. In this chapter, I would like us to reflect on that verdict, and to think if we can find sources for both a more positive defence of celibacy and also for a whole-hearted and joyful celebration of human relationships, marriage and sexuality. So this chapter is both about reconceiving the motives and pattern of celibacy but much more widely, it is about a positive affirmation of our bodiliness, our natural createdness, our sensuality, our sexuality, and our human relationships.

This is part of a deeper question. How do we imagine God relating to the most intimate aspects of our lives? Does he avert his gaze? Should we hope for, eventually, freedom from the desires and messiness of our bodies? Or is there something in our doctrine of God which affirms our physical sexuality? Even more deeply, how seriously do we believe that God really loves us as we are; that we are in some sense, as he wishes us to be, in our created humanness? Most profoundly of all, what happens if we really believe that God is love and what are some of the risks of trying to believe that? If we were really to believe that God is love, how might our lives and our Church change?

To help with this journey, I want to choose two different topics in the history of spirituality and look at them very briefly. They are first, an exploration of the sense of the love of God, but experienced in the context of a celibate life; second, an exploration of the sense of the love of God experienced in the context of married life. Then we will look at a passage from Luke where Jesus is in relationship with a woman.

Humane celibacy – Julian of Norwich

I never read women's glossy magazines. Very occasionally in the dentist's perhaps ... But I remember a little while ago a phase when celibacy was fashionable. I suspect it was 99 per cent marketing but there was the germ of the idea that it was possible to be a fulfilled and healthy human being and not be in a sexual relationship. I think the Church may be one of the last places where this wisdom will be retained and lived out and – call me old-fashioned – you may be surprised to hear that I think we need to say it a little more loudly. For while there are terrible examples of the destruction of human beings by enforced celibacy, there are also positive examples to be celebrated.[17]

A good one is Julian of Norwich.[18] I have chosen her for two reasons. First, over the last twenty years she has become increasingly popular and the depth and power of her theological thinking have been increasingly honoured. She is thus a very contemporary figure. Second, because her whole being was infused with a sense of the love of God; and that is really the underlying theological theme for this chapter.

Now in some ways this is a nonsensical choice. We know so little about Julian. She was born about 1342 – the time of the Black Death – and died some time after 1413. We know that she became very ill as a young woman – it seems that she regarded this as an answer to prayer as she had wished to be tested – during which time she had 16 visions. She recovered, wrote two accounts of these visions and lived the rest of her life as an anchorite in Norwich.

From another perspective as well, using Julian as an example of celibacy as life-giving is nonsensical. At times she seems to have regarded her body in a deeply negative light. She writes:

During this time I saw a body lying on the earth. It looked heavy and horrible, shapeless and formless, like a swollen mound of stinking compost. And suddenly out of this body there sprang a most beautiful creature, a little child, perfectly shaped and formed, agile and lively, and whiter than a lily, who at once glided up into heaven. The swollen body stood for the awful wretchedness of our mortal flesh and the smallness of the child for the utter purity of the soul. I thought: 'Nothing of this child's beauty is left behind on this body, and the child is uncontaminated by the body's filth'. [19]

This runs against so much of what we have been arguing for in this book. It is understandable from one perspective. A diseased or even a decaying human body is an ugly sight and there is therefore a strong sense of longing to be away from it. But there is little acceptance here of the potential for a healthy human life and for the good which that embodies. And yet, despite her profound sense of sin and mortality, Julian also had a great vision of the splendour of what it is to be a human being. Earlier she writes of God's generous work in nature and in grace: 'He has put some sort of nature on all the different creatures, but in man the parts all come together. Man's nature is whole, with all its powers. It is completely beautiful, good, kingly and noble. It is everything that is magnificent, precious and glorious.'[20] For her – and this is one of the examples of her remarkable theological breadth – the glory of humanity is that Christ was destined to be human and humanity was destined to be drawn into the love and bliss of Christ: 'This lovely human nature was made for Christ so that man could be created in glory and beauty, and saved for joy and bliss.'[21] This is an immensely positive vision of what it is to be human.

My instinct is that it was precisely the depth of her experience of God's love that overcame the risks of her negative conception of human physicality. This must remain one of the defences of celibacy. That there is a depth and quality of the experience of God's love which can so consume people that there is a form of sufficiency in it. Now, I might want to argue – and I do so very cautiously because I am married – that this celibacy needs mostly to be held within the bonds of affectionate human communities. Julian, while an anchorite, was not divorced from human contact and even friendship and family. Further, it is not to try to impose some hyper-spiritual expectation on the celibate, whose lives are every bit as human and complex as the married. This includes the recognition that much modern 'singleness' is not chosen and can therefore feel like enforced celibacy and therefore that some pastoral reticence and flexibility is appropriate here: unless we still really believe in our guts that sexual 'sins' are the most serious. But it is to recognise that, as well as the ordinary human choices and circumstances which contribute to celibacy, there is the potential for a different sort of freedom from the married. Within this freedom, there is the potential for a depth of commitment, experience and witness that has its own unique quality. There is an interesting question, which I will touch on briefly in a moment when we look at Luther and Jeremy Taylor, as to how a married couple can in their way also share this depth of experience of the love of God. But first a reflection on Julian's experience of the love of God.

Julian finishes her manuscript with a dialogue with God about the purpose of her visions:

> From the time it was first revealed to me, I often longed to know what our Lord meant. More than fifteen years later I was answered. Spiritual enlightenment came with the words, 'Do you want to know what our Lord meant in all this? Learn it well: love was what he meant. Who showed it you? Love. What did he show you? Love. Why did he show it? Out of love ... So I was taught that love was what our Lord meant.[22]

Unerringly Julian, earlier in her writing, pinpoints the objection that many people, especially those coming from a more conservative Evangelical background, bring to her ideas. There is not enough 'wrath' here. We will return to this crucial point a little later, but hear her on this: 'I could not see any kind of anger in

God, neither short-lived nor longer-lasting – indeed if God were angry even for a moment we could never live, we should simply cease to be.'[23] When we imagine God to be angry with us, it is precisely that – our distorted and sin-corrupted imagination. God loves us even in our sin, in Julian's beautiful phrase, 'with pity not with blame'. This does not mean Julian is blind to or complacent about her own sin. Far from it. But she is absolutely certain that God's love is absolute and certain. It is an entirely different conception from the God who fiercely waits to punish us if we have not dealt with the legacy of original sin in our lives. It is a vision of the Christian life fundamentally driven by love, not by fear. It fits well with the vision of trying to live the Christian life in this world for positive and not negative reasons.

The joy of sex in marriage – Luther and Taylor

You may think it is quite a jump from Julian to Luther – it is. But behind Luther's angst and temper and unpredictability was a man who had a profound sense of the love of God and also of human love. For Luther, through his marriage to Kate the ex-nun, warmth and humanity came into his life, which was marked by such turbulence and depression. We know this not just from the stories of Luther and Kate, but also from Luther's own comments, recorded by his students in his *Table Talk*.[24] He said simply: 'The state of matrimony is the chief in the world after religion …'[25] In other words, marriage only comes second to being a Christian in what is of value to human beings. One of the great undervalued achievements of the Reformation – undervalued in part because the Reformers were still so deeply bound into a view of the world which saw human desire as sinful[26] – was to return marriage, and thereby human relationships, human love, human sexuality, to the centre of the Christian spiritual life. As Luther himself remarked: 'It is written in the first book of Moses, concerning matrimony: God created a man and a woman, and blessed them. Now, although this sentence was chiefly spoken of human creatures, yet we may apply it to all the creatures of the world ... wherein we find a male and a female consorting together, engendering and increasing.'[27]

Luther's marriage was not initially a love match. Kate was the last of a batch of nuns whom Luther had helped to leave their convent. He had arranged marriages for them, apart from Kate, and she and he were sort of 'last choices'. Luther said he married to please his father, to spite the pope and the devil and to witness to his faith before his martyrdom.[28] But he grew to love her deeply (he said he would not swap her for France or Venice, though he rather spoiled the effect by saying that in any event, other women had worse faults), even though he found married life, with noisy children, financial worries and a firm wife, something of a trial. Indeed he went on to argue that living in a family was the best 'school for character', replacing the monastery.[29]

In his down-to-earth way, Luther seems to have had a humorous attitude to human relationships and sexuality. He later joked: 'The reproduction of mankind is a great marvel and mystery. Had God consulted me in the matter, I should have advised him to continue the generation of the species by fashioning them of clay ...'[30] And he seems to have known something of the real sexual rhythms of marriage: 'The first love [that is, the first period of marriage] is drunken. When the intoxication wears off, then comes the real marriage love.'[31] Above all Luther clearly experienced deep tenderness in his marriage, writing that a wife or husband was not just to be loved, but was to be the 'dearest friend' and a companion not just of the flesh but of the mind as well.[32]

In theory at least, the return of marriage to centre-stage at the Reformation marked the restoration of human physical love as part of the intended purposes of God (though how this could be forgotten in a community with the Songs of Songs amongst its Scriptures, only Bernard of Clairvaux could answer[33]). This was to be picked up and covered more fully and creatively in the work of Jeremy Taylor. We have already learned that Taylor was a staunch Royalist but in this chapter we study him because he is crucial to the development of a Christian spirituality for marriage in that he wrote so passionately about the goodness of being married. He was a married priest and tragically lost his first wife Phoebe and a number of his children to sickness. A recent book, *Muskets and Altars*, has emphasised his impact. Reginald Askew writes of him: 'The candour and realism of a happily married priest of the Church of England rescued Christian teaching from its very long history of theological distress over concupiscence, and its exaltation of virginity. Would *Holy Living* be the first sensible Christian handbook about married love in English?'[34] Askew discerns in Taylor a new understanding of chastity: 'Wasn't chastity the tenderest expression of mutual love and understanding between partners, and the antithesis of sexual exploitation by either side?'[35]

So sexual love really is a good gift of God that enriches and enables marriage. While Taylor writes about the detail of married life in *Holy Living*, it is in his sermon 'The Marriage Ring' that we hear him at his lyrical best: 'Marriage was ordained by God, instituted in paradise, was the relief of a natural necessity and the first blessing from the Lord; he gave to man not a friend but a wife, that is, a friend and a wife too …'[36] While we must not inappropriately modernise Taylor – the woman is clearly to obey, though it is an obedience of love and under love – the sense of genuine joy in his account of married sexual life is infectious (well, at least it is to me as a man and I am conscious that I write this as a not very reconstructed husband and father): 'When a man dwells in love, then the breasts of his wife are pleasant as the droppings upon the hill of Hermon, her eyes are fair as the light of heaven, she is a fountain sealed, and he can quench his thirst, and ease his cares, and lay his sorrows down upon her lap, and can retire home as to his sanctuary and refectory, and his gardens of sweetness and chaste refreshments.'[37] Here the Song of Songs is being put to its proper use.

Like Luther, Taylor becomes polemical in his defence of marriage: 'Single life makes men in one instance to be like angels, but marriage in very many things makes the chaste pair to be like to Christ.'[38] But what does it mean that in marriage, we are 'like to Christ'? Without falling into sugary sentimentality – impossible for me after twenty years of marriage – it is simply about love: the love that holds on in the hard times; the love that will bear the pain (though not the abuse, unlike Christ) of holding on; the love that is more intimate with this other person than with any other; the love expressed in every part of our personalities and our bodies. God communicates his love in the love, including the sexual love, we have for one another – real, earthy, embodied, human love. In all of this, marriage is simply the most visible and structured of our human relationships, all of which, when in good health, reveal and communicate the love of God, that fills his world.[39]

Gospel reflection: Jesus for women

And so to Luke: this story is from 7:36–50 and it challenges us very profoundly about male attitudes to women and the Church's attitudes to sexual sinners.

> One of the Pharisees asked Jesus to eat with him, and he went into the Pharisee's house and took his place at the table. And a woman in the city, who was a sinner, having learned that he was eating in the Pharisee's house, brought an alabaster jar of ointment. She stood behind him at his feet, weeping, and began to bathe his feet with her tears and to dry them with her hair. Then she continued kissing his feet and anointing them with the ointment. Now when the Pharisee who had invited him saw it, he said to himself, 'If this man were a prophet, he would have known who and what kind of woman this is who is touching him – that she is a sinner.' Jesus spoke up and said to him, 'Simon, I have something to say to you.' 'Teacher,' he replied, 'speak.'
>
> 'A certain creditor had two debtors; one owed five hundred denarii, and the other fifty. When they could not pay, he cancelled the debts for both of them. Now which of

them will love him more?' Simon answered, 'I suppose the one for whom he cancelled the greater debt.' And Jesus said to him, 'You have judged rightly.' Then turning towards the woman, he said to Simon, 'Do you see this woman? I entered your house; you gave me no water for my feet, but she has bathed my feet with her tears and dried them with her hair. You gave me no kiss, but from the time I came in she has not stopped kissing my feet. You did not anoint my head with oil, but she has anointed my feet with ointment. Therefore, I tell you, her sins, which were many, have been forgiven; hence she has shown great love. But the one to whom little is forgiven, loves little.' Then he said to her, 'Your sins are forgiven.' But those who were at the table with him began to say among themselves, 'Who is this who even forgives sins?' And he said to the woman, 'Your faith has saved you; go in peace.'

Points to ponder
- First, some reflections on the text of the story. It is particularly complex, the most complex of the four which we have looked at so far. There are similar stories in Matthew 26:6–13, Mark 14:3–9 and John 12:1–8, though for these three they form part of the beginning of the Passion narrative. There, Jesus is anointed as preparation for his death and burial. Luke does not have this story at that point but has this story much earlier in his gospel. So, at first sight this looks like a Lucan rewriting of a traditional story, which Luke links to the parable of the two sinners. It is possible that Luke had this as a separate story and does not want to confuse the reader by using a similar story twice.[40]
- The verbal links indicate some connection between the text of the stories, but it is difficult to be clear about which is influencing which. Matthew, Mark and Luke tell us that the jar is alabaster. Only Mark and John tell us it is pure nard with which she anoints Jesus. Only Luke and John tell us that the woman anoints Jesus' feet and wipes them with her hair. But

Luke has some distinctive features: only Luke tells us that the house is that of a Pharisee; only Luke tells us that the woman washes Jesus' feet with her tears and kisses them; only Luke tells us she is a notorious sinner; only Luke stresses her love and Jesus' love and forgiveness. This is a very distinctively Lucan story.

- The commentators are fun on this. Some go all round the houses to avoid the obvious sensuality, even the frank sexuality of this story. One goes so far as to suggest that the woman anoints Jesus' feet because they are the only part of him to be touched by fallen human beings.[41] I am tempted to see such a commentator as a Pharisee of the Pharisees. We are not told what sort of a 'sinner' this woman was. She is seemingly well known in the city as a sinner. The most likely guess is that she is a prostitute, a class of women who were visually and socially segregated.[42] It must be something embarrassing and disreputable to account for Simon's reaction of distaste.

- The point of the story as Luke tells it, and reinforces it with the parable, is to show us the difference between a forgiven sinner and a self-righteous religious person, between someone who is responding with love to the love of God and someone who, whatever they say, has not experienced and feels no need of such love. But I want to highlight the sexuality and sensuality of the story. I do not think Nolland's phrase, 'affectionate gratitude' gets anywhere near the passion and intimacy of these events.[43] There has been some deeply offensive material written about Jesus' sexuality, as well as much foolish speculation, but I am reminded constantly of Dorothy Sayers' heartfelt tribute to Jesus:

> Perhaps it is no wonder that the women were first at the Cradle and last at the Cross. They had never known a man like this Man ... A prophet and teacher who never nagged at them, never flattered or coaxed or patronised; who never made arch jokes about them ... who rebuked without querulousness and praised without condescension; who took their questions and arguments seriously;

who never mapped out their sphere for them, never urged them to be feminine or jeered at them for being female; who had no axe to grind and no uneasy male dignity to defend; who took them as he found them and was completely unselfconscious.[44]

Jesus was at ease with women and they with him. How can his Church have so deeply forgotten this?

• Why does the woman weep? Is it simple sorrow for her sins or is there already some sense of acceptance by Jesus? He could presumably have had her ushered away. This is a very public and raw display of emotion. Jesus accuses Simon of profound discourtesy in not bringing him water to wash his feet; a basic breach of manners in a hot and dusty climate. But the woman is weeping enough to wash Jesus' feet with her tears. And then she dries his feet with her hair. This is the sort of thing we see only in continental art movies. It is very intimate and Barclay reminds us of the significance for a Jewish woman, presumably even a fallen women, of letting her hair down in public.[45] Then she kisses Jesus' feet and anoints them with this very expensive perfume. John, in one of those intriguing vivid little sensual comments that mark his gospel, says that the perfume filled the house. Touch, smell, look, as well as words. Deep emotions of love and tenderness between a man and a woman. But this is the Son of God being loved and touched.

• Luke reminds us of the shock of this. Simon the Pharisee goes straight to the spiritual point. This is a dangerous woman. She is a sexual sinner and we have been reminded only recently with the Taliban, of the ferocity with which such loose uncontrolled women are punished. There is a particular 'threat' and a particular 'contamination' that comes from contact with a 'fallen woman'. Hence Simon's frank disgust and therefore his dismissal of Jesus. Anyone who lets this woman touch him is not of God. It is an open and shut case. But it is of course the opposite that is true. This woman really loves Jesus and through Jesus, his Father. So she touches him.

(How can my Church, the Church of England, ever have allowed the language of 'taint' to be used of the ministry and physical presence and touch of women?)

• This is not some sanitised sinner, as we find in those rather implausible Christian autobiographies. Her familiarity with men, with touching men, is embarrassingly evident. Goodness knows how much of her life she had sorted out. What was she going to go back to doing afterwards? We hope she had a new life but none of this is worked through yet. This is a profound and yet impulsive welcoming of a dangerous sensual sinner back into the family of God, long before she is safe. If Jesus can take such risks, even with sexual sinners about whom we remain so neurotic, why can not his Church follow? If we are nervous for our reputations and our respectability, then we are sitting with Simon the Pharisee. John Drury describes the type sharply: 'cold', 'envious resentment', 'well-preserved lives which are too comfortably self-concerned to go out to others except in criticism'.[46] Why do so many hard-line Christians only become gentle when their own lives, or the lives of their families, have been broken?

A Response

We get endless catalogues of books sent to us in College. One of our jobs is to decide which books to buy for the library. Last summer I saw a book that I had to buy for myself just because of the title: *Saving Jesus from Those Who Are Right*.[47] It is by Carter Heyward, an American woman theologian who seems to have ticked most of the boxes on the politically correct list. She is gay, a green, shares a farm as well as teaching theology, is anti-racist, a feminist, a recovering alcoholic. Half the time her book drives me mad with frustration, but at its heart, I heard a profoundly important message, that God means love. She uses God as a verb. So we 'god' somebody when we love them, more precisely when we are in right relationship to them. (You can see why I get frustrated.) But she is of course absolutely right. If John can talk of 'doing the truth' (1 John 1:6), then we can talk of 'doing god'. I'd like to quote one of her paragraphs and you can hear the impact which she has had on my own thinking: 'I am suggesting that authoritarian, moralistic (self-righteous), adversarial posturing that requires obedience does little to help create, redeem, or sustain the work of justice, the vitality of loving relationships, or the general well-being of God's people and creatures. As an alternative to authoritarian understandings of social/relational power, I propose *mutual relation* as a way *to god* (verb).'[48] Reflecting on those who have opposed the consecration of Rowan Williams as Archbishop of Canterbury, however much I might question Heyward's theology and her exegesis, there is no doubt for me about whose image of the Church is closer to Jesus and will prove to be more life-giving and attractive. God is always the life-bringer.

Prayer

> Tender God, touch us.
> Be touched by us.
> Make us lovers of humanity,
> Compassionate friends of all creation.
> Gracious God, hear us into speech;
> Speak us into acting,
> And through us, reach the world.
> Amen.

Carter Heyward[49]

CHAPTER FIVE

From Stability to Patience

Inhumane busyness

The desperate need today is not for a greater number of intelligent people, or gifted people, but for deep people.[1]

So wrote Richard Foster over twenty years ago when he lamented, with David Watson's passionate support, that 'superficiality is the curse of our age'. I fear our situation has not improved a great deal. 'Poor little talkative Christianity'[2] does not have a good reputation at the moment as a place to go for 'depth'. A vicar of my acquaintance overheard two of his older female parishioners chatting:

'I'm going to start yoga classes soon', says the first.
'Why's that?', says the second.
'Because I want to learn about how to meditate. I think it would help slow me down. Might help me to pray.'
'Why don't you go and see the Vicar to talk about it?'
'Oh, he wouldn't know anything about that sort of thing', finished the first.

'He wouldn't know anything about that sort of thing.' How often do people come to the 'vicar' if they have a spiritual need, or just want to 'slow down'? Do 'they' instinctively feel that the 'vicar' is someone who understands spiritual things, from the inside, and could help them to go further in their search? Or are they more likely to go to the New Age shelves in the book shop, or buy a crystal; or go up into the hills, dig the garden, take up yoga? Occasionally a monastic retreat house will feature in the Sunday supplements as one of a range of places to go to chill out. I have met this sort of spiritual searcher at retreat houses, attracted and bemused by the depth and the discipline of these Christian communities. But I do not think such people are very common. One of the attractions of Westernised Bhuddism, or of Eastern Bhuddism seen through Western eyes, is that it communicates a sense of depth and space but, apparently, without the 'dogma' that shapes Western monasticism – caricatures again, but confirmed monthly on our TV screens, in the cinema and in our daily papers.

It is another cliché to note that we live in a busy society. At a personal level, with the advent of e-mails and text messaging, information can be shared and decisions taken at much greater speed than ever before. But at what cost? A recent novel brought home to me where the cost can be at its sharpest, with 'working mums'. Allison Pearson's popular novel *I don't know how she does it*, describes the life of Kate, a City fund manager and mother of two, whose life is a constant juggling act of international travel and missed meetings with her children. In the end, of course, the pressure is too much and her marriage breaks (temporarily) and she narrowly avoids an affair. The combination of frantic busyness, guilt and a kind but ineffectual husband is at times hilarious, but mostly 'achingly sad'. In one of the most famous passages, Kate reflects on the lives of her female friends, and her own life:

> Home. I look at the word for a long time. Home. Hear its rounded centre. Picture what it means. I am married but am not a wife, have children but am not a mother.
>
> What am I?
>
> I know a woman who wakes her baby at 5.30 every morning so that she can have some time with him.
>
> I know a woman who went on a TV discussion programme and talked about doing the school run. Her nanny told me she barely knew where her kids' school was.

I know a woman who heard that her baby boy took his first steps from a babysitter down the phone.

I know a woman who found out her husband left her from a note that was read out to her by a nanny.[3]

There are, of course, huge issues lying behind this passage about lifestyles choices and gender roles, but speaking as an ineffectual husband, despite our wealth of labour-saving devices, we seem to have less time to do good things together than in my own childhood. Poignantly, Kate has a fleeting experience of peace during a snatched family holiday:

St David's is one of the few places that bids me be still. And here in the nave I realise that, these days, stillness is an unaccustomed, even an uncomfortable sensation. The cathedral is timeless, and my life … my life is nothing but time. Rich has taken Emily and Ben to explore the gift shop. Left alone, I find my mouth forming words no one can hear: 'Help me'. Asking a God I'm not sure I believe in to get me out of a mess I don't understand. Oh, very good, Kate, very good.[4]

It would be great to be able to say that we do things differently in the Church; that we don't breed workaholics; that our structures facilitate a good quality of life, not least for our families. But for those carrying leadership responsibilities in the front line of the Church – the 'parochial' clergy – the speed and pressure of work seems to be increasing exponentially, not least as parishes or chapels are amalgamated together. (I occasionally worry that we are exaggerating our plight when compared to previous generations. The workload of a nineteenth-century slum priest makes me feel ill just looking at it.[5] But they were bachelors and had housekeepers …) When surveys of the clergy reveal what tiny amounts of time they are spending in prayer,[6] then it is not an exaggeration to say that both externally and internally there is a crisis of spirituality in the Church. It is, in part, that we are not asked to speak of the deep things of God. It is, in part, that when we do speak, we can sound shrill and shallow. And it is, in part, that we may be trying to speak too much. One of Cardinal Basil Hume's great gifts was not just communicating a sense of a person rooted in the presence of God, but also rationing his public statements.

There is another aspect to this sense of speed – the 'quick fix'. Whether it is losing weight, or curing a cold, or recovering from a personal trauma, we want things done quickly. We can't afford to spend too long getting better or changing our behaviour. Again the Church has found itself, often unconsciously, drawn into this way of feeling and behaving. It is as if (and I speak as someone who has been knocking around in Evangelical circles since the mid-1970s) every couple of years another 'craze' arrives. The latest spiritual technique which will – this time – provide the short-cut to a sustained dynamic spiritual life: whether it is speaking in tongues, power evangelism, being slain in the Spirit, learning to prophesy, or more prosaically, leg-lengthening. I have seen people's lives changed for good by some of these experiences. People changed so that they become more ready to take on responsibility in leadership and care for others. I have also seen people cruelly hurt as their hopes were built up only to be smashed on the rocks of reality: continued ill health, psychological turmoil, ongoing spiritual battles. At the risk of another huge generalisation, I wonder if this longing for a spiritual 'quick fix' has become quite so dominant in our churches in the West only in the past two hundred years and especially since World War II, exactly in parallel with wider social changes. The irony is that the very groups within the Church who most vociferously portray themselves as being 'counter-cultural' are those most deeply seduced by 'quick-fix spirituality'. Who is being culturally conditioned now?

In this chapter and the final one I hope that we may explore together the fundamental nature of the Christian life. How do we grow in faith and love? How are we weaned away from destructive and sinful patterns of behaviour? And most deeply, what is the purpose of the Christian life? What is all this for? In this chapter, I am trying to make one simple point, which is that real growth takes time. Given the topics that we have already

covered, you can probably foresee some of the underlying theological convictions that will shape my answer to these
questions. If God, crudely speaking, helps rather than controls,
then our journey of change will inevitably be slow. If we recognise that God has made us as integrated human beings, where
mind, body and spirit are inextricable, then the speed at which
we really change will be shaped by the interaction of all aspects
of our humanity together, and therefore by the pace of change
of the 'slowest' parts of our human nature – our embodied
psyche, our 'guts'. Nor do we undergo change in isolation from
other people. We are always beings who live in community, and
we are profoundly shaped not just by what goes on 'inside our
heads' but by the communities to which we belong. I have had
to learn that my conscious mind often runs on ahead, assuming
that something is 'sorted' when my 'guts' are moving along at
their own completely different timetable. And when I am not in
touch with my 'guts' then I speak inauthentically and
unrealistically.

Stability and patience – Benedict and the people of the Desert

To help us to reflect on all this, we will look back to the Desert
Fathers and Mothers, the first Christian monks and nuns, whose
sense of space and time was almost at the opposite end of the
spectrum to ours. Then we will study one of Jesus' sharpest and
most subversive parables, which should undermine any
complacent or self-righteous belief that we have, at last, 'got it
right'.

But first, to return to one of the constants of this book, I noted
earlier that one of the vows that a new Benedictine monk took
was of 'stability'. There was a careful process of discernment
before someone was allowed to join a monastery. Indeed, a
potential recruit was actively discouraged. An applicant was
supposed to be kept waiting outside the monastery for four or
five days and then only admitted to the guest-house. Thereafter
there was a lengthy novitiate and before being finally accepted

the prospective monk had the Rule read to him several times so that he was under no illusions. But once someone had made a clear-eyed decision to join, this was a decision to stay. 'But let him understand that according to the law of the Rule he is no longer free to leave the monastery, or to withdraw his neck from under the yoke ...'[7] The idea of flitting from monastery to monastery until one found the place that suited was not part of the deal.[8] Stability meant not running away from challenge, discipline and struggle in this particular place with this specific group of people. It was a very down-to-earth understanding of stability. (Anyone who has lived in a family or a community will know what a tough discipline this is.) Esther de Waal reminds us very helpfully of the fundamental significance of stability: 'Benedict puts stability first since without it the other two [obedience, conversion] lose much of their meaning.'[9] It was within 'the enclosure of the monastery' – within these walls – and in this group of people that the monk was to learn holiness and the love of Christ.[10] (Immediately, some of us may be feeling uncomfortable about the sort of 'church-hopping' that is so fashionable now. Why do we imagine so easily that the problem with the Church is 'them' and not 'us', or forget that there may be good to be released through staying, enduring and growing through struggle?)

Strikingly, to our eyes, Benedict was moderating the fiercer and perhaps more interior understanding of 'stability' which the Desert Fathers and Mothers had followed. From the middle of the third century, Christians began to move out of the urban centres of Egypt and the Holy Land, to make their home in the 'deserts' and wildernesses. They had a range of motives: escaping persecution; escaping the increasing complacency of the Church, especially after the conversion of the Roman Empire; finding a place of spiritual warfare (they believed that demons lived in the desert) and even a form of martyrdom, when this was no longer a real possibility.[11] Within a couple of generations, thousands of people had chosen to follow this way of life: partly because of the quality of the lives of the Desert Fathers and Mothers; partly because their example was promoted by key bishops. (So Anthony came out of the desert to support Athanasius in his fight with heretics, who in turn (probably) wrote the life of Anthony, making him the most famous of the early Desert Fathers, partly to uphold his own theological and spiritual convictions against the heretics.[12]) In due course, through the work of a Western monk, John Cassian, their ideas and practices were spread to the West, including Benedict.[13]

The spirituality of the Desert Fathers and Mothers is attractive for a range of reasons. For example, it was not rigid. Their pattern of life varied. Some lived as solitary hermits. Others in more or less formal communities, gathered around an individual *Abba* or, less frequently, *Amma*.[14] There is a sort of slightly anarchic egalitarianism about them. Many seem to have come from socially humble backgrounds. They were not the highly educated monks of developed monasticism. Chitty retells the story of Abba Macarius, who would ignore those who came to him with reverence, but if someone approached him, calling him an ex-camel trader and thief, then he would welcome them warmly.[15] There is a sort of topsy-turvy foolishness about them that is deeply subversive of our 'normal' expectations. So Abba Anthony was quizzing a group of monks about a passage of Scripture. They each tried to explain it but to them all, Anthony replied, 'You have not understood it'. 'Last of all he said to Abba Joseph, "How would you explain this saying?", and he replied, "I do not know". Then Abba Anthony said, "Indeed Abba Joseph has found the way, for he has said, 'I do not know'"'.[16] For me, teaching in an academic community where knowledge is expected and honoured, this humility is a healthy perspective. Sister Benedicta Ward highlights the story of two old monks who, having lived together for many years, decided to try to have an argument to be like other men: 'The first said to him, "Look I will put a brick between us, and will say it is mine, and you say, 'No it is mine', and so the fight will begin." So they put a brick between them and the first said, "This brick is mine", and the other said, "No it is mine", and the first responded, "If it is yours, take it and go" – so they gave it up without being able to find an occasion for argument.'[17] It is not often in reading a spiritual classic that I laugh out loud, but that is a common experience with the sayings and stories of these people.

Candidly, I find some aspects of their life at best baffling and at worst unacceptable. Lust appears – perhaps surprisingly (or not) given the relative absence of women – to have been a huge problem. Many of the sayings are devoted to how to overcome it. Some appear rather strange: 'Meeting some nuns on the road, a monk made a detour. The superior said to him, "If you were a perfect monk, you would not have noticed we were women".'[18] A classic 'Catch 22'! And there is a lurking undercurrent that sex is entirely bad. The story is told of two monks who wished to discover how far they had advanced spiritually, so God sent them to visit a shepherd and his wife. At first their piety seemed modest but then they revealed: 'Since I married my wife, we have not had intercourse with one another, for she is a virgin: we each live alone. At night we wear hair shirts and ordinary clothes by day.'[19] It was sexual restraint, even in marriage, that proved their holiness. This is in complete opposition to the case I argued in Chapter 4. At times the paranoia about women is deeply troubling:

> A brother was walking with his own mother, who was old. When they came to the river she could not cross it. Taking his cloak, her son covered his hands with it, so as not to touch his mother's body, and carrying her in this way brought her to the other bank. And his mother said to him: 'My child, why did you cover your hands?' He said to her, 'A woman's body is a fire and from it comes remembrance of other women: that is why I did that'.[20]

Overall, there can be a refreshing realism in the sayings about the pitfalls of asceticism. Anthony himself said: 'Some have afflicted their bodies by asceticism, but they lack discernment and so they are far from God.'[21]We could also note the counter-arguments of more expert scholars who do not think that the Desert Fathers and Mothers were 'flesh-hating'.[22] A good example of wisdom in this area is from Abba Poemen: 'Abba

Issac came to see Abba Poemen and found him washing his feet. As he enjoyed freedom of speech with him he said, "How is it that others practice austerity and treat their bodies hardly?" Abba Poemen said to him, "We have not been taught to kill our bodies, but to kill our passions".' [23]

However, it is difficult not to be very cautious about their focus on bodily asceticism, which they saw as a, sometimes *the*, key tool to spiritual growth. Training the body to go without sleep, or a comfortable home, or nice food, or even food itself, were all seen as ways of reducing the control of the 'flesh' and liberating the soul for prayer and spiritual growth. These disciplines might often be penitential and go on for years. At its worst it seems almost competitive. Who can fast longest? Who can live the longest distance from water? Who can live on their own for longest?[24] At its most extreme, who can live on top of the tallest pillar for longest? (For example, the Syrian monks were reputed to be the most extreme and it is true that Simeon Stylites lived on a platform on a pillar for 36 years. The motive was to be free to pray but ironically it tended to have the effect of drawing more people who came to wonder and seek advice ...) In evaluating all of this we must again be honest about how we have changed as churches, and why.

But it is in their understanding of 'stability' and of the need for time to grow, that the Desert Fathers and Mothers do appear to have something special to teach us. Anthony was famous for leaving his home and village, and after an initial experiment of living in a hut as a hermit on the edge of a village, going out to a ruined fort in the desert and staying there on his own. According to Athanasius, Anthony was physically, mentally and spiritually whole when he emerged.

> And when they saw his body, they marvelled at his sweet-ness, for he had not exercised and yet he was not weak as though he had come out from fasting and fighting with demons ... They saw that the thought of his soul was pure, and he was not sorrowful and suffering; he had neither been disturbed by pleasures, nor had laughter or sadness

111

ruled over him. Moreover, when he saw the crowd, he was not disturbed, nor was he delighted when they greeted him. Rather he maintained complete equilibrium because reason was guiding him.[25]

(Given that Anthony lived to be over 100, he had clearly done something right.) Athanasius believed that this extended period of solitude had so purified Anthony that he had been remade into the image of God, just as had originally been intended. But it had taken over twenty years. Many of the sayings describe periods of years of spiritual struggle, temptation and *accidie* (that resonant word for spiritual and emotional depression and listlessness which they had coined) before a monk came to a place of peace and resolution. Leaving aside our hurried secular culture, how many Christians plan seriously for years of disciplined struggle in the spiritual life?

It was the conviction that solitude and silence meant that there was no escape from confronting the reality of themselves and of God which shaped the lives of the Desert Fathers and Mothers; though we should note that many lived in community and most lived under the direction of a senior *Abba* or *Amma*. Their word *hesychia* was almost a technical term for the combination of outward solitude and silence, which lead to an interior stillness and centredness on God.[26] They had discovered that if a person could not find holiness and peace within the four walls of their cell, they would not find it anywhere. Sister Benedicta sums this up crisply:

> The cell was of central importance in their asceticism. 'Sit in your cell and it will teach you everything', they said. The point was that unless a man could find God *here*, in this one place, in his cell, he would not find him by going somewhere else. But they had no illusions about what it meant to stay in the cell: it meant to stay there in mind as well as in body. To stay there in body, but to think about the outside world, was already to have left it.[27]

One story provides a sharp example of this reality, but also of the way the Desert Fathers and Mothers sought to undercut the risk of spiritual élitism:

> There was a brother who was a *hesychast* [solitary hermit] in a monastery, and he often got angry. So he said within himself, 'I will go and live apart, alone, and the fact of having nothing to do with anyone will assuage my passion.' So he went away and lived in solitude in a cave. Now one day when he had filled his jug with water he put it on the ground, and suddenly it fell over. He picked it up, filled it, and it fell over again. Having filled it a third time, he put it down and it fell over again. He was furious and picked it up and broke it. Coming to his senses, he recognised that he had been deceived by the enemy, and he said, 'Since I have been overcome, even after withdrawing into solitude, I will go back to the monastery, for everywhere there is warfare, endurance, and the help of God.' So he arose and returned to his place.[28]

I am writing this chapter having spent several weeks living on my own in a solitary fashion in a quiet valley in the Lake District. I can vouch for the fact that my bad temper had travelled with me, even in the absence of wife and family. For here there was no escape from confronting my own character and temperament. Solitude is not, of course, an infallible route to spiritual wisdom. Abba Poemen expressed this crisply: 'He said that Abba Ammonas said, "A man may remain for a hundred years in his cell without learning how to live in the cell."'[29] But it was my own experience, and that of others who have travelled far further down this road, that the longer the period of solitude, the greater the sense of how far there is still to travel on the road to Christlikeness.

If I can permit myself another huge generalisation, we probably live in a noisier world than any previous generation. On the one hand, our houses and cars are emptier and quieter. On the other hand, we have many more houses and cars, and we seem to fill them with constant noise from radios, CD-players, TVs and the ubiquitous mobile phones. Going into silence can be like a sort of detoxifying process. It takes time to slow down and learn again to hear. Once that deeper hearing has begun, the next step feels even slower, that of focusing the mind, body and spirit on the encounter with God.

One of the strengths of the Desert Fathers and Mothers was precisely that they held mind, body and spirit together. I have worried already about when this became an excessive asceticism, but at least it took the body seriously. And it seems as if common sense constantly broke into the extremes. For example, Anthony tried to distinguish between three forms of temptation. One was simply the result of the natural rhythms of the body. A second was the consequence of just eating and drinking – 'the warming of the body'. Wise words for those prone to lengthy and regular fasting. Only the third was, in Anthony's mind, the direct temptation of the demons.[30] They knew what it was to have a wandering mind and spirit and found wisdom in the discipline of the cell:

> A brother questioned an old man, saying, 'My thoughts wander and I am troubled by this'. The old man said to him, 'Remain sitting in your cell and your thoughts will come to rest. For truly, just as when the she-ass is tied her colt runs here and there but always comes back to his mother wherever she is, so it is with the thoughts of him who for God's sake remains steadfast in his cell: even if they wander a little they will always come back to him.'[31]

There is another aspect of their 'stability' that bears on the question of patience in the spiritual life. We have noted their sense of direct conflict with demons and the stories and sayings frequently describe a monk seeing demons, most famously if not frequently as beautiful women.[32] Strangely we read of Anthony being physically injured by demons coming to him in the form of beasts.[33] They were also credited with miracles. Indeed Anthony was reputed to have healed many when he emerged from his 20-year solitude.[34] But the aspect of his ministry he was most renowned for was attracting others to the ascetic life. The role of miracles was never to short-cut the spiritual journey. Sister Benedicta makes a strong case that this movement was 'ascetic rather than mystic ... concerned with action – behaviour – not mystical experience'.[35] They were cautious about claiming to have had visions and the accepted response from the monk was that he or she was not worthy of such a vision. Indeed the core spiritual virtue, which defeated the demons, was not some supernatural one, but humility. This is an absolutely typical example:

> When Abba Macarius was returning from the marsh to his cell one day carrying some palm leaves, he met the devil on the road with a scythe. The latter struck at him as much as he pleased, but in vain, and he said to him, 'What is your power, Macarius, that makes me powerless against you? All that you do, I do, too; you fast, so do I; you keep vigil, and I do not sleep at all; in one thing only do you beat me.' Abba Macarius asked what that was. He said, 'Your humility. Because of that I can do nothing against you.'[36]

This is not a virtue or a spiritual reality that I hear being commonly exalted in our modern supernaturalist church circles.

The point of the desert way of life was to deepen love for God and in God. It seems to me we can sum Anthony up in two of his sayings. The first encompasses the spirituality of the desert: harsh God, ferocious renunciation, rigorous repentance, terrifying discipline.

> He also said, '*Always have the fear of God before your eyes*. Remember him who gives death and life. *Hate the world and all that is in it*. Hate all peace that comes from the flesh. *Renounce this life, so that you may be alive to God*. Remember what you have promised God, for it will be required of you on the day of judgement. Suffer hunger, thirst, nakedness, be watchful and sorrowful; weep and groan in your heart; test yourselves, to see if you are worthy of God; *despise the flesh so that you may preserve your souls*.'[37]

This could in fact be a summary of inhumane Christianity. But a deep irony is revealed in the second saying, that at the end of this, as with the Rule of Benedict, there was a profound sense of the love of God. 'Abba Anthony said, "I no longer fear God, but I love Him. For love casts out fear" (1 John 4:18).'[38] I note this, not to justify actions and beliefs which I find unacceptable, but first, to remind myself that God's grace is active often even in the midst of error-strewn faith, and second, that criticism of these Desert Fathers and Mothers sometimes sounds like a fly buzzing in a vast cool silent cathedral.

Our response

We cannot and should not go back to this world of the third and fourth centuries; just as when we reflect on Jesus of Nazareth, there is a gulf of understanding and life-context to be crossed. My wife would not take kindly to being placed in a convent should I decide to answer a call to the monastery. One of the stories of the monks raises very sharply the questions that came back to the fore at the Reformation. Where is the Christian life to be lived?

> It was said that there were three friends who were not afraid of hard work. The first chose to reconcile those who were fighting each other, as it is said, 'Blessed are the peace-makers' (Matt. 5). The second chose to visit the sick. The third went to live in prayer and stillness in the desert. Now in spite of all his labours, the first could not make peace in all men's quarrels; and in his sorrow he went to him who was serving the sick, and he found him also disheartened, for he could not fulfil that commandment either. So they went together to see him who was living in the stillness of prayer. They told him their difficulties and begged him to tell them what to do. After a short silence, he poured some water into a bowl and said to them 'Look at the water', and it was disturbed. After a little while he said to them again, 'Look how still the water is now', and as they looked into the water, they saw their own faces reflected in it as in a mirror. Then he said to them, 'It is the

same for those who live among men; disturbances prevent them from seeing their faults. But when a man is still, especially in the desert, then he sees his failings.' [39]

There are a variety of ways of responding to this story. We could argue that this is a story of self-indulgence, individualised salvation at its worst. The key thing is to know and save my own soul, and when contrasted with peace-making or caring for the sick, it is an unattractive choice. Or we could argue that it is a story of despair. The 'world' is unsaveable – withdraw from it. Or, I think, we could try to humanise it by converting it into an argument for balance: either as a warning to the activists not to neglect their inner life or as an encouragement to many of us to undergo serious preparation before public ministry. But I cannot find it in me to affirm it simply as it stands, and that locates me – and I guess most readers – in a fundamentally world-affirming and engaged vision of the Christian life.

But one of the striking features of encountering either the Desert Fathers and Mothers, or Benedict – at least for a modern Evangelical – is to hear people who take Scripture with utter seriousness: but different bits of Scripture to those which I have been encouraged to follow. This takes us back again to the example of Jesus of Nazareth. We have already noted that Jesus lived a life marked by a fairly radical rejection of aspects of first-century mainstream Jewish life. He never married. He owned little if any property. Most disturbingly, he appears to have undermined the normal expectations of family life: 'Then his mother and his brothers came to him, but they could not reach him because of the crowd. And he was told, "Your mother and your brothers are standing outside, wanting to see you." But he said to them, "My mother and my brothers are those who hear the word of God and do it"' (Luke 8:19–21).[40]

This renunciation of normal family life was a key feature of the life of the Desert: as was the commitment to giving up everything, including almost all possessions, to live a life of radical dependence on God and physical hardship. The verse that Anthony heard as a direct word from God to him during the Eucharist was: 'If you want to be perfect go and sell all your possessions and give them to the poor and come and follow me, and you will have treasure in heaven' (Matt. 19:21).[41] He took this literally, sold up, and followed Christ out into the wilderness. For these Desert Fathers and Mothers saw themselves following Christ out into the desert to fight the demons. The temptation narrative (Luke 4:1–14) was central to their understanding of the spiritual life and they imitated Christ in a straightforward way, not least by going to these 'deserted places' to pray.[42] (It is always worth asking ourselves why 'we' invest some parts of Scripture with non-negotiable authority when there are other Christians who invest other parts of Scripture with a similar absolute authority.)

I am not arguing here that we should all follow Christ into the wilderness and take up celibacy and poverty. That would be counter to the arguments of Chapter 1 about how we are to imitate Jesus of Nazareth and about the value of life in this world. But there may be principles here for us to ponder. For example, Jesus spent, arguably, thirty years preparing for his brief public ministry of perhaps three years. The Church gives our ordinands two or three years to prepare for a working life of twenty, thirty or even forty years; and we wonder that so many clergy 'burn out'. What might the rule of 'stability' (understood in its widest sense of taking time, persistence, and the value of the inner life) have to say to us about this part of modern ecclesiastical policy?

We have heard a lot from the Desert Fathers and Mothers about 'hearing'. Towards the end of Pearson's novel, *I don't know how she does it*, when Kate and Rich are being reconciled, Kate talks about 'hearing'. She has learned to liken the busyness in her life to the noise of a giant waterfall that drowns out all other sounds:

> He pushes his right hand across the table so it's near mine. The hands lie next to each other as if waiting for a child to draw round them.
>
> 'There's nothing left to love, Rich, I'm all hollowed out.

Kate doesn't live here any more.'

The hand is on mine now.

'You were saying about moving away from the water-fall?'

'I thought if I, if we moved away from the waterfall we could hear again and then we could decide if –'

'If it was the noise that stopped us hearing or the fact that we didn't have anything to say to each other any more?'[43]

Kate has learned this metaphor from a black-cab driver doing a philosophy degree, not from the Church, even though Christian faith is clearly in her roots and has spoken to her at times. But the cab driver has communicated because he lives his faith. He lives differently. Do we?

We have seen how some of the ideas and actions of the Desert Fathers and Mothers, and Benedict after them, in their working out of 'stability' were extreme and, at times, even deathly. If we have chosen (been called) to life 'in the world', or in marriage, then spiritual disciplines like living in a cell for twenty years are not feasible. But there are things to learn which we can weave into 'Humane Christianity', into a different way of living, full of time and spaciousness. That it takes time to grow in faith and hope and love. That it takes time to get to know ourselves. That spiritual 'highs' may not be the best indicator or even method of spiritual growth. That even short periods of time when we are alone with ourselves with God may provide elements of the 'nowhere to hide' spirituality which the people of the Desert prized so highly. And that almost all of us will have people to live with, who will provide some of the grit that may help pearls to grow, as we face honestly why we find it difficult to live with them. For, ironically, given the criticisms of Benedict's understanding of humility that I made in Chapter 3, it is truthfulness about ourselves and the consequent realistic self-knowledge that will preserve us from some of the worst and most dangerous excesses of inhumane Christianity.

Gospel reflection: Jesus against self-righteousness

These thoughts lead me to the parable of Jesus that most subverts our self-satisfaction:

> He also told this parable to some who trusted in themselves that they were righteous and regarded others with contempt: 'Two men went up to the temple to pray, one a Pharisee and the other a tax-collector. The Pharisee, standing by himself, was praying thus, 'God, I thank you that I am not like other people: thieves, rogues, adulterers, or even like this tax-collector. I fast twice a week; I give a tenth of all my income.' But the tax-collector, standing far off, would not even look up to heaven, but was beating his breast and saying, 'God be merciful to me a sinner!' I tell you, this man went down to his home justified, rather than the other; for all who exalt themselves will be humbled, but all who humble themselves will be exalted.' (Luke 18: 9–14)

Points to ponder
- I spent some time wrestling with the question of which passage to choose for this chapter. Not because much of Jesus' life and teaching is not directly about the values of 'stability' but rather because I wanted to get to the core of the issue. This parable is about our self-perception and self-understanding. 'Know thyself' is at the heart of 'stability'.
- Parables are dynamic events. We approach them now in a written form but they were originally spoken, and spoken to have an impact on the hearers there and then. The hearer (reader) is drawn into the story, becomes part of it, and identifies with certain characters or feelings, so that the parable gets in underneath our conscious screening processes, into our 'guts'.[44] This parable in particular is not an intellectual exercise, but in our responses to it, we are revealed and challenged.
- It has an introductory editorial comment (from Luke). 'Jesus

told this parable to some who trusted in themselves that they were righteous and regarded others with contempt.' It is almost universally accepted as a parable that goes back to Jesus but it is unique to Luke's gospel and he may have placed it here as part of a sequence of teaching outlining the unexpected nature of God's kingdom and especially of those welcomed into it. It has this very precise introduction. We could hear it as a warning against any 'self'-righteousness. Is it then meant to imply that we are all such sinners that our moral behaviour is of little or no value? Or is it a more specific warning against the inner attitudes that can go with actually keeping (part of) the will of God? That a person can come to have a superior sense of their own importance and value, and of the relative value-less-ness of (all the) others, thus losing sight of the super-abundant love and grace of God which undergirds everyone? Again, it is not quite as simple – or as safely boxed away – as a critique of 'works-righteousness' in the old Protestant sense.

- How are we supposed to react to the Pharisee? We are conditioned now to see Pharisees as legalistic hypocrites but we need to remember again that at its heart the Pharisaic movement was trying to 'democratise' Judaism, by taking standards of holiness and applying them to everyday life for everyone, so that Israel would be saved. ('Holiness exalteth a nation' as the station posters so often proclaim.) So some commentators argue that the instinctive response of the hearers would be initial sympathy, especially as, for example, the Pharisee fasts far more than was required and tithes very seriously.[45] Others argue that this is a caricature of a self-righteous Pharisee, which would have been heard as such in the first century.[46] But whichever is the case, for Jesus and to early Christian eyes, the Pharisees had got righteousness completely, absolutely, wrong. Theirs was a false and deceptive righteousness, for despite keeping so much of the (moral) Law of the Old Testament, they had lost its essence. I wonder if movements that aspire to holiness do not carry within themselves the seeds of their own deep inner corruption and destruction – spiritual superiority. Aspiring to holiness, when not held within a dominant framework of love and humility, can lead to inhumanity. Perhaps one of the realities of flawed humanity is that we cannot manage the gift of holiness: just as we seem to warp so many other gifts of God, such as beauty, creativity, sexuality, love. And warped holiness may stray towards blasphemy as it tempts its possessors to claim for themselves a status that is not ours to claim, only to receive, and in parallel attempts to rubbish the status of others.[47] As Nolland comments: 'his [the Pharisee's] love for God does not move him to have compassion for his fellows; his righteousness, rather, drives him away from others'.[48] How often do we see and hear this in our Church, and tragically how often does the world see this in our Church? It seems as if those most passionate for the truth of the Gospel of Grace fall not infrequently into this sin of spiritual superiority.

• Notice how the Pharisee stands 'on his own', aloof, separate, superior.[49] Does he pray out loud as was the normal practice?[50] Is he deliberately praying so that he can be heard? We might react by feeling 'how can anyone pray in this way, telling God that they are superior to other people?' But the list of people includes those it is surely right to feel superior too: 'thieves (extortioners), rogues (evil-doers), adulterers, tax-collectors.' (We can imagine the list being targeted at the tax collector.) There was much material in the Psalms and later Jewish tradition where the righteous thanked God that he had saved them from unrighteousness (and the unrighteous) and made them holy;[51] and tax collectors were a really special case of uncleanness.[52] They made their money by taking a percentage of the local taxes. Because in Judea they were working for the army of occupation they were also traitors, but traitors who could ultimately call on the power of the feared Roman army. They therefore had the chance to be seriously crooked, and rich. Who would not despise them?

• So why has the tax collector gone to pray? It looks like a bad attack of guilt. He stands 'far off', perhaps in the corner of the

Temple, in the shadows, too ashamed to be seen there. Frightened perhaps. He cannot even bring himself to raise his head to look up to God, but can only say repeatedly, 'God be merciful to me a sinner', while rhythmically and publicly beating his chest in a very un-English sort of way.[53] He is in a desperate mood. Ruth Etchells writes insightfully: 'No wonder that his body language is that of despair. The task of redemption is impossible. So he does not stand erect with hands uplifted, the classic pose of praise to God. Instead he stands in the posture of grief, despair and penitence, with bowed head and with hands beating his breast.'[54]

- We might note, with Bailey, that he could be attending the Temple during one of the twice-daily atonement sacrifices and so, translating *hilaskomai* as 'make an atonement for me' (cf. Rom. 3:25), he is appealing for God to 'apply' the atonement sacrifice to him. There may be a strong ritual element lurking behind this parable, which might just remind us that ritual and grace are not the absolute opposites as in some Protestant theology.[55]

- But, the tax collector is the one who is 'justified'. This is a big word, but how big? First we note that there is another parable told to those who wanted to 'justify' themselves – the Good Samaritan (Luke 10:29). We should note that both parables have deeply unrespectable 'heroes' and were told to undermine the confidence of the religious and spiritual élites. It also has echoes of Pauline understandings of salvation – to be vindicated, declared justified in a court of law by God. While most commentators do not see a direct linkage to Paul's own more technical teaching on justification, the core theology and spirituality is the same.[56] It is astounding. That a crooked quisling with a broken heart was declared to be in the right with God whereas a highly self-disciplined and spiritual Pharisee was not, because of his arrogance. This might alert us to the fact that the parable is about inner attitudes rather than outward practices. We might believe in 'justification by faith' and pronounce 'Jesus is Lord' but be as deeply corrupted by arrogance as this Pharisee. The unsound and immoral might simply trust in the mercy of God and so be justified by God and before 'us'.

- It is interesting to note that the tax collector is 'justified' before he has changed his life. The parable is a parable not a real life story, so we must not try to read too much into it. For a lived-out example we have to wait until chapter 19 and the story of Zacchaeus, who is 'saved' when he repents and more than restores the money he has stolen and gives yet more to the poor. While in Chapter 6 I will wrestle with the issue of 'conversion', it is clear that Luke regards repentance and trust as the heart of salvation. The dying thief has no chance for amendment of life, only gasped out public repentance, but he is destined for paradise that very day.

- So who do we identify with? The tax collector of course. We recognise our own sinfulness, our failings, our guilt, our fear to look God in the face. And we are, of course, truthful and honest. We would not claim to be righteous, or superior to other people – at least not out loud like that self-righteous Pharisee. What a good job we are not like him – despising other people … The jaws of the parable spring shut. We have fallen into the trap of spiritual and moral superiority. Suddenly we have to see ourselves as the 'Pharisee' that we are, judging others. Instead of standing as we should, focused only on God and our own selves, not risking to 'judge others so that we may not be judged ourselves' (Luke 6:37).

- I wonder, dear reader, if you feel a bit short-changed. Here is a book about 'Humane Christianity' and yet sin and judgement have been reintroduced – 'same old story'. But this most subversive of parables should stop us drifting into that sense of moral superiority over the 'bad' Christians who have lived inhumane Christianity. The point of 'Humane Christianity' is not to gloss over our 'fallenness', but it is to make us deeply careful about how we regard other human beings, and ourselves, so that we 'treat no one with contempt'. We no longer have to strain after moral and spiritual superiority because we are in Christ now. Our 'status' is secure. It is enough for us to try to discern how to be like him.

How different would our Church look if we, individually and as a community, focused more on our own frailties and on the gift we have in God in Christ and less on denouncing the shortcomings of others? We might sound less judgemental, angry, superior and more truthful, humble, attractive.

A patient response

'It is better to wear out than to rust out.'[57] Evangelicals, more than most, are prone to activism, though it can afflict all Christians. It is as if everything depends on us. Add to that even a moderated version of 'a million dying a day without God in China'[58] and this can be a recipe for chronic overwork. That drive to overwork allied to the longing that, 'please God this time', we will find the solution for our spiritual problems, can be a deadly *chimera*. Worst of all, when we think we have found 'it', we can breed in ourselves a sense of spiritual superiority. Truly inhumane Christianity. Better to be patient with ourselves and others, as God is. For God is always the life-bringer.

I finish this chapter with a story rather than with a prayer, although you might like to weave it into your prayers.

> A hunter in the desert saw Abba Anthony enjoying himself with the brethren and was shocked. Wanting to show that it was necessary sometimes to meet the needs of the brethren, the old man said to him, 'Put an arrow in your bow and shoot it'. So he did. The old man said, 'Shoot another', and he did so. Then the old man said, 'Shoot yet again', and the hunter replied 'If I bend my bow so much I will break it'. Then the old man said to him, 'It is the same with the work of God. If we stretch the brethren beyond measure they will soon break. Sometimes it is necessary to come down to meet their needs.' When he heard these words the hunter was pierced by compunction and, greatly edified by the old man, he went away. As for the brethren, they went home strengthened.[59]
> Amen.

CHAPTER SIX

From Conversion to Christ

A humane cross

So what is all this for? Crudely put, why does God make Christians? Indeed, more profoundly, why does God make human beings? I don't want to fall into too facile a caricature, but in some parts of the Church, it can feel as if the whole point of being a Christian is to make other people Christians – a gigantic spiritual version of pyramid selling. The richness and breadth of the Christian faith compressed into repetitive hackneyed evangelism: 'Ten thousand thousand are their texts, but all their sermons one.'[1] But if we were to go back to Irenaeus again, 'the glory of God is a human being fully alive',[2] then we would give a bigger answer. God is most profoundly committed to human flourishing in this life as well as in the next. God is always the life-bringer. God's will is that we are the best that we can be as human beings; that we are so drawn into him that we begin to, and will end in, sharing his glory. So it is never just a matter of being 'converted' but of being made Christlike.

There are two interrelated issues that flow into this final chapter. The first is this question which I have just opened up: what is life for? And within that, echoing the title of another recent novel: how are we to be good?[3] Partly, what is it to 'be good'? But more, how do we find the energy to 'be good'? The second issue, I hope, will help us to begin to answer that question. What about the cross of Christ? I have deliberately kept the cross in the background of this book. In theological terms I have wanted to stress creation and the incarnation as convictions and understandings which can resource 'Humane Christianity'. But this has been a struggle. Temperamentally, and because of my Evangelical shaping, the cross feels central to everything. But our teaching about the cross of Christ is so swamped by the language of human sinfulness, that it has become, tragically, a key feature of inhumane Christianity, used to browbeat people into submission or to generate unhealthy feelings of guilt and unworthiness. The cross is a scandal when we make it into a verbal weapon to undermine other human beings, and above all when the source of renewed life is made an instrument for oppression and the status quo. At its most extreme, the cross is for many Jews a symbol of prejudice and violence, but a classic example of this sort of oppression of those within the Church is from a sermon to secondary-school boys in Joyce's *A Portrait of the Artist as a Young Man*. When I read this as a (Christian) sixth former I remember feeling both guilty and manipulated:

> O my dear little brethren in Christ Jesus, will we then offend that good Redeemer and provoke his anger? Will we trample upon that torn and mangled corpse? Will we spit upon that face so full of sorrow and love? Will we too, like the cruel Jews and the brutal soldiers, mock that gentle and compassionate Saviour? Who trod alone for our sake the awful winepress of sorrow? Every word of sin is a wound in his tender side. Every sinful act is a thorn piercing his head. Every impure thought, deliberately yielded to, is a keen lance transfixing that sacred and loving heart. No, no. It is impossible for any human being to do that which offends so deeply the divine majesty, that which is punished by an eternity of agony, that which crucifies again the Son of God and makes a mockery of him. [4]

This is tragic because the cross is, above all, life-giving: 'The tree of shame was made the tree of glory; and where life was lost, there life has been restored.'[5] In that most bizarre way, an instrument of brutal torture has become a symbol of celebration, of life. A 'humane' cross?

I am aware that, for some people, the journey that this book has taken will be seen as profoundly misguided. How can anyone, let alone a Christian, talk of the celebration of the goodness and potential of humanity in the aftermath of the most murderous – and most secular – century in human history? Surely, now above all, we need to be pressing home the message of the essential sinfulness of human beings, their need for the forgiveness and the ontologically new life of the convert in Christ: the Gospel of the cross. With qualifications, part of me agrees. If the twentieth century has taught us anything, it is that all human dreams of heaven on earth will go wrong. The passionate justice of *The Communist Manifesto* ends in the Gulag. The longing for simplicity of the Cambodian revolution ends in the 'Killing Fields'. The 'American Dream' ends in 'imperial' wars. We need to orientate ourselves again by Jesus of Nazareth.

But 'preaching the cross' is not as simple as we might like to think.[6] First, the 'cross' is, of course, a piece of theological shorthand. In places I will put 'the cross and the empty tomb' to remind us that the cross and resurrection are inseparable.[7] The resurrection was portrayed by the earliest Christians as the vindication of Jesus' life, teaching and death as well as being the demonstration of the triumph of God over sin and death. To try to be a Christian without belief in the resurrection is to cut out from ourselves confidence in the face of death and hope for the future of the world. So I would argue that a key feature of 'Humane Christianity' is to remain hopeful because the resurrection is a vibrant part of our faith – without falling into a foolish over-realised eschatology which holds that God has already won and all is triumph for us now. But space requires that all this is taken as read.

As foundations for this chapter, which is in truth more cross- than resurrection-shaped, I note here my convictions that the cross has a threefold significance. First, it is the place where God 'deals with' human sin and evil. Second, it is where he shows us he is immersed in the suffering of this world, and above all, third, where he shows us that he loves us. Because human sin and suffering are in reality impossible to disentangle – however much conceptual clarity about the existence of innocent suffering is essential – for us to have faith in God requires that all three aspects of our relationship with him are handled and kept together. For all this to 'work' theologically, it is essential that Jesus of Nazareth was both 'truly God' and 'fully human'. There is a further point to stress: the cross is not to be seen merely as the point of entry into the Christian faith, for it is, when carefully expressed, a model for our own lives. So, the cross is not just a form of words but a reality within God, which happened to a real flesh and blood human being, and whose purpose is to renew human living.

In this chapter I hope to reflect a little on the meaning of the death of Jesus of Nazareth building on our earlier work on creation and incarnation, so that we have a genuine sense of the activity of God all holding together, remembering that God is always the life-bringer. Note again the wisdom of *The Mystery of Salvation* here: 'Both the continuity of creation and salvation, which an emphasis on incarnation highlights, and the discontinuity, which is emphasised by attention to the cross and resurrection, are important. The Christian view of the world makes sense only if neither is absolutised.'[8] In this chapter we will look at what the cross has 'achieved', but vitally, without surrendering to fantasy about ourselves as Christians. We will encounter Luther again and also hear Jeremy Taylor as he tried to help the Royalists of the English Civil War live converted Christlike lives. We will finish by walking with Jesus the 'way of the cross', to reflect on the nature and power of sacrificial love.

Atonement

Time for another cliché: our society finds it difficult to deal with issues of failure, guilt and redemption. We have a healthy scepticism about those who too glibly claim to have seen the error of their ways and reformed. But if there is no chance of repentance – that is, change of life as well as remorse – then we

are at risk of extensive dishonesty ('don't get caught'), of devaluation of moral standards ('well it doesn't matter that much
anyway'), and of scapegoating ('well at least I am not like him
over there and he can carry the can anyway'). I worry that the
apparent impossibility in our public political life of acknowl-
edging a mistake or failure creates a climate of bland denials
over against a self-righteous, harassing media: there is no
honest, common recognition of human fallibility. More fundamentally, how are we to put right that which goes wrong? Yes,
this includes the enabling of moral change and the delivery of
justice and forgiveness, but where does the evil 'go' and who
deals with its consequences, its residue and ongoing existence?
The issue is one of *atonement* as well as repentance.

I am fascinated that a novel with this title by one of Britain's
leading novelists has been in the best-seller lists for months. Ian
McEwan's book *Atonement*, set mostly in the 1930s and 1940s,
tells the story of Briony, unhappy younger sister to Cecilia, who
distorts the story of the rape of one of her cousins so that
Cecilia's 'boyfriend' (Robbie) is convicted of the crime. The
ramifications of this ravage the rest of her 'life' and that of her
family (including incongruously her cousin who later marries
the rapist). As the novel moves on Briony tries to atone. She
turns down a place at Cambridge and follows in Cecilia's footsteps as a wartime nurse. As Cecilia notes: 'She's saying that she
wants to be useful in a practical way. But I get the impression
that she's taken on nursing as a sort of penance.'[9] Briony confirms this: 'Whatever skivvying or humble nursing she did, and
however well or hard she did it, whatever illumination in
tutorial she had relinquished, or lifetime moment on a college
lawn, she would never undo the damage. She was unforgiv-
able.'[10] In the end Briony – having in some sense made partial
atonement by nursing horrifically wounded soldiers – does
make contact with Cecilia again. As expected, it is a difficult
meeting:

> She stood where Cecilia had stood, with her back to the
> sink and, unable to meet her sister's eye, said 'What I did

was terrible. I don't expect you to forgive me.'

'Don't worry about that', she said soothingly, and in the second or two during which she drew deeply on her cigarette, Briony flinched as her hopes lifted unreally. 'Don't worry', her sister resumed. 'I won't ever forgive you'.[11]

The moment is super-charged because of Robbie's unexpected presence and it is saved only by Cecilia's love for Robbie. She holds him and kisses him passionately to keep him from sinking into revenge. For Briony the experience of being excluded as the couple kiss in front of her is one of punishment, almost penance, a form of atonement: 'she felt obliterated, expunged from the room, and was relieved'.[12] Taken together this is serious repentance: Briony publicly recounts her wrong-doing (including writing a new statement and confessing face to face to her parents); she feels it very deeply; she suffers herself; she makes reparations; she gives love super-abundantly to those who need it. It is almost enough to make atonement.[13] But the real source of redemption for Robbie is Cecilia's trusting and unconditional love.

All this is set against Robbie's experiences of the horrors of war, as a soldier at Dunkirk. As he waits to escape the beaches, he muses on Briony's decision to admit her guilt so that he would be declared innocent:

> But what was guilt these days? It was cheap. Everyone was guilty, and no one was. No one would be redeemed by a change of evidence, for there weren't enough people, enough paper and pens, enough patience and peace, to take down the statements of all the witnesses and gather in the facts. The witnesses were guilty too. All day we've witnessed each other's crimes. You killed no one today? But how many did you leave to die?[14]

This is an exquisite account of the moral despair of post-modernity. It is not that nothing is wrong – Robbie frets over leaving the mangled body of a dead child unburied – but that so much is wrong and who is there left to judge and put it right?[15]

This is the fundamental basis for the book's complex dénouement. Briony 'becomes' a successful novelist and the last chapter is her epilogue as she faces her own death as an old woman. But McEwan, using Briony as a mouthpiece, then begins to remind us that this is a novel. It is a literary construct. Is it true or not, Briony muses, that both Robbie and Cecilia were 'in fact' killed in 1940, without a reconciliation, and has she shielded us, the readers, from this, saving us from this 'bleakest realism'? In other words, 'we' cannot bear stories without a just resolution. But as a novelist McEwan has shown us by his terrible account of the random cruelty of war that there is no justice in life – just harsh tragedy, occasionally mitigated by human love. I take it that this has led McEwan to the atheism he mentions on the penultimate page. But then, if there is, obviously, no God in this disordered cruel universe, then there is also no justice and no possibility of atonement. 'There is no one, no entity or higher form that she can appeal to, or be reconciled with, or that can forgive her.'[16] I read McEwan as saying that it may be that all we can do is to imagine justice, dream of 'happy endings', create them in art. For 'atonement was always an impossible task, and that was precisely the point'. But, 'the attempt was all'.

I recommend this novel and hope that if you read it, you will reflect for yourself on whether 'atonement' is 'possible'. I have found my reaction to this novel swinging back and forth. From one perspective, it is a brave and truthful answer to the question of atonement. In a universe with no external guarantor, where the innocent suffer without hope of salvation or justice, where life can appear to be monstrous, we might just give up. But McEwan appears to be saying that we must keep striving for justice and that love remains a vehicle of redemption, even if a very fragile one. It strikes me as courageous hope in the face of such overwhelming meaninglessness. Christians must beware of rushing too soon to give answers that point back to God. Our spiritual ancestors may have found it easier to believe in a God of love and justice in the face of the tragedy of life but our era does not. There appears to be something about our industrialised cruelty, and of innocent suffering in the presence of the huge potential for well-being that our technology has brought, that is causing modern, and postmodern, thinkers to find the possibility of faith in God, as we used to express it, impossible.

But what is it about human beings that enables them still to hope and love in the face of the awfulness of life, as we know that they do? It seems both irrational, but also absolutely right and inescapable. It is how we are. It is how we have 'been made'. And there are times when love and justice do seem to bear fruit, to resonate with the structure of the universe. The universe is not entirely inhumane. Christian celebration of the goodness of the created world (even if it has been 'warped') and of humanity in it – the beautiful blue sky this morning and my capacity to enjoy it, even as the radio describes war in Iraq – stops us from surrendering to an unbalanced gloom about our world.

But I wonder if, ultimately, the alternative to belief in divine justice is not, in strict logic, either mad despair or hedonism? Wrongdoing leaves a need for restitution, even punishment. If there is no justice, ever, even in the 'next life', for the innocents, then how is this to be borne? It is too painful to contemplate this 'bleak reality'. It makes a mockery of all our longing and language of justice.

The cross and atonement

In the face of this 'bleak reality', Christians will find themselves hanging on to the cross. Our most precious symbol of God is an instrument of unjust torture. After Dostoevsky, a facile appeal to the soothing hope of heaven is immoral,[17] and so is incredible, but we believe that on the cross, God endured the reality of human agony, including evil. He shows that he is with us in the mess. But more, we believe that on the cross (and through the empty tomb), ontologically (if not yet and far from fully) God broke the power of evil, dealt with some of the requirements of justice, gave us a glimpse of the glorious future, and showed us that the engine for these achievements is love, expressed in an 'ordinary' human being.

There is something both horrific and wonderful about the diverse theologies of how Jesus of Nazareth 'bore our sins' on the cross.[18] The horror is an angry, punitive, even apparently self-hating God, who has to vent on someone the punishment for wrongdoing and who sends his own Son to be the innocent victim. The doctrine of 'penal substitutionary atonement' has been shaped not just by Scripture but also by an odd inheritance of medieval feudalism and the legalistic world of early modern Europe. If for a moment we think of relationships within a family, how could a parent shun their child – as we are meant to believe the wrathful Father shuns us and even his Son – if the child simply repents and asks for forgiveness? A judge or a feudal monarch might require 'satisfaction', but a loving father? But despite its problems, I want to acknowledge the sense of grace present in the belief that God 'deals with' the sin (and punishment) of those who cannot deal with it.[19] And God deals with it through real suffering, not by treating it as unimportant. Evil is acknowledged as evil and as hugely costly; yet because it is 'dealt with' there is always space for mercy – hence the penitent thief on the cross. This is the immense theological, spiritual, psychological and emotional freedom which 'justification by grace through faith' brings.

I want to emphasise strongly here that God's motivation in all of this is love, not anger. Though neither Scripture nor tradition would quite express things this way (because blame for the Fall was always placed very squarely on human shoulders), I would argue that the cross is about God absorbing the consequences – evil, punishment, and mortality – of a creation that had the potential to become flawed and that did 'fall', becoming 'warped'. This costly 'absorbing' by God of these 'consequences' is the atonement. Further, if we remember the discussion in Chapter 1 about God and time and God's interaction with creation, then the cross is not just about sorting 'the past', it is at the same time about shaping the present and the future, about liberating human beings now and for eternity. It is about how God always is towards humankind – ready to bear the cost and welcome us home. God is always the life-bringer.

If a previous huge generalisation was even a quarter right – that the Church has been on the back foot in terms of human moral development in the last century – then part of the agenda for the Church must be to regain its moral passion. I am not convinced that the theology of 'justification' will do this on its own. If human moral growth is of such little importance in the journey of salvation, then why bother? 'Justification' on its own could be seen as producing a rather static spirituality. But if the journey of salvation is towards full humanity in Christ, which means not less than striving to be Christlike, then, theologically, we have to hold justification and sanctification inextricably together.[20] (This has the additional merit of addressing the charge that 'substitutionary atonement' – selectively applied and appropriated – is in fact immoral and tends towards undermining individual moral responsibility.) The cross is not only about the process of coming to Christ in conversion (and managing the falls that we experience thereafter), it is fundamentally about becoming truly human in Christ. But how can an instrument of death become a means of becoming fully human?

I would argue that it does so in three ways. First, by providing a place – the foot of the cross – to take our guilt (as well as our grief, our anger, our despair) and to hear the words, 'Father forgive them', as the One through whom the universe was created[21] endures some of the worst suffering which humankind can inflict. If part of this sense of forgiveness is the conviction that God in Christ, out of sheer love, takes the blame and the punishment that human beings in some sense deserve but otherwise cannot escape, then I believe we can celebrate that reality. Earlier, I asked where does the evil 'go'? In part it goes on to God in Christ's body on the cross. He is, terribly, the scapegoat. Second, by giving us a motive to live and love generously ourselves, by demonstrating in a concrete way the depth of God's love for us. Third, by giving us an example of what it is to walk the way of self-discipline and self-sacrifice for others and crucially to reassure us that this way of living is never wasted. The rest of this chapter will explore different reflections on these three spiritual realities, but woven together, which is how they should be held. We need to do this both for the Church but also for God's world, where 'how to be good' is a pressing question.

For if this is 'atonement', we might be asked, does it make anything better, now? Does this reality change actual lives? Sometimes Christians treat the cross as if it is a 'get out of jail free' card. How do we make sure that our gratitude for the guarantee of God's loving forgiveness of us, which is achieved and demonstrated on the cross, does not slither into being a way of constantly letting us off the sharp hook of moral growth and conflict? The easy assumption that 'God will forgive me' (and therefore 'I need do no more'), whether expressed in a medieval indulgence or a revivalist experience, is a dangerous spirituality. And no modern Christian can forget Bonhoeffer's warning about the Church's offer of 'cheap grace'; with the dire consequences this had in not enabling a more robust and courageous opposition to Nazism:

> Cheap grace is the deadly enemy of the Church. We are fighting today for costly grace … Cheap grace is the preaching of forgiveness without requiring repentance … Cheap grace is grace without discipleship, grace without the cross, grace without Jesus Christ, living and incarnate … The upshot of it all is that my only duty as a Christian is to leave the world for an hour or so on Sunday morning and go to church to be assured that my sins are forgiven.[22]

If the cross is not changing lives, it is mere sentimentality or a deceptive placebo.

Conversion

We have had a funny reminder of the complicated effects of conversion and lack of realism in a most insightful book on modern Britain. In Nick Hornby's novel *How to be Good*, David, a caustic, even bitter journalist whose marriage is on the rocks, undergoes a 'conversion' experience at the hands of an 'alternative' healer with the revealing name of GoodNews.[23] The account of David's 'conversion', which is explicitly *not* a Christian conversion, should make Christians think. (Try putting 'Jesus Christ' in place of 'he' …)

> 'He's changed my life.'
>
> 'He seems to have sucked everything out of you.'
>
> 'Yes, he did. Every bad thing. I could almost see it coming out of me, like a black mist. I didn't realise I was so full of all this stuff.'
>
> 'He touched my temples again, when I was talking to him, and I just felt this amazing warmth flood right through me, and he said it was pure love. And that's what it felt like.'

The story is told from the perspective of David's wife, Katie, a GP, who has just embarked on an affair as the novel begins. Katie likes to think of herself as a basically 'good' person:

> Listen: I'm not a bad person. I'm a doctor. One of the reasons I wanted to become a doctor was because I thought it would be a good – as in Good, rather than exciting or well-paid or glamorous – thing to do.'[24]

As Katie ruefully recognises, having an affair and telling your husband on a mobile phone that you want a divorce are not actions normally associated with being 'good', but she is basically secure in her side of the row. And then David is 'converted'. At first it is simply shocking that he is kind and considerate, forgiving and calm, having lost his caustic core. But then the extent of his conversion becomes apparent when he gives £80 to a rough sleeper in a doorway, gives some of the children's toys to a women's refuge, tries to give away a Sunday lunch and finally sets up a scheme to persuade his neighbours in this leafy patch of North London each to take in a homeless person. Why? In his own words: 'All I know is that I want to live a better life. I want to live a better life.'[25] And more precisely: 'We don't care enough. We look after ourselves and ignore the weak and poor. We despise our politicians for doing nothing, and think that this is somehow enough to show we care, and meanwhile we live in centrally-heated houses that are too big for us ...'[26] It is an acutely observed critique of 'Islington' self-righteousness – lots of political correctness but cocooned in (in world terms) considerable wealth and with minimal personal cost. Not surprisingly, Katie is thrown, and reacts with bewildered rage.

It is a shrewdly written book. David's conversion, while in some ways challenging and attractive – Katie wonders if it is like living with Jesus, or Bob Geldof[27] – is also alienating and rigid. He loses his sense of humour, indeed his sense of irony. Whilst it would be inaccurate to describe him as lacking in humility – he is all too ready to admit his faults – there is, simply, a lack of realism about himself and others. Katie's character portrait of him can stand as a warning to any 'convert': 'How could I have forgotten that this is what always happens with zealots? They go too far, they lose all sense of appropriateness and logic and ultimately they are interested in nobody but themselves, nothing but their own piousness.'[28] In desperation Katie goes to church to find an alternative spirituality to compete with David. In common with all the novels that we have looked at in this book, the Church gets a satirical treatment. (Hornby, like de Bernières, Harris and McEwan, is not a neutral observer of Christianity. The last sentence of the book reads to me like a statement of atheism.[29]) But Katie's account of her visit to church ought to be compulsory reading for Christians. The vicar in charge of the slightly run-down, cold, inner-London parish church, with an ageing congregation, is, of course, undergoing a crisis of faith and (a true sign of desperation this) sings both the latest chart song and also 'Getting to know you' from *The King and I* during the service. The most telling observation is the deep embarrassment Katie and her brother share when they find they have both been to church.[30]

There are, however, signs of good news from a Church – and Katie's – perspective. One is that the vicar's sermon is about not being 'artificially good' and she cites 1 Corinthians 13 on the true self-forgetful nature of love. (Katie is almost converted because it gives her such a good weapon in her fight with David.) A second occurs when the vicar comes for a consultation with Katie and is forced by Katie to give a judgement on Katie's marriage before getting her prescription. The 'nice lady vicar' tells her to stay. Katie does so, and is in the end grateful for the advice. But fundamentally, Christianity is just too implausible and crumbling to sustain its place in the novel. So, as the heart of the problem gradually becomes clearer, Hornby offers an interesting diagnosis and, to my mind, an unsatisfactory solution.

In the end David realises that he has lost faith in GoodNews and is feeling empty and depressed. The crunch happens when, during a process of reconciliation with people whom they have hurt in the past, GoodNews completely fails to be reconciled to his sister and has a furious public row. Katie reflects (and this goes to the heart of 'Humane Christianity'):

> Who are these people, that they want to save the world and yet they are incapable of forming proper relationships with anybody? As GoodNews so eloquently puts it, it's love this and love that, but of course it's easy to love someone you don't know ... Staying civil to someone with whom you've ever shared Christmas turkey – now there's a miracle.[31]

(I am reminded of both Benedict and Luther.) As Katie tells David when he laments GoodNews' frailty: 'You were human all the time. You just forgot.'[32] This could be seen simply as an argument for complacency, but I hear it as an insight into our human condition: that we are flawed and complex; that we grow and change slowly, without miraculously discarding parts of our personalities or histories; that just living quietly and decently can take a lot of energy. In a climactic speech Katie says: 'If in twenty years' time, we're all still speaking, and Molly's not an anorexic, and Tom's not inside, and I'm not hooked on tranquillisers, and you're not an alcoholic, and you and I are still together, well, that'll be a bloody miracle in itself.'[33] But is it enough? Katie has known all through the novel that she is tired, without hope, without richness in her life. Hornby has a vivid metaphor for both Katie and David. They have a 'flat battery' inside.[34] They are 'soul-dead'.[35] But they still have to 'drive the car', get through life. In a very moving passage Katie reflects that what she – and everyone she knows – has lost, is 'love':

> Oh, I'm not talking about romantic love, the mad hunger for someone you don't know very well … I'm talking about that love which used to feel something like optimism, benignity … Where did that go? I just seemed to run out of steam somewhere along the line. I ended up disappointed with my work, and my marriage, and myself, and I turned into someone who didn't know what to hope for.[36]

Katie's (Hornby's) answer is the richness that comes from reading good books, listening to beautiful music, little bits of space without 'stale' air. Katie thinks this will be enough to keep her alive and able to care for her family, without striving to 'be good'. She does not, of course, turn to the discredited, absent or non-existent God.

When I first read this, and it was my reaction also to McEwan, I was angry, and sad. Angry that the riches of life in Christ had been overlooked. Sad that these people did not know, had not even glimpsed, the reality of Christian life. But a second reaction is that I, and my friends and colleagues, are not immune from these feelings of emptiness. Burnt-out clergy are only a cliché because there are so many of them. At least for clergy, we have the structures of the Church to retain us. Our lay people just drift away.[37] Have we really got the resources of life that will give us the energy and the love we need in order to keep trying to 'be good'?

Back to the cross and love – Benedict and then Luther.

Benedict and conversion

We have already seen that the key vow of the Benedictine monk was to 'conversion of life'. Through the hard discipline of the Rule, the monk was to become Christlike, by receiving grace and by disciplining selfish egotism out of himself. Chapter 4 of the Rule described how to do this, listing the 'tools of the good works'. These are God's moral and spiritual commandments. Benedict gathers together the Ten Commandments and many instructions from the New Testament, and later traditions, such as 'love one's enemies' or 'listen gladly to holy reading', and says that if the monk faithfully uses these 'tools', then on the Day of Judgement he will receive the Lord's reward.[38] We might be tempted to ask where is the 'grace' in this? Where is God's generous giving of new life and the spiritual resources to live it, not to mention forgiveness for the inevitable failures? I think they are just simply and fundamentally assumed to be in place by Benedict. It is God who has called the monk to the monastery.[39] It is God who will forgive, through the ministry of the abbot.[40] God will give the grace.[41] But the 'tools' are called 'tools' because the purpose is not just to produce people who will keep these commandments, but who have been shaped to be Christlike in their very selves. Esther de Waal has also wrestled with this chapter and concludes:

> These tools for my spiritual life are not so very different from the tools for my day-to-day life at work in garden or kitchen; they have been issued to me, I am responsible for using them and on the day of judgement I shall have to return them and render account ... And then comes the moment when the good worker claims his or her wages. But they are not wages that the world might chalk up, based on any outward achievement. 'What the eye hath not seen nor the ear heard' surely brings me back to the *disposition of the heart*, to the secret intentions known to God alone.[42]

As we have seen, the pinnacle of this interior disposition is love

141

for God in Christ, and for one's neighbour; a wonderful vision of salvation resulting in mutual love between Christ and monk. But, the journey to that inner place is, in Benedict's experience, very tough and requires of the monk, immense effort. Again, we come back to the sheer realism of these ancient saints about the nature of change in a human being. The 'way of the cross' – understanding it according to Antony, Benedict and Francis – of disciplining the self and of self-sacrificial love is slow, not fast. For if God simply changes us by 'zapping' us then we will not have really changed at all. So where do we get the energy for this moral and spiritual change? From the cross. And the motive for walking the 'way of the cross' is fundamentally, love.

Luther, the cross and grace

The 'theology of the cross' is often portrayed as a negative blast. A 'no' to merely human effort (hence Luther's fierce rejection of his monastic background).[43] I have already argued that it is often used as a mechanism to grind guilt into people. So how are love and the cross to be related? Can they be? Luther may seem an odd choice to converse with about God's love. As we have noted, he seems to have suffered from depression and the last quarter of his life, after 1530, is often portrayed as a sad decline, marked by increasingly intemperate outbursts.[44] But Luther had grasped, or been grasped by (possibly because of his depressions) a profound sense of the love of God, shown most clearly in the brutal reality of the cross. Again, this needs careful expression. Luther lived with and taught a ferociously severe God of judgement. The cross revealed this more clearly than anything else:

> They contemplate Christ's passion aright who view it with a terror-stricken heart and a despairing conscience. This terror must be felt as you witness the stern wrath and the unchanging earnestness with which God looks upon sin and sinners, so much so that he was unwilling to release sinners even for his only and dearest Son without his pay-

ment of the severest penalty for them ... And if you seriously consider that it is God's very own Son, the eternal wisdom of God, who suffers you will be terrified indeed. The more you think about it, the more intensely you will be frightened.[45]

It is important to hear this undiluted because it is this sort of description of the atonement that has caused such offence for the last three hundred years in the West.[46] But for Luther this was paradoxically the place where God's love is most clearly revealed. In some ways this is simply standard Christian preaching. Jesus dying for us, shows the depth of his love for us. But Luther goes further: 'You will see that Christ would not have shown this love for you if God in his eternal love had not wanted this ... Thus you will find the divine and kind paternal heart, and, as Christ says, you will be drawn to the Father through him ... *We know God aright when we grasp him not in his might or wisdom (for then he proves terrifying), but in his kindness and love.*'[47]

We must not misrepresent Luther. For him, God always retained a fierce judging aspect and it is often to be heard in his writing and preaching as he threatened others, but behind it was a passionate love, made all the more poignant because Luther placed such a strong emphasis on the real humanity of Christ.[48] Bainton finishes his biography with a paraphrase of Luther's own writing. Luther asks how can we know that the 'All Terrible' is also the 'All Merciful':

> In Christ, only in Christ. In the Lord of life, born in the squalor of a cow stall and dying as a malefactor under the desertion and the derision of men, crying unto God and receiving for answer only the trembling of the earth and the blinding of the sun, even by God forsaken, and in that hour taking to himself and annihilating our iniquity, trampling down the hosts of hell and disclosing within the wrath of the All Terrible the love that will not let us go.[49]

The joy of the doctrine of justification is that it reveals to us precisely this receptive, loving, forgiving, self-sacrificing God. At its most radical it should tempt us to antinomianism – living without the restraints of the moral law – because 'I am so loved and saved by God that I can keep on sinning because he will always forgive me'.[50] And it provides the best motive for loving others – sheer gratitude rather than the need to earn God's love. So Luther writes: 'Why should I not therefore freely, joyfully, with all my heart, and with an eager will do all things which I know are pleasing and acceptable to such a Father who has overwhelmed me with his inestimable riches? I will therefore give myself as a Christ to my neighbour, just as Christ offered himself to me …'[51] As Lutheran theologians stress, this is truly a religion of grace.[52] But, does this religion of grace have to be posited on – as it was absolutely for Luther – the negation of all human qualities? Luther believed that it was only by first convincing people of the extent of their need, by completely destroying their attempts, even their hope, to 'justify' themselves, that they would come to appreciate God's generosity. Hence, in soteriological matters, his ferocious rubbishing of human reason and wisdom and moral endeavour. God only justifies sinners who cling to him in faith, which is a process entirely separate from any human moral effort.[53]

But what if God's generous grace is more extensive and more connected to the whole of human living? We cannot storm the gates of heaven or arrive there with a perfect checklist of virtues. But I am not trying to do that and I suspect few modern British people are either. The cause of their disenchantment with God and the Church is more likely to lie in what is heard as an antiquated and authoritarian language of sin, rather than a stress on the gracious generosity of God. God gives to us across the whole of our human life – in his creating and in his redeeming together – and it is the same God active in both sorts of activity. All is grace, all coheres together; so all is gratitude. God is always the life-bringer. Therefore, is Christ's mission best served by a verbal assault from the Church on human complacency or by a communal life and language in the Church shaped by gratitude for God's goodness to us?

A pastoral note: clergy often agonise in funeral sermons about how to talk of the deceased, especially when their knowledge of the faith of the deceased is thin. But it is possible both to give thanks warmly to God for the qualities evident in a life and the good things that a person has enjoyed but also to stress that death is the door to direct encounter with God, and that we go to him trusting in his character of love – shown best in Jesus – not trying to bribe him to love us. All is grace.

A suffering God

There are two final points to make on Luther. First, one of the aspects of Luther that has been picked up by modern theologians is the depth of his understanding of Christ's suffering: the God-forsakeness of Christ as the truest revelation of God. A key part of Luther's *theologia crucis* was the conviction that only on the cross do we truly see God (and then only the back – *posteriora Dei* – of God). For while God is paradoxically most clearly revealed in 'the humility and shame of the cross'[54] ('clearly' is perhaps the wrong word because God's revelation even here is concealed, partial, open only to faith), this is the *absconditus Deus* – the hidden God. 'Hidden' because the God revealed in a dying helpless man is not the God of power and glory, though he in some sense stands behind it, but a God of absence and weakness and humility. Thus this revelation, to Luther's mind, contradicts the God constructed by human reason. If we want to see God, we look to the passion of Christ, even in his God-forsakeness, which Luther explored more fully than had ever been done before. Bainton in his biography of Luther, paraphrases poignantly Luther's understanding of the death of Jesus: 'In old age the angel of death often muffles his wings and permits us to slip peacefully away. Jesus went to his death in full possession of his faculties ... Christ at this point was simply a man, and it was for Him as it is for me when the Devil comes and says "You are mine".'[55] While Luther drew profound pastoral implications from this,[56] it is in post-World War II theology that this theme has been amplified far beyond Luther's own vision.

The theologian who has forged the way in this is Jürgen Moltmann, who was a German soldier and then POW. He argues passionately against the traditional view that the divine part ('nature') of Jesus of Nazareth did not suffer on the cross, only the human. He makes a technical theological point first: 'If this divine nature in the person of the eternal Son of God is the centre which creates a person in Christ, then it too suffered and died.'[57] But from this technical base he builds a profound theology opening to us the nature of God's suffering on the cross:

> To understand what happened between Jesus and his God and Father on the cross, it is necessary to talk in Trinitarian terms. The Son suffers dying, the Fathers suffers the death of the Son. The grief of the Father here is just as important as the death of the Son. The Fatherlessness of the Son is matched by the Sonlessness of the Father and if God has constituted himself as the Father of Jesus Christ, then he also suffers the death of his Fatherhood in the death of the Son.[58]

And he applies this in the most terrible of circumstances, drawing, rightly and essentially, also on Jewish insights into the character of God:

> A shattering expression of the *theologia crucis* which is suggested in the rabbinic theology of God's humiliation of himself is to be found in *Night*, a book written by E. Wiesel, a survivor of Auschwitz: 'The SS hanged two Jewish men and a youth in front of the whole camp. The men died quickly, but the death throes of the youth lasted for half an hour. "Where is God? Where is He?" someone asked behind me. As the youth still hung in torment in the noose after a long time, I heard the man call again, "Where is God now?" And I heard a voice in myself answer: "Where is he? He is here. He is hanging there on the gallows ..." Any other answer would be blasphemy. There cannot be any other answer to the question of this torment. To speak here

146

of a God who could not suffer would make God a demon. To speak here of an absolute God would make God an annihilating nothingness. To speak here of an indifferent God would condemn men to indifference.[59]

Moltmann goes on from this to a solid hope for the future, rooted again in the work of the Triune God:

As Paul says in I Cor. 15, only with the resurrection of the dead, the murdered and the gassed, only with the healing of those in despair who bear lifelong wounds, only with the abolition of all rule and authority, only with the annihilation of death will the Son hand over the kingdom to the Father. Then God will turn his sorrow into eternal joy. This will be the sign of the completion of the Trinitarian history of God and the end of world history, the overcoming of the history of man's sorrow and the fulfilment of his history of hope.[60]

This combination of searing realism and hope is crucial to the spirituality of 'Humane Christianity'.

I am often surprised – perhaps I should not be surprised, given many generations of prayers beginning 'Almighty God' – by how little of this theology of a 'suffering' God, who does not run the world like a clockwork toy, has permeated out beyond the confines of academic theology. So many funeral visits come up against the conviction that 'God has done this'. The response of the bereaved can then be anger or disbelief. Our alternative language that 'God is in this with you' is so slow to take hold. Perhaps we need to reshape our liturgies and preaching even more to witness to the gentleness and reticence of God, his silent suffering presence and his love known only in and through this silent presence.

Back to Luther and conversion

Second, despite his stress on grace, Luther was never naïve. He was absolutely convinced that the power and habits of selfish behaviour – sin – ran deep in humankind and needed to be confronted in a disciplined manner, even after justification. Indeed – and this is a measure of the realism of Luther's theology – we remain for the whole of our lives *simul iustus, simul peccator*: at the same time both sinner and justified.[61] But I struggle with Luther's understanding of the journey of sanctification. He regarded those who were justified as having been already redeemed in their inner selves but he believed that this needed to be worked out in the 'flesh', because the body had a tendency to revolt against the Spirit:

> Although, as I have said, a man is abundantly and sufficiently justified by faith inwardly, in his spirit, and so has all that he needs, except insofar as this faith and these riches must grow from day to day even to the future life; yet he remains in this mortal life on earth. In this life he must control his body and have dealings with men ... he must indeed take care to discipline his body by fastings, watchings, labour, and other reasonable discipline and to subject it to the Spirit so that it will obey and conform to the inner man and faith and not revolt against faith and hinder the inner man, as it is the nature of the body to do if it is not held in check.[62]

Shades of the old enemy 'dualism' again.

I am convinced that humankind is 'in trouble' (self-preoccupied, wilfully and inadvertently 'blind', destructive, as well as being creative and full of life), but I am convinced that God's overriding purpose is to rescue, not to condemn. Christ is the key to renewed human living but it is a mystery how he comes to people and it is not open to our fallible judgement to discern who has responded and who has not. So I conceive of salvation as being about a 'more' rather than being about an 'either/or'. I am passionately committed to a soteriology that takes human moral action seriously but is undergirded with mercy. So I am very hesitant about clear divisions between 'saved' and 'unsaved' and I want to read biblical metaphors about 'sheep and goats' always through the lens of the 'wheat and tares'. I am positive about the potential life-giving quality of following Christ but fiercely agnostic about those who 'reject' him. I reflect that Hooker argued that even excommunication from the Church could not be an infallible guide to someone's eternal destiny: 'As for the act of excommunication, it neither shutteth out from the mystical, nor clean from the visible, but only from fellowship with the visible in holy duties.'[63]

This neatly highlights why the language of 'conversion' can be so problematic: not because God does not wonderfully help people to turn around, but because we interpret language like 'born again'[64] to mean a particular inner or emotional experience to which we give the label 'spiritual' and then the rest of life struggles to catch up. But 'rebirth' is a metaphor not a rigid law. It is a mystery often not clearly accessible to our eyes. Yes, the more we stress the 'deadness' of human beings outside Christ, the more we will have to use the language of stark rebirth, but the New Testament is rich in metaphors about coming into Christ. To take a small selection which the New Testament weaves seamlessly together: 'salvation' (with its roots in *soteria* meaning healing);[65] entering the 'Kingdom of God/heaven';[66] 'redemption' (from the slavery of sin and to the devil (Col. 2:11–15)); 'reconciliation of enemies' (2 Cor. 5:18–20). We do immense pastoral harm by trying to shoe-horn people (and God) into a certain very narrow range.[67] But above all, this is so because being converted, as in true *metanoia*, is a turning round of the whole of life – spirit, mind, body, behaviour – to follow Christ. It may be, for some, initially or dominantly, experiential, but we are to be converted to Christ, made Christlike as we are incorporated into him – not merely converted.[68] It is to be embodied and embedded conversion, not dehumanising conversion. This is the purpose of salvation. It is a far more dynamic and humanly realistic and humane understanding of the Christian life. But it is not a soft option. And this is where Jeremy Taylor is such a wise guide.

Taylor: grace, discipline and becoming Christlike

Taylor truly is one of the lost treasures of the Church of

England. His books on *Holy Living* and *Holy Dying* were, until well into the nineteenth century, standards of English Christian spiritual reading. His own life, marked by serious discipleship and much personal suffering, combined with his voluptuous and sometimes wonderfully witty English prose, make him enriching to read (if occasionally a little long-winded). What is often forgotten is that he wrote the first English-language life of Christ, *The Great Exemplar*, published in 1649, and thought rigorously about how we are enabled to grow in faith and wisdom. Taylor's work is slowly coming back into view and a recent fine article intriguingly compares his ideas to those of Nick Hornby.[69] Andy Griffiths reminds us that the problem Hornby identified was a 'flat battery' and he relates this to Taylor's understanding that progress in the spiritual and moral life is only produced as God restores a right 'deliciousness' to our desires – which is of course the appropriate response to the attractiveness of God. In other words God helps us to begin to want the right things in life. The kick-start happens when God gives us a 'new heart'. This is not in Taylor a synonym for conversion (he was a fierce anti-Puritan and convinced sacramentalist), rather it is a spiritual re-energising and renewal. What it does do is stress that it is God's grace in Christ that enlivens and sensitises us so that we can encounter and hear him. Using Taylor's own words: 'He calls himself "the way, the truth, and the life"; that as he redeems our souls from death to life, by becoming life to our person; so he is truth to our understandings, and the way to our will, and affections …'[70] But the journey thereafter is a slow one. Taylor has a wise understanding of how human beings are motivated. It is not primarily through our intellect. Rather it is through our imaginations and our emotions, our desires.[71]

These are shaped in part by careful attention to the life of Christ because we are to imitate him both as God incarnate and as our 'eldest brother':

> In the great counsel of eternity, when God set down laws and knit fast the eternal bands of predestination, he made

it *one of his great purposes to make his Son like us, that we also might be like his holy Son; he by taking our nature; we by imitating his holiness*: 'God hath predestined us to be conformable to the image of his Son [Rom. 8:29] ... And therefore it was a precept of the apostle ... 'put ye on the Lord Jesus Christ' [Rom. 13:14]: the similitude declares the duty: as a garment is composed and made of the same fashion [shape] with the body, and is applied to each part in its true figure and commensuration; so should we put on Christ, and imitate the whole body of his sanctity, conforming to every integral part, and express him in our lives, that God, seeing our impresses, may know whose image and superscription we bear, and may be acknowledged for sons, when we have the air, and features, and resemblances, of our elder brother.[72]

Taylor could not believe that Christ had given so much 'only' to 'justify' us when what was needed was for us to become like him – according to God's original intention for humanity.

Taylor's portrayal of Jesus is rooted in the seventeenth century, and we would not write it like this now. His Jesus is not out to shake the social and political order, as would fit, for example, a Jesus in a Royalist mode. Therefore, specifically, I would argue that it is often more difficult to imitate Jesus than Taylor allows for. He softens some of Jesus' radicalism. Nonetheless, Taylor's Jesus is described as being sufficiently human, in some aspects of his behaviour, for it to be possible for us to conceive of imitating him, and his portrait of Jesus is often deeply attractive: 'he did so converse with men, that men, after that example, might for ever converse with him.'[73] There is a sense of realism that this imitation takes time and grace from God, but it works with our humanity, as well as challenging and resourcing it:

For as in the acquisition of habits, the very exercise of the action does produce a facility to the action, and in some proportion becomes the cause of itself; so does every exercise of the life of Christ kindle its own fires ... so when our lives are formed into the imitation of the holiest Jesus, the Spirit of God returns into us, not only by the efficacy of imitation, but by the merit ... of the actions of Jesus.[74]

So we grow good habits in ourselves by imitating Christ, but also, as we imitate him, so he helps us directly, not least by the spiritual power ['merit'] of his whole life, not just his death and resurrection.[75] Most fundamentally, our imitation of him is driven by grateful love: 'there being no better imitation of him than in such actions as do him pleasure, however he hath expressed or intimated the precedent.'[76] There is a profound sense of spiritual union running through Taylor's imitation of Christ. Most beautifully expressed in his own words: 'We lead Jesus into the recesses of our heart by holy meditations; and we enter into his heart, when we express him in our actions ...'[77]

Our desires are also trained as we perform our 'routine' religious duties of prayer, Bible reading, worship, use of the sacraments and care for others.[78] Indeed one of the surprising things for a modern reader of *Holy Living*, as Askew has stressed, is that it starts with some of the ordinary aspects of life – personal habits, money, use of time, sex, health – and only later goes on to the 'spiritual' aspects of life.[79] Taylor is ruthless at working in detail through a human life to illuminate how we are to become Christlike.

To take a current issue as an example, hear him reflecting on the relative de-merits of gluttony and drunkenness:

> because intemperance in eating is not so soon perceived by others as immoderate drinking, and the outward visible effects of it are not either so notorious or so ridiculous, therefore gluttony is not of so great disreputation amongst men as drunkenness; yet according to its degree it puts on the greatness of the sin before God, and is most strictly to be attended to ... and the intemperance is alike criminal in both, according as the affections are either meat or drink.[80]

Indeed, Taylor argues that intemperance is condemned in

Scripture more frequently only because it affects the thinking part of a man or a woman, not because it is intrinsically more serious. But his approach to alcohol is rounded and balanced: 'Drunkenness is an immoderate affection and use of drink. That I call immoderate, that is besides or beyond that order of good things for which God hath given us the use of drink. The ends are, digestion of our meat, cheerfulness and refreshment of our spirits, or any end of health …'[81] Notice that Taylor includes as 'an end of health', 'cheerfulness and refreshment'. In other words God has given us alcohol to help us to be happy. There is a form of common sense self-love here, for he describes 'surfeiting' as 'uncharitable' to the body. Taylor argues again and again that a holy life is a healthy one, because it is a 'natural' one, lived according to God's created order. (Interestingly, in his arguments Taylor often cites Classical Greek and Roman authors to show that this is a widely perceived natural wisdom.) But it is not just the occasions of drunkenness that Taylor is concerned about – and its consequences which he spells out in graphic detail[82] – but it is the 'affection' to it. So even someone who can 'hold their drink' may be guilty of drunkenness in Taylor's eyes because if they drink too much they may be damaging their body, as well as disobeying Jesus' command to 'be sober and ready' (Luke 21:34), and undermining their love for him and the presence of his Spirit in them. It is about allowing a distracting love to enter the heart, which then takes a bigger place than that which is appropriate.

Taylor is at his most lyrical, however, when writing about the spiritual life. We will look at one brief example. The heart of the spiritual life was, for Taylor, reception of the Holy Communion (though as Askew reminds us, Taylor actually kept this till last in his spiritual exercises and stressed other elements of the Christian life because under the Commonwealth receiving Communion according to the Book of Common Prayer was sometimes difficult and technically illegal). In Taylor's words: 'This is the sum of the greatest mystery of our religion; it is the copy of the passion and the ministration of the great mystery of our redemption …'[83]

In a very famous passage he spells out what happens during the Communion service:

> When the holy man stands at the table of blessing and min-
> isters the rite of consecration, *then do as the angels do, who*
> *behold, and love, and wonder* that the Son of God should
> become food to the souls of his servants; that he who can-
> not suffer any change or lessening, should be broken into
> pieces, and enter into the body to support and nourish the
> spirit, and yet at the same time remain in heaven while he
> descends to thee upon earth; that he who hath essential
> felicity should become miserable and die for thee, and then
> give himself to thee for ever to redeem thee from sin and
> misery; that by his wounds he should procure health to
> thee, by his affronts should entitle thee to glory, by his
> death should bring thee to life, *and by becoming a man he*
> *should make thee a partaker of the divine nature.* These are such
> glories, that although they are made so obvious that each
> eye may behold them, yet they are also so deep that no
> thought can fathom them; but so it hath pleased him, to
> make these mysteries to be sensible [appreciable through
> our senses] because the excellency and depth of the mercy
> is not intelligible; that whilst we are ravished and compre-
> hended within the infiniteness of so vast and mysterious a
> mercy, yet we may be as sure of it as of that thing we see
> and feel and smell and taste, but yet is so great that we can-
> not understand it.[84]

This paragraph has a number of key elements of 'Humane Christianity'. First, the focus is on the immense love of God in Christ and on Christ's humility in winning salvation for humankind. And this salvation is to make us 'partakers' of his own divine nature. The response to this is simply to love and wonder. But God in Christ's gentle humility goes further. He conforms his way of communicating to how we communicate as physical beings. So he comes to us in a form we can tangibly appreciate, as we see, feel, touch and taste the bread and wine in Communion.[85] It is of course a profoundly sacramental –

material and spiritual working together – vision of encountering Christ.

This is such a mystery, such a close encounter with the divine and such a privilege, that Taylor provides a lengthy list of ways for us to prepare for this Communion. So before coming to Communion, we are to have our sins dealt with, make peace with our neighbours, and have done so with some little time in advance to show that this is a serious repentance and not an overnight emotional change.[86] This takes the slowness of our human nature realistically. On the day of Communion itself the communicant is to rise early to pray, receive Communion fasting (including from sex the night before), give alms, and not rush back to the 'world' afterwards. It is a formidable discipline. It is a bodily, spiritual, personal and communal discipline, but all shot through with thankfulness. Without this it could tend to legalism. Through all of this there is a passionate love from Christ and stirring love in us, which takes us to the heart of the meaning of the cross. This is best summed up for me in an 'act of love' [prayer] in *Holy Living*:

> O most gracious and eternal God, the helper of the help-less, the comforter of the comfortless, the hope of the afflicted, the bread of the hungry, the drink of the thirsty, and the Saviour of all them that wait upon thee; I bless and glorify thy name, and adore thy goodness, *and delight in thy love*, that thou hast once more given me the opportunity of receiving the greatest favour which I can receive in this world, even the body and blood of my dearest Saviour. O take from me all affection to sin or vanity; let not my affec-tions dwell below, *but soar upwards to the element of love*, to the seat of God, to the regions of glory, and the inheritance of Jesus; that I may hunger and thirst for the bread of life, and the wine of elect souls, *and may know no loves but the love of God, and the most merciful Jesus*. Amen.[87]

It is no more appropriate to be naïve about Taylor than it is to be naïve about any of our other Christian saints, and there are elements of this spirituality from which we would need to distance ourselves – for example, one of his standard tactics is to persuade the reader to focus on the ephemeral aspects of human life and pleasure, so that they appear much less valuable than heavenly ones[88] – but the experience of love that runs through this prayer gives us our deepest clue as to the source of the energy we need to 'be good': the love of Christ for us, shown most clearly on the cross.

As Griffiths points out, it is in doing that we are shaped so that we become different people who want more of God, and so on, in a beneficial spiral. He also points out that this is in line with much modern educational theory about how we learn as human beings. In other words, to grow spiritually and morally we need a 'big' piece of motivation – having our love for God stimulated by his love for us – but this must be worked out in 'small' day-to-day mundane spiritual disciplines. This is the 'way of the cross'. Griffiths' conclusion is both broad and positive:

> The important question in the moral formation both of individuals and communities, in short, is not how they can derive the rules to live by, but how they can become people whose dispositions and desires will naturally lead them to act in a Christ-like manner. If Anglicanism is designed to point us to God's grace until we forget ourselves in it, to 'shape' us until our disciplines overwhelm and transform us, to start our flat batteries of desire, it might turn out to be a way to be Good after all.[89]

To put this very simply in my own words: however seriously we need to face the reality of our sinfulness, the best and most effective motivation for the Christian life is receiving God's love and the best way to do that is to spend time with Jesus of Nazareth, especially on the cross, and see how he loved 'us' and then to try to model ourselves on his way of life.

Gospel reflection: Jesus the life-giver

And so for one last time to Luke. Sacred territory this time, the heart of 'Humane Christianity': Luke 23:32–46.

Two others also, who were criminals, were led away to be put to death with him. When they came to the place that is called The Skull, they crucified Jesus there with the criminals, one on his right and one on his left. Then Jesus said, 'Father, forgive them; for they do not know what they are doing.' And they cast lots to divide his clothing. And the people stood by, watching; but the leaders scoffed at him, saying, 'He saved others; let him save himself if he is the Messiah of God, his chosen one!' The soldiers also mocked him, coming up and offering him sour wine, and saying, 'If you are the King of the Jews, save yourself!' There was also an inscription over him, 'This is the King of the Jews.'

One of the criminals who were hanged there kept deriding him and saying, 'Are you not the Messiah? Save yourself and us!' But the other rebuked him, saying, 'Do you not fear God, since you are under the same sentence of condemnation? And we indeed have been condemned justly, for we are getting what we deserve for our deeds, but this man has done nothing wrong.' Then he said, 'Jesus, remember me when you come into your kingdom.' He replied, 'Truly I tell you, today you will be with me in Paradise.'

It was now about noon, and darkness came over the whole land until three in the afternoon, while the sun's light failed; and the curtain of the temple was torn in two. Then Jesus, crying with a loud voice, said, 'Father, into your hands I commend my spirit.' Having said this, he breathed his last.

Points to ponder
- For the key interpretative framework for this passage I am indebted to a very influential article by the Revd Dr Walter Moberly.[90] He argues that we have for generations, rightly in some ways, lived out of a harmonised account of the crucifixion, weaving together an apparently seamless story, but that this has had the effect of obscuring the quite different

emphases that each gospel gives to its account, and that this has had very important theological and spiritual consequences. In particular, Luke's distinctive presentation of the meaning of the death of Jesus has got lost, especially from Evangelicalism. Moberly writes:

> In Mark, Jesus is an anguished figure, abandoned by both man and God, speaking only in loud cries. There is absolutely nothing to relieve the agony except perhaps the centurion's words, by which time Jesus is already dead. In Luke, Jesus is a compassionate figure, forgiving Man, trusting God, and peaceful throughout. The nature of the difference may be well expressed by an artistic analogy. Mark's portrayal is like Grünewald's famous crucifixion in the Isenheim altarpiece – a stark, agonizing, disturbing picture. Luke's portrayal is like any of the crucifixion scenes of Fra Angelico – always peaceful, dignified, moving.[91]

- Specifically, whilst Mark lends itself to a substitutionary atonement reading: 'Luke's portrayal looks something like a mixture of Aulen's *Christus Victor* thesis, which sees the cross as a victory over sin, death and the devil, and Abelard's "moral influence" thesis, which stresses the moving and transforming effects of Christ's supreme demonstration of how life under God should be lived.'[92] In other words, Luke stresses Jesus' own loving humanity as the location of God's victory and the model for how we are to live and die. I do not see these different gospel theologies as contradictory emphases, but this biblical reflection will seek to explore specifically Luke's theological spirituality.
- There are some textual issues to address. I have made a slightly arbitrary choice of which verses to read. We could well have included Jesus' words to the weeping women of Jerusalem as part of Luke's distinctive Passion narrative. Much of the material in Luke 23:32–46 is uniquely Lucan, certainly in content and partly in vocabulary, possibly from a distinct Lucan source, but it is also clear that he has taken

Mark and adapted it for his own purposes. The most famous words in this section – 'Father, forgive them' – have a very uncertain textual history, being absent from many early manuscripts. But as, Marshall and Nolland argue, these words fit so well into Luke's portrait of Jesus and prefigure Luke's account of Stephen's martyrdom (Acts 7:60), that it is most likely that the words were omitted by some early Christian copyists because they could not conceive of the crucifixion being forgiveable.[93]

- The essential shape of the story is similar to the other Passion narratives. The following elements are common to all four and may be said to have particular status as 'historical facts'[94]: Jesus is crucified on a Friday, the day before the Passover; at the place of 'The Skull'; with two other criminals; on an official charge of claiming to be the 'King of the Jews'; his clothes were divided up by the soldiers; before he died he was offered sour wine to drink; he died in the afternoon before sunset and was buried by Joseph of Arimathea. Distinctive to Luke are the following: Jesus' words of forgiveness from the cross; the watching people do not mock (unlike the rulers); the penitent criminal and Jesus' conversation with him; Jesus' last words from the cross. Luke also stresses Jesus' innocence of the charges more than the other gospels (23:4, 14–15, 22, 41, 47) and underplays his abandonment by the disciples (he omits the account of the disciples fleeing in Gethsemane and they are present at a distance at the crucifixion). It is, if this can be so expressed, a less traumatic account of his death. And as Moberly stresses, these are not random alterations but are consistent with the account of Jesus given in the respective gospels. So, just as one example, Luke does not include the saying of Jesus about giving his life as a 'ransom' (Mark 10:45), which for Mark is the key to interpreting Jesus' death.
- I noted at the beginning of this reflection that this is 'sacred territory' and I find it immensely uncomfortable spiritually to think about why the Passion narratives contain such significant differences both of detail and of overall theology. In

simple terms, how can we know what 'really happened'?
And what might be the relationship between what, say, Luke
tells us and what 'really happened'? Is Luke (or Mark,
Matthew or John) simply 'making things up' or 'leaving
other things out'? It is not just that it is difficult to harmonise
all of the Passion narrative details, but that when read in the
light of the whole portrayal of Jesus in a particular gospel, the
respective Passion narratives fit so well. In other words, what
we read is the product of a strongly intentional (editorially),
piece of writing. It is possible to an extent to conceive of different sources lying behind the different Passion narratives,
but again, given that there is clear evidence of some knowledge of the other traditions by most of the gospel writers,
how can we imagine them leaving out or playing down some
of these momentous and moving words and stories? To short-
cut a long discussion, I will quote Moberly again:

> Each gospel consists *both* of certain sayings and doings
> of the historical Jesus and of the interpretation that has
> been put upon these by the evangelist … If a doctrine of
> the authority of scripture is to be meaningful, it must be
> primarily the gospels as we have them, and not some
> historical (and usually debatable) reconstruction that
> goes behind the text, that is authoritative for the com-
> munity of faith. This means that to regard each gospel as
> inspired and authoritative entails according inspired
> and authoritative status to each gospel's interpretation
> of Jesus.[95]

• Traditionally, Luke is said not to have a theology of the atonement. So Drury writes: 'There is a certain lack of doctrinal
  punch since he sees the event of salvation in terms of the
  whole story, and particularly the resurrection and ascension,
  rather than in a stark focus on the passion alone (24:26).'[96]
  Very briefly, to help us to discern Luke's purposes, we can
  note that Jesus goes to the cross in obedience to the Father
  (22:42) and to fulfil the Scriptures (18:31; 22:37; 24:27, 45; cf.
  Acts 3:18; 17:2–3; 26:22–3). But also in conflict with Satan

(22:3, 31, 53) from whom Jesus is rescuing humankind (Acts 26:18). It is a time of trial, of testing (22:40, 46, cf. 21:19 and 22:28, 32). That Jesus is an innocent man is affirmed again and again and Luke especially stresses this by rewording the centurion's verdict after Jesus' death (23:47). That Jesus is the King of the Jews, Messiah, Chosen One, Son of Man, Son of God is also heavily emphasised by Luke in his passion narrative (22:22, 48, 67, 69, 70; 23:2, 3, 35, 37, 38, 39, 42) but uniquely qualified by the re-interpretation of authority which Luke includes after the Last Supper, rather than on the road to Jerusalem (Matthew/Mark). So Jesus is the Messiah, but a humble, loving, serving, subversive Messiah. But Jesus does have authority, above all authority to welcome people into the kingdom of God, giving forgiveness and new life in the Spirit (3:16; 4:18–19; 23:43; 24:49; cf. Acts 1:5, 8; 2:4, 33, 38-39; 3:19–20). He redeems not just Israel but all the nations (24:47; cf. Acts 4:12; crucially 10:34–43; 11:18; 13:47; 15:11; 26:17–18; 28:28), opening the Kingdom to all through forgiveness and trust in him. And in his resurrection and ascension, he is not just vindicated but is both forerunner for all who will be saved (Acts 26:23) and is also shown to be 'Godlike' in his new mode of working. So, I think the heart of Luke's understanding of Jesus is that he is the One who can offer forgiveness and acceptance to all, which is entry into the renewed life of God's inclusive kingdom (1:77–80; cf. Acts 13:38–39; 16:31; 20:21). This new kingdom is rooted in God's character, but Jesus is the 'earthly' representative and implementer of this new kingdom.

- What part specifically does Jesus' death play in this? It reveals and discredits those – the powerful and righteous of this world – who do not want God's humble and humbling way of salvation so they reject him (20:17–19; 23:35; cf. Acts 4:10–11; 7:51–3). Jesus' continued innocence, love and faith during his time of trial proves that he is who he claimed to be (23:47). So he is the suffering and vindicated Messiah (24:26; cf. Acts 2:23–4, 36; 5:30–31; 17:31). His death seals with his own blood the new covenant which has reconstituted God's people as anyone who repents and trusts (22:19, 20). But fundamentally, as Messiah he simply has to die. A crucial passage seems to me to be Philip's encounter with the Ethiopian eunuch where they study Isaiah 53:7–8. Jesus as the 'suffering servant', the 'scapegoat', lies behind all of Luke's portrayal of Jesus. But even this does not tell us 'how' atonement works – just that it was 'necessary' and that from now on forgiveness is to be preached in his name (24:26 and 46–7). Luke simply puts these two statements together. Perhaps Luke's wisest teaching on the 'atonement' is just that it has happened. It leaves us free to make little runs at understanding 'how' without claiming that we 'know'.

- Luke's account of the crucifixion proper begins with the mention of the two criminals. He describes them as *kakourgous*, or criminals, as opposed to Mark's *lestas*, bandits (possibly Zealot revolutionaries). This may reflect Luke's sensitivity to a Roman context. He moves this to an earlier point in the narrative compared to Mark and Matthew. Along with the unique story of the repentant criminal, this gives us strong clues as to the meaning of the cross in Luke. It is focused in forgiveness and heaven offered to all, even, or especially, from the cross. The penitent thief is both a figure full of hope for us but also fraught with ambiguity. He appears to have faith in Jesus as the Messiah – extraordinary that he should have this faith when he is a 'bad' person, outside the community of faith, and in such personal torment – but it is a very incomplete faith, focused perhaps on the future: 'When you come …' And there is no time for amendment of life. But it is enough: 'Today, you will be with me in Paradise.'[97] When we are in despair with ourselves and feel trapped in our human frailty, we can remember these words and cling to them: 'Today, you will be with me in Paradise.' Walking with Christ in the garden. It is enough for us. Trust and rest in the love of God, for anyone.

- Jesus gives forgiveness from the cross: 'Father forgive them, they don't know what they are doing.' Even here, at the moment of utter blasphemy when the Son of God is taunted and his power thrown back into his face, teased with bitter wine, unjustly tortured to death, he pleads for forgiveness, he pleads in mitigation – 'they don't know'. Do we believe his prayer was heard? If the Church had heard these words, rather than Matthew's (27:25) might it have restrained the anti-Semitism which has so stained the reputation of the Church and scoured the life of the Jews? These words of forgiveness haunt us when confronted by evil. Can or should we, or the victim, always forgive the torturer or the terrorist or the abuser? 'Be merciful, just as your Father is merciful' (Luke 6:36), Jesus tells us. Do we have to set this against 'Be perfect, therefore, as your heavenly Father is perfect' (Matt. 5:48)? Might 'Humane Christianity' remind us that we are to err always on the side of forgiveness because that is how God in Christ treats us?

- It is often noted, in contrast to later sermons and devotional works, how little is said about the crucifixion. 'And they crucified him' is all that is said. The restraint is understandable in people for whom crucifixion was a continuing and probably common horrific reality. They did not need to tell their readers what actually happened to Jesus: nails in hands or forearms, possibly a nail through the feet or the heel bones, etc. (Nolland wonders whether, as was common in Judea, the Roman soldiers might not have fitted the small ledge on which the crucified could sit. The ledge enabled the crucified to support themselves and so live for longer – that is, die more slowly.[98]) Later generations, unfamiliar with the reality of crucifixion, might need to have the details spelt out. But I can't help wondering if the focus on the details of Jesus' suffering does not have a pathological, even macabre, element to it, especially when it is used, classically, to increase our feelings of guilt. Reticence may have spiritual and emotional benefits here. And the contrast between how Christians have relished the details of the crucifixion compared to our slow journey away from supporting state execution is remarkable. As a young ordinand, I had written a fiery essay on theodicy, using the cross to justify the ways of God. The professor asked quietly what was the main thing we should learn from the crucifixion. I waffled on. She said simply: 'Never again. That we should never again let a human being suffer like this.' I had never thought like that before. I had never heard anyone say that before. Why do we in the Church focus so much on increasing human guilt and so little on changing human suffering? Why does the death of this Man of Love on the cross not fire our compassion for other human beings, rather than fuel our anger at 'them' for their 'unbelief'? Notice how in Luke, the people don't mock. They look on in sad wonder. We don't have to despise 'them'. They will wonder and love with us if we tell the story well, as Luke does.

- Even in death, Jesus trusts. There is an argument about how we should translate v. 46. Is it 'Jesus, crying with a loud voice, said …', or 'Jesus, crying with a loud voice, then said …'. It is partly a minor quibble because these last words are the opposite end of the spectrum to 'My God, my God, why have you abandoned me?' This Jesus dies confident in God's love and purposes for him. Barclay tells us that the words of Psalm 31:5, with which Jesus died, were the words Jewish children were taught to say as their night prayers: 'Even on a cross Jesus dies like a child falling asleep in his father's arms.'[99] (On the cross in Luke, God is always Jesus' 'Father'.) In this Jesus models a 'dry death' for us.[100] In Luke's day, this telling of the story helped other Christians to face a cross, or fire, or sword, or crazed animals of the arena, with some courage and hope. Later, our ancestors prayed regularly for a 'good death', meaning one with little pain, of course, but also with time to prepare and full of faith. If Luke was all we had, I wonder if it would be enough for the moments of darkness and terror and isolation? I suspect not. But it is still a wonderful model for us. So we pray for a Lucan death and perhaps work that others may have one too.

- Even in death, Jesus trusts. He has drunk deeply from the dregs of human evil and suffering. Betrayed, tortured, subject to a mock trial, public humiliation, public weakness as he stumbles with the weight of the cross, as he is stripped; mockery even in his death agony. And yet he trusts and loves. In this sense he reigns from the cross. This is how Jesus is the 'King of the Jews'. Luke makes us stop and think. Could I do this? How did this man do this? Why? What did he achieve? The more we take Jesus' humanity seriously, the more we will see this as a triumph of trust and love over apparent abject failure. This absorbing of hatred without returning hatred, and so overturning it, is Luke's understanding of God. Like the humble father in the parable of the prodigal son, he waits, poised to run to us to welcome us home. It is because Jesus knows that God is a Father like this that he lives a life welcoming all-comers but especially those despised and excluded by the powerful and the righteous. It is because Jesus knows that God is a Father like this that he does not lose hope, even in the midst of terrible suffering. It is because Jesus knows that God is a Father like this, that he takes into his own body the pain of hatred and evil, trusting that in this he will be vindicated. It is because Jesus knows that God is a Father like this that he continues to love till the end, and in that loving is the triumph of God over evil made visible.

A Summary of Humane Christianity

In closing this book, I want to try to summarise some of its key points. The crucial mind-set is summed up in that wonderful quotation from John Drury that the 'past is not the preserve of the conservatives'.[101] We have begun to explore some of the good memories from our Christian past which have tended to be overlaid by the combined legacy of theological and ecclesiastical totalitarianism but there is so much more to explore. We need to keep doing this re-creative historical and theological work, to redeem our past, reading it in the light of 'Humane Christianity's' theological principles:

• God's creation, and humanity as the pinnacle of it, is still essentially good and its future is glorious. Yes, of course humankind is fallen and flawed – sometimes so terribly flawed that we have the potential utterly to ruin the good creation which God is giving us – but still immensely valuable and destined, with creation, for a beautiful future. So we are to love creation and our fellow human beings and be wary of any attempt to slip contempt for humanity back in under the guise of describing sinfulness. The Western Church has been very profoundly shaped by the legacy of Augustine. I have tried to avoid slipping facile criticisms of him into this book, but I cannot help wishing that someone like Irenaeus had come to greater prominence: because he places such a huge value on humankind, because of Christ, who is both creator and redeemer, 'recapitulating' humankind by his incarnation. It is a warmer, more humane, account of the Christian faith. The Western Church has mostly fought shy of the Eastern Orthodox doctrine of *theosis*, that human beings are to be made Godlike.[102] The Orthodox, of course, have managed the hugeness of this theological claim very carefully, arguing that we will come to share the divine attributes or energies but not the divine essence. But they have a much stronger sense than we do that our destiny is to be incorporated into God. In Irenaeus' incomparable phrase: '... following the only sure and true Teacher, the Word of God, Jesus Christ our Lord, who because of his immeasurable love became what we are in order to make us what he is.'[103] Athanasius, the hammer of the heretics, was even more succinct and shocking: 'He [Christ], indeed assumed humanity that we might become God.'[104] Therefore we must always keep before us the huge value and dignity of human beings now and for eternity.

• The core of God and of his action is love. If we run the risk of allowing love, not judgement, as being the driving force in God, this is not a soft option. William Barclay used an intriguing phrase – 'the wrath of love'.[105] Having all our actions and worse, our motives, exposed to the unblinking gaze of pure love is not a prospect to be contemplated without awe. But we so easily acquire our inner demons which we project on to God, that we need to return again and again to this simple truth: 'God is love'. I was struck by a saying from Isaac of Nineveh, also known as Isaac the Syrian, a seventh-century Assyrian bishop who became a hermit in what we now call Iraq. He said of God: 'Just because the terms 'wrath', 'anger', 'hatred' and the rest are used of the Creator in the Bible, we should not imagine that he does anything in anger, or hatred or zeal. Many figurative terms are used of God in the Scriptures, terms which are far removed from his true nature.'[106] There are strong echoes here of Julian of Norwich. If, as I have tried to argue, the essence of sinfulness is not some abstract quality of pride, but rather our indifference to the love of God and the needs of others, then salvation is about freeing us to love. I come back again and again to the Epistle of John: 'So we have known and believe the love that God has for us. God is love, and those who abide in love abide in God, and God abides in them … Those who say 'I love God', and hate their brothers or sisters, are liars; for those who do not love a brother or sister whom they have seen, cannot love God whom they have not seen' (1 John 4:16, 20).

- Even allowing for the style of drawing very stark contrasts which John uses in these Epistles, the words cannot be softened: 'love', 'liar', 'brother and sister', 'God', 'seen and unseen'. Yes, the cross, atonement, is about bringing forgiveness and new beginnings, but the purpose of all this is to generate and sustain people of love and justice. Yes, the cross and the empty tomb are the place where God is seen most profoundly at work, but even here, God's ways are not alien to the world he is creating.[107] By absorbing sin and overcoming death, through sacrificial love, God is renewing creation. But the point of all this, crucially, is that to be part of this renewed creation is to be liberated to live a life of love. Without real demonstrated practical love for our fellow human beings, John is clear that our claims to love God are false.

- If we want to see a human life that shows what love in

human form is like, then we look at the life of Jesus of
Nazareth. Here we need to combine both a Patristic stress on
Jesus as the incarnate Son of God with a much more modern
stress on Jesus as fully human. It is not a matter of looking to
an infallible Jesus but looking to see how a life can be lived
that is truly loving in the midst of all the complexity of being
a travelling first-century Jewish rabbi. Real love. This is why
it is so dangerous when we stop spending time with the life
of Jesus of Nazareth. This is why too much time preaching
Paul (on sin rather than Paul on love) and not preaching the
Synoptic Jesus can leave us arguing about the mechanics of
the process of salvation and distract us from its content and
purpose.

- This touches on a side current that yet needs stressing: Jesus
  Christ is the pinnacle, purpose and plumb-line of Scripture.
  While the Church of England is committed in its formularies
  to the authority of Scripture, the nature of this authority has
  always been a matter of interpretation. As long ago as the sixteenth century, Richard Hooker was arguing for criteria to
  evaluate different parts of Scripture. He argued that key
  features were discerning the nature of the 'law' in Scripture
  (i.e., whether it was an unchangeable moral principle, or a
  changeable application of a principle, or a temporary legal or
  liturgical practice) and the purpose for which the law was
  originally given, i.e. whether the circumstances had subsequently changed requiring a change in the 'law' itself. [108]
  The key criterion for interpretation was and is, of course, the
  standard of the life of Christ.[109] So, if a passage of Scripture
  appears to portray God in a less than Christlike light, we are
  free – more, we are required – to evaluate this passage of
  Scripture accordingly. Bishop Nazir Ali makes the point
  comprehensively but very clearly:

> In spite of his [Jesus'] great reverence for Scripture, he
> was able decisively to set aside the levitical *lex talionis*
> (law of retaliation) in favour of his characteristic
> teaching on loving our enemies and praying for our

persecutors … Not everything in Scripture has the same significance and not everything has the same significance for us as it might have had for previous generations. Not only is Jesus Christ the exegesis of God, he is also the exegesis of Scripture.[110]

This frees us from being bound hand and foot to clearly sub-Christian passages of Scripture (or even imagining that Scripture will give us a rule-book for handling new situations), but without allowing us to sit light to Scripture, because it is always the Scripture of Jesus.

• We are destined for eternity. There will come a time when this body will wear out. (It already is wearing out, according to Mrs Bartlett!) As Paul reminds us, if we hope only for this world, then we are 'sad' (loose paraphrase of 1 Corinthians 15:19). We will not be able to make everything alright in our lifetimes. People will still suffer both immense wrongs and also the random hardship of our mortality. The point of eternal life and heaven is not to console us so that we sit on our behinds, but without the hope of eternal justice, the current and past injustices and sufferings of the innocent of this world make life here unendurable. This hope is not a reason to rest now, but a promise that even failure now is not the end.

• But we live life to the full now, as God intends us to; living positively for others not from negative restrictions. I think this is the most difficult part of this summary to get right. I am drawn back to the caricature of an Anglican. I want to say 'both/and'. For the good gifts of God in creation – beauty, fun, excitement, pleasure – are to be enjoyed. To do other than that is to deny God's generosity to us. But love will temper our freedom to enjoy these gifts, when others don't share them. Nor should we be naïve in assuming that we will find it easy to manage our desires and pleasures. Further, life often contains nasty surprises and costly choices. So as well as 'life in all its abundance' we also walk 'the way of the cross'. Yet again we come back to Jesus of Nazareth, not because he shows us exactly how we are to live, but because his values and behaviour act like a searchlight exposing our self-deceptions and our neuroses. Do I make excuses for what I do with my money? Jesus will shine through them. Do I abstain from a pleasure but really out of fear? Jesus will shine into that darkness as well. There will not be one neat and tidy right answer for us. But Jesus models what it is to be fully human: sensual as well as spiritual, fun-loving and cross-carrying.

- This is related to a crucial point, which we need to stress amidst all this language of love. The combination of late twentieth-century Western medicine and the Charismatic Revival has been very dangerous for the wisdom and the health of parts of the Church. We take the miracle stories of Jesus and we feed them into our longings for release and victory in a world of suffering, throw in a little dose of 'Freudian' father-figures, and we have the recipe for trying to believe that which is not true. God's love for us did not, does not, will not mean safety from the routine heartbreaks of human life. His actions are far more mysterious than we might like them to be. It seems to me evident, despite much advocacy from other points of view, that miracles remain miracles because they are rare and that much of the time God's influence on us and on his world is restrained and hidden. Our ancestors knew this without having to have it explained to them because they buried their children so regularly.
- I want to finish by returning to sayings from three very different sources. First, that profound vision of hope from Julian of Norwich: 'all shall be well'. The incarnation, cross and resurrection show us the future. In Jesus we have God's guarantee that the best of humanity will be saved for ever. Second, to quote the much maligned Paul again: 'For it is the God who said, "Let light shine out of darkness", who has shone in our hearts to give the light of the knowledge of the glory of God in the face of Jesus Christ' (2 Cor. 4:6).

It is into our hearts that God the creator has shone through Jesus of Nazareth. (The reference is in part to Paul's own conversion but has a wider sense of God's mode of revelation to all of us.) Creation and revelation and salvation are inseparable. And what is revealed to human hearts? It is a human face full of the divine glory which is revealed in and to human beings that are like fragile and humble clay pots.[111] This is 'Humane Christianity'. Third, and finally, why does God do all this? So that, in the words of the Shorter Catechism of the Westminster Confession, we may 'glorify God and *enjoy* him forever', because God is always the life-bringer.[112]

Prayer

For our closing prayer, we have a prayer of love and gratitude for all that God in Christ has given us. It is a prayer of the Franciscans (slightly adapted).

> We adore you, most loving friend and master, Jesus Christ,
> Here and in all your churches
> Throughout the world,
> And we bless you
> Because by your holy cross,
> You have redeemed the world.
>> May the life-giving cross
>> Be the source of all our joy and peace.
> Amen.

NOTES

Introduction

1. The first was written by Edmund Campion, the Jesuit, the second by John Penry, the separatist. See E. Ives, *God in History* (Tring, Lion, 1979), p. 108.
2. See especially the work of Jonathan Riley-Smith. Try for starters, *The Oxford Illustrated History of the Crusades* (Oxford, Oxford University Press, 1999), especially ch. 1.
3. S. Runciman, *A History of the Crusades* (Cambridge, Cambridge University Press, 1954), vol. 3, *The Kingdom of Acre*, p. 123.
4. Runciman, *Kingdom of Acre*, p. 480.
5. T. Jones and A. Ereira, *The Crusades* (London, Penguin/BBC, 1996). This might be thought to indicate something of the ignorance and insensitivity of the modern Western intelligentsia about religious faith. Would Saladin have wanted to be called a 'model Christian'?
6. See his debates with the Cardinal of Milan in U. Eco and M. Montini, *Belief or Nonbelief* (New York, Arcadia, 2001).
7. U. Eco, *Baudolino* (London, QPD edn, 2002), p. 16. This is not an exaggeration. See Runciman, *Kingdom of Acre*, p. 123 for an account that mirrors that of Eco.
8. See S. Runciman, *The Fall of Constantinople* (Cambridge, Cambridge University Press, 1965), Appendix 2.
9. 1 Tim. 6:13: ʐoo-govovτos, a participle meaning '(the one) who keeps alive'.
10. See further material from this conference on the website: <www.evangelism.uk.net>.
11. J. Drane, *The McDonaldization of the Church* (London, Darton, Longman & Todd, 1998), p. 11.
12. The C. of E. has just produced [yet another] report on the future of theological education and one of its minor reflections is that if the Church wishes to use its theological educators for serious research and writing, then the pace of, for example, theological college life has to be restrained. So that is my excuse for this not being as polished as I would like it to be. *Formation for Ministry within a Learning Church: the Structure and Funding of Ordination Training*, Report of a Working Part of the Archbishops' Council, 2003, para. 2.12 v), p.12, and crucially paras. 2.13 and 2.12, pp.20–21: 'Thus, a further issue for our agenda is an institutional basis for research that enables the Church to think deeply about its mission in and to the world.'

Chapter 1: Inhumane Christianity

1. Callum G. Brown, *The Death of Christian Britain* (London, Routledge, 2001), p. 188.
2. Brown, *Christian Britain*, pp. 7 and 175ff.

173

3. P. Brierley, *The Tide is Running Out* (London, Christian Research, 2000). The title says it all.

4. See H. McLeod, *Religion and the People of Western Europe* (2nd edn, Oxford, Oxford University Press, 1997): 'In the early 1960s, the pace of religious change began to speed up and in the years 1965–75 it reached a speed which some found overwhelmingly exhilarating and others found terrifying. The changes included ... above all, in the latter part of this period, a dramatic fall in the number of people belonging to churches or attending services' (p. 136).

Between 1967 and 76, attendance at mass among Belgian Roman Catholics fell from 43 to 30 per cent; in France between 1966 and 1972 from 23 to 17 per cent; in Sweden between 1955 and 1970 a third of people described themselves as 'less religious'. See pp. 138–9 and 141.

5. Brown, *Christian Britain*, p. 198.

6. Seven out of 26 footnotes in chapter 1 come from newspapers, mostly the *Guardian* and the *Observer* – not the most objective commentators on church life. I think a more balanced guide to modern British religious life is G. Davie, *Believing without Belonging. Religion in Britain since 1945* (Oxford, Blackwell, 1994). The figure of 72 per cent of the British population (see <www.statistics.gov.uk/census2001>) claiming to be Christian has, rightly, rather rocked some of the Church's glib and ill-informed secular opponents, but we cannot presume on this residual faith surviving. Cf. R. Gill, *Churchgoing and Christian Ethics* (Cambridge, Cambridge University Press, 1999), pp. 87–93, where he summarises statistics about the fall in churchgoing related to the decline of Christian beliefs among young people: 'A cultural theory of churchgoing contends that Christian beliefs and values do depend upon churchgoing. Yet the evidence just reviewed suggests that churchgoing is declining fast in a number of countries, especially amongst young people' (p. 91). Brierley (*Tide is Running Out*, p. 98) produced the shock-horror headline figure of the churches 'losing' 1,000 young people per week.

7. Brown, *Christian Britain*, p. 2.

8. B. Cornwell, *Harlequin* (London, HarperCollins, 2000).

9. B. Cornwell, *The Winter King*, *The Enemy of God*, *Excalibur*. In the end I became so fed up with the crass portrayal of Christians in these novels that I had to give up reading them.

10. L. de Bernières, *The Troublesome Offspring of Cardinal Guzman* (London, Vintage, 1998). We should note that he is a committed agnostic who has been involved in a serious and genuine public debate with the Church. See for example his debate with the Bishop of Oxford which touches on many of the issues of this book at <www.fish.co.uk>. Also on this theme, see R. Harries, *God Outside the Box* (London, SPCK, 2002).

11. de Bernières, *Cardinal Guzman*, p. 258.

12. Thomas Aquinas, *Summa Theologiae*, 2a2a, 11, 3, ed. T. Gilby (Cambridge, Blackfriars, 1975), p. 89. Aquinas continues: 'But on the side of the Church is mercy which seeks the conversion of the wandered, and she condemns not at once, but after the first and second admonition, as the Apostle directs [Titus 3:10]. Afterwards, however, if he is stubborn, the Church no longer confident of his conversion, takes care of the salvation of others by separating him from the Church by excommunication, and furthermore

delivers him to the secular court to be removed from this world by death.'

13. de Bernières, *Cardinal Guzman*, p. 258.
14. de Bernières, *Cardinal Guzman*, p. 378.
15. See also L. de Bernières, *The War of Don Emmanuel's Nether Parts*, first published 1990. I used the Vintage impression, London, 1998.
16. de Bernières, *Cardinal Guzman*, p. 377.
17. Matthew 23:27–28 and 23. Cf. Luke 11:42 and 44, where Jesus describes them as 'unmarked graves': i.e. they make people unknowingly 'unclean'.
18. L. D. Benson (ed.), *The Riverside Chaucer* (3rd edn, Oxford, Oxford University Press, 1988), p. 128.
19. See, J. Dolan (ed.), *The Essential Erasmus* (London, NEL, 1964), p. 158.
20. A. Trollope, *Barchester Towers* (first pub. 1857), pp. 22–3. (London and Glasgow, Blackie and Sons, no date).
21. R. Tressell, *The Ragged Trousered Philanthropists* (first pub. 1914, 1965 edn), p. 171. (London, Granada, 1965).
22. J. Winterson, *Oranges Are Not the Only Fruit* (London, Vintage, 1991), pp. 81 and 132.
23. See the national evangelism conference website, <www.evangelism.uk.net>, and J. Drane, *The McDonaldization of the Church* (London, Darton, Longman & Todd, 2000). Also books as varied as P. Richter and L. Francis, *Gone but not Forgotten* (London, Darton, Longman & Todd, 1998) or Brierley, *The Tide is Running Out* or indeed any study of 'Generation X'.
24. *Observer Review*, 2 February 2003.
25. Augustine hugely and tragically compounded this by connecting sexual intercourse and reproduction with the passing on of 'original sin'. The complexity of Augustine's thinking is well-expressed in G. Bonner, *St Augustine of Hippo. Life and Controversies* (Canterbury Press, Norwich, 1986), p. 378. 'It is from, and by, concupiscence that the guilt of Original Sin is conveyed from the parents to the child. Concupiscence itself is not Original Sin; it is a wound and vice of human nature, making it a slave to the devil; can be the occasion of sin, even in the baptized; and is the means whereby Original Sin is transmitted. *It is an infection which conveys an inherited legal liability*' (my italics). Bonner also crisply explains Augustine's (and Jerome's) mistranslation of Romans 5:12 which drove him to stress that human guilt was transmitted seminally (literally) from Adam rather than being an issue of repeated human falling. For a gentle defence of Augustine and an illuminating placement of him in his context, which does much to undermine modern 'demonising' of him, see C. Harrison, *Augustine. Christian Truth and Fractured Humanity* (Oxford, Oxford University Press, 2000).
26. See the crucial discussion in J. D. G. Dunn, *The Theology of Paul the Apostle* (Edinburgh, T & T Clark, 1998, pp. 51–73) for an extensive and insightful review of the range of meanings of *soma*, 'embodiment', and *sarx*, 'flesh', in Paul's writing. Briefly, Dunn argues for the continued translation of *sarx* by 'flesh' because it is a technical term for Paul (p. 70), but stresses that whereas *sarx* encompasses a range of meaning tending towards the negative – human physicality, mortality and frailty vulnerable to the pressures of sin – *soma* gives potential for a positive celebration of our embodied createdness. He writes: 'we could say that Paul's distinction between *soma*

and *sarx* made possible a positive affirmation of human createdness and creation and of the interdependence of humanity within its created environment' (p. 73). I am indebted to conversation with my colleague Dr Mark Bonnington on this point.

27. In J. Fife, *To Be Honest* (London, Darton, Longman & Todd, 1993), p. x. I am indebted to my colleague the Revd Charles Read for this reference.

28. Strictly speaking, the sin in Genesis 3 is disobedience, not pride as such. Hence metaphors of 'rebellion' in much Christian evangelism. But the root cause of this 'rebellion' is often portrayed as pride, or a human unwillingness to remain in an appropriately creaturely, humble situation with respect to God's authority. Hence the language of pride is the most apt. But, more broadly, if we read the Genesis narrative not as a paradigmatic Fall – Genesis 3 – followed by examples of its consequences in 'real' life, but rather as one (if crucial) account of what it is to be 'sinful', but amplified by other insights into human sinfulness, then we find ourselves with a range of interpretations: the jealousy and resentment leading Cain to violence (Genesis 4); the marriage of the 'sons of God' to the daughters of men suggesting a crossing of God-given boundaries and a rivalry with God, which resulted in evil and especially violence (Genesis 6); the Tower of Babel suggesting arrogance and competition with God (Genesis 11).

29. This is a good point to mention that I do not see myself as following the argument of Matthew Fox for a 'creation-centred' spirituality, to the exclusion of a 'fall-centred' spirituality, but rather to redress the balance between the two. Fox's work is, however, very symptomatic of the urgent need for the churches to address these questions. See M. Fox, *Original Blessing: A primer in creation spirituality* (Santa Fe, NM, Bear and Co., 1983) and the excellent article, R. Bauckham: 'The new age theology of Matthew Fox', *Anvil*, vol. 31 (1996), no. 2.

30. It was not just a question of whether 'matter' was morally flawed, but that it was imperfect and by definition, prone to change. Over against this, the divine was held to be by definition 'impassible' – changeless. This was of course particularly significant in the christological debates where the idea of the divine being incarnated was highly problematic. Modern theologians remain divided as to whether the credal christological formulae, Nicene and Chalcedonian, successfully resolve this problem, especially when read against the Synoptic Gospels. But note Gunton's comment: 'Orthodox Christology was able to emerge only as a result of a critique of certain, virtually unquestionable, philosophical dogmas about the nature of deity, so that in its essential claims, particularly those concerning God's involvement in the material world in Jesus of Nazareth, orthodox Christology contradicts the heart of the mainstream Greek philosophical tradition.' C. Gunton, 'Christ the Wisdom of God', in S. Barton (ed.), *Where Shall Wisdom Be Found?* (Edinburgh, T & T Clark, 1999), p. 249.

31. Irenaeus, *Against Heresies*, Bk 2, ch. x., section 3, (hereafter *AH*), in *Ante-Nicene Fathers* (American edn, 1995 reprint, Massachusetts, Hendrikson, Peabody), vol 1, p. 370 (my italics). Where possible, I have checked the translation against Grant (see following). It is staggering, to a non-specialist, how neglected Irenaeus has been as a creative theologian, as opposed to, more narrowly, a smiter of heretics. For further reading see some fine recent publications: J. Behr, *Asceticism and Anthropology in*

Irenaeus and Clement (Oxford, Oxford University Press, 2000), esp. pp. 23–34; R. M. Grant, *Irenaeus of Lyons* (London, Routledge, 1997) and I. M. MacKenzie, *Irenaeus's Demonstration of the Apostolic Preaching* (Aldershot, Ashgate, 2002).

32. *AH*, 2.ix.1, p. 369.

33. For this section I have drawn heavily on Gunton's use of Francis Watson's book, *Text, Church and World* (Edinburgh, T & T Clark, 1994), cited in Gunton, *Wisdom*, pp. 249–61.

34. I am indebted to Dr Walter Moberly for this question.

35. Gunton, *Wisdom*, p. 258.

36. Gunton, *Wisdom*, p. 259 (italics mine).

37. These arguments, I think, are valid whether the Christology is seen as being shaped by the 'wisdom' tradition or by a more overtly trinitarian tradition.

38. Gunton, *Wisdom*, p. 259.

39. Doctrine Commission of the General Synod of the Church of England, *The Mystery of Salvation* (London, Church House Publishing, 1995), p. 52. Much of the thinking of this Report has fed into this book.

40. This renewed theology is at last finding its way into (English Anglican) liturgy. Note in Eucharistic Prayer G in *Common Worship* (London, Church House Publishing, 2000): 'In the fullness of time you made us in your own image, the crown of all creation.'

41. The meaning of the phrase 'image of God' is highly complex and surprisingly uncertain in modern commentaries. For example see G. Wenham, *Genesis 1-15* (Waco, Texas, Word, 1987), pp. 28–32.

42. Genesis 1:26–27. The word *bara*, to create, is used three times in verse 27 and has not been used since verse 1 where it describes the whole of God's creative work and verse 21 where it refers to God creating living breathing creatures. G. von Rad, *Genesis* (London, SCM Press, 1972), p. 57: 'God participates more intimately and intensively in this than in the earlier works of creation.' I find the similarities between the theology of the two creation narratives more striking than any differences suggested by the 'documentary hypothesis'.

43. von Rad, *Genesis*, pp. 57ff. Though as Dr Moberly points out this specific word for 'idol' is not used in condemnations of idolatry elsewhere in the Old Testament.

44. W. Brueggemann, *Genesis* (Atlanta, Georgia, John Knox Press, 1982), p. 32.

45. von Rad, *Genesis*, p. 58. Italics original.

46. D. Wilkinson, *The Message of Salvation* (Leicester, InterVarsity Press, 2002), p. 36.

47. Wilkinson, *Message*, pp. 37ff.

48. See Behr, *Asceticism*, pp. 114–5, expounding *AH*, 5.xvi.2.

49. Wenham, *Genesis*, p. 31.

50. Again the phrase 'breath of life' is a topic of much discussion. Wenham, *Genesis*, p. 61, confirms the sense of the uniqueness of this mode of creation.

51. Psalm 8. This is the NRSV translation, which is the Bible version used normally in this book. 'God' is the now widely agreed translation of *elohim*, which used to be translated 'angels'. P. Craigie, *Psalms 1-50* (Waco, Texas, Word, 1983), p. 108.

52. Behr, *Asceticism*, p. 38.
53. P. Seddon, unpublished paper 'Evangelical Sacraments', citing J. Moltmann, *God in Creation. An Ecological Doctrine of Creation* (London, SCM Press, 1985), ch. x (italics original).
54. *AH*, 5.vi.2, p. 532.
55. We must note here that in Paul's language we will have 'spiritual bodies' and as Dunn reminds us (*Paul the Apostle*, p. 61) we can 'hardly begin to say' what Paul envisaged. But we also remember that Christians have believed that Christ keeps his body for ever. So Gregory argued passionately that Christ keeps his flesh for ever. 'For where is his body now, if not with him who assumed it?' See Letter 101 in *Cyril of Jerusalem, Gregory Nazianzen*, Nicene and Post-Nicene Fathers, vol. 7, (Peabody, Mass., Hendrickson, 1995 reprint of 1894 edn), p. 440. And it was a key feature of Cranmer's polemic against transubstantiation that Christ is in heaven with his body and therefore could not be physically present in the bread and wine. See Article 29 of the 1553 Forty-Two Articles. See G. Bray (ed.), *Documents of the English Reformation* (Cambridge, James Clarke, 1994), p. 302.
56. From an unpublished paper, but see G. Morley, *John Macquarrie's Natural Theology: The Grace of Being* (Aldershot, Ashgate, 2003). Italics in original. Morley (and Macquarrie) are also making a technical christological point here that stresses a Christology 'from below' rather than 'from above'. I prefer a kenotic Christology 'from above' but recognise the affirmation of God's good creation present in the Macquarrie/Morley argument.
57. This is an appropriate place to note that I will use the masculine personal pronoun when referring to the activity of God. This is mostly for ease and to avoid some of the rather inelegant circumlocutions we fall into when trying to avoid this usage, but it is worth stressing that except for direct references to Jesus of Nazareth, all language of gender as applied to God is entirely metaphorical, as even a moment's thought will confirm. If 'God the Father' is unseen, invisible, even incorporeal (1 John 4:12, Col. 1:15, John 4:24) how then can we literalistically use male language to describe him? Obviously, Christianity has a complex history when trying to describe divinity in terms of gender – a discussion best left for another place – but the reminder that we relate to 'God' through metaphor is one of the fundamentals of this book.
58. C. S. Lewis, *The Screwtape Letters* (Glasgow, Collins, first pub. 1942, 24th impression, 1976), p. 44. Screwtape continues: 'The Enemy's determination to produce such a revolting hybrid was one of the things that determined Our Father to withdraw his support from him.' Lewis was a strong defender of the fundamental goodness of creation and human pleasure within it, as befitted a beer-drinking pipe smoker.
59. I am particularly grateful to Bishop Alex Graham for pushing me to think this through more fully. For a succinct introduction see B. Lohse, *A Short History of Christian Doctrine* (Philadelphia, Fortress Press, 1985), chs. 2 and 3. Also J. D. G. Dunn, *Jesus: Teacher of Wisdom or Wisdom Incarnate?*, in Barton (ed.), *Wisdom*, pp. 75–92.
60. I recognise that this short-cuts an immense theological and philosophical debate. All I want to assert here is that we can encounter God in this world, though I would argue that this is always in a mediated rather than a direct manner. In other words, we meet God through a range of media –

our senses, words, symbols, emotions, actions – rather than in some immediate, non-mediated way.

61. D. Hardy, 'The Grace of God and Earthly Wisdom' in Barton (ed.), *Wisdom*, p. 237. This book contains a wide-ranging reflection on wisdom, including arguments that there is a sharp discontinuity between Christian and non-Christian wisdom. See especially the essay by R. Hays, 'Wisdom according to Paul'. I will return to some of these issues in Chapter 6.

62. D. Hardy, 'The Grace of God and Earthly Wisdom', in *Finding the Church* (London, SCM Press, 2001), p. 264, n. 16, citing K. Nerburn and L. Medelkoch (eds.), *Native American Wisdom* (Navato CA, New World Library, 1991).

63. Matthew 5:26. I am indebted to Philip Seddon's article for an exposition of this point.

64. For a fuller account of my reading of Hooker's theology and its relevance see my article 'What has Richard Hooker to say to modern Evangelical Anglicanism?', *Anvil*, vol. 15, no. 3 (1998). Note that a recent essay by Rowan Williams stresses Hooker's identity and value as a theologian of wisdom. R. Williams; 'Hooker: Philosopher, Anglican, Contemporary', in A. S. McGrade (ed.), *Richard Hooker and the Construction of Christian Community* (Medieval and Renaissance Texts and Studies, Tempe, AZ, 1997). Note esp. his conclusion (p. 383): 'But the final comment I'd want to make is to underline the significance of a sapiential theology in an age when the theological debate so readily polarizes between one or another variety of positivism (biblically fundamentalist, ecclesiastically authoritarian, or whatever) and a liberalism without critical or self-critical edge.'

65. R. Hooker, *Of the Laws of Ecclesiastical Polity*, bk 2, ch. VII, section 6, p. 271. Currently the most straightforward way to read Hooker is to find a second-hand Everyman edition of Books I–V of the *Laws*, first published in the 1590s (C. Morris, London, Dent, 1965, first published 1907). The outstanding critical edition is the recent Folger edition. My quotations are normally taken from the Everyman edn, but checked against the Folger edn.

66. W. David Neelands, 'Hooker on Scripture, Reason and "Tradition"', in McGrade (ed.), *Richard Hooker*, p. 80.

67. We owe this crisp formulation to Thomas Aquinas. Aquinas, *Summa Theologiae*, 1a, 1, 8, ed. T. Gilby (Cambridge, Blackfriars, 1964), p. 31. The whole sentence reads: 'All the same, holy teaching also uses human reasoning, not indeed to prove the faith, for that would take away the merit of believing, but to make manifest some implications of its message. Since grace does not scrap nature but brings it to perfection, so also natural reason should assist faith as the loving bent of the will yields to charity.' Cf. Neelands 'Hooker on Scripture', p. 80: 'For Hooker as for Thomas, grace does not destroy but perfects nature, and Scripture does not obliterate but perfects reason. "Supernatural endowments are an advancement, they are not an extinguishment of that nature whereto they are given"' (*Laws*, bk 5. ch. 6, p. 221). Neelands also gives a reference in the *Dublin Fragments* (13, 4:113.12–13) where Hooker cites Pseudo-Dionysius 'for to destroy nature is not the part of Providence'. Neelands argues that this is counter to mainstream Calvinism in the sixteenth century.

68. Neelands, 'Hooker on Scripture', p. 85.

69. From Hooker's response to 'Puritan' critiques of the *Laws*. Cited by J.

Booty, 'Hooker and Anglicanism' in W. Speed Hill, *Studies in Richard Hooker* (Cleveland and London, Press of Case Western Reserve University, 1972), p. 218.

70. *Laws*, bk 1. ii. 3, p. 152. The quotation is from Wisdom 8:1.
71. The word comes from the hymn about Christ, which Paul cites in Philippians 2:6–11, where Christ is described as having 'emptied Himself' (*heauton ekenoson*). This is both a wonderful and a complex passage of Scripture. I am taking a particular line – no longer widely accepted amongst biblical scholars – in interpreting 'emptied himself' to mean the pre-existent Christ divesting himself of the attributes and consciousness of his divine nature, when he became a human being. Cf. J. D. G. Dunn, *Christology in the Making* (2nd edn, London, SCM Press, 1989), pp. 114–21.
72. Gregory Nazianzen, one of the great Cappadocian theologians of the fourth century, wrote: 'Whatever has not been assumed cannot be restored [healed]; it is what is united with God that is saved.' J. N. D. Kelly, *Early Christian Doctrines* (5th edn, London, A. and C. Black, 1977), p. 297.
73. The classic Chalcedonian formulary has, to my mind, proved least helpful here: the human and divine natures in Christ were to be 'acknowledged' but 'without confusion, without change, without division, without separation' and 'the characteristic property of each nature being preserved, and concurring into one Person …' (See J. Stevenson, *Creeds, Councils and Controversies* (London, SPCK, 1986), p. 337.) In keeping distinctive but united the divine and human attributes in Christ, it leaves unsettled the question of what Jesus was actually thinking (how could an omniscient divine consciousness remain separate from his human self-consciousness) and is not always helpful in exegeting the gospels. Key works for me in this area have been Dunn's *Christology* and N. T. Wright's *Jesus and the Victory of God* (London, SPCK, 1996), both of which wrestle faithfully with the humanity of Jesus of Nazareth as the way in to his divine sonship. For all sorts of people, including many in the churches, meeting the complexities of the real Jesus of Nazareth is too threatening. Poignantly Wright writes: 'The Divine Saviour to whom they pray has only a tangential relationship to first-century Palestine, and they intend to keep it that way. He can, it seems be worshipped, but if he ever actually lived he was a very strange figure, clothed in white while all around wore drab, on his face a perpetual faraway expression of pious solemnity' (p. 9).
74. R. W. L. Moberly, *The Bible, Theology and Faith* (Cambridge, Cambridge University Press, 2000), p. 224 (italics mine).
75. Because I will be using Luke's gospel in this book, we should note at this stage the following helpful reflection on the transfiguration as described by Luke: 'When Jesus overtly has the visible characteristic of the divine realm in the form of transformative light, it may still be possible to miss seeing it. Thus the "glory", the divine realm into which Jesus has entered in his prayer, is something accessible to human perception, but not straightforwardly so' (Moberly, *Bible, Theology and Faith*, p. 55).
76. Lewis, *Screwtape*, p. 46.
77. Moberly, *Bible, Theology and Faith*, p. 235.
78. *AH*, 4. xx. 7, p. 490.
79. Behr, *Asceticism*, p. 56.
80. *AH*, 3. xviii. 5, p. 447.

81. *AH*, 3. xviii. 1, p. 446. Cf. Grant, *Irenaeus*, p. 52.
82. I am citing Behr, *Asceticism*, p. 63, citing *AH*, 3. xxi. 10 (italics mine).
83. *AH*, 4. xxxviii. 3, p. 522.
84. Behr, *Asceticism*, pp. 60–61.
85. *AH*, 3. xx. 2, p. 450.
86. Hooker, *Laws*, bk 5, liv.5, p. 215.
87. For contrasting ways to moderate the simple grammatical literal meaning of the 'Sermon on the Mount' see: A. Harvey, *Strenuous Commands* (London, SCM Press, 1990) and J. Stott, *Christian Counter Culture* (Leicester, IVP, 1978).
88. To my mind, Irenaeus took the doctrine of the assumption of the human condition by Jesus in a strange direction. For example he believed Jesus lived until he was fifty, because he thereby reached and included 'old age'. He wrote: 'Being a Master, therefore, he also possessed the age of a Master, not despising or evading any condition of humanity, nor setting aside in himself that law which he had appointed for the human race, but sanctifying every age, by that period corresponding to it which belonged to himself. For he came to save all through means of himself – all, I say, who through him are born again to God – infants, and children and boys, and youths, and old men. He therefore passed through every age, becoming an infant for infants, this sanctifying infants ...' *AH*, 2. xxii. 4, p. 391. It is quite an attractive image if a little gender specific. Grant includes the following phrase in his translation of this passage: 'and did not abolish in his person the law of human growth' (*Irenaeus*, p. 114). This reinforces for us the principle of proper development embedded by God in human nature.
89. Cf. 1 Cor. 7.
90. John 10:10. I am deliberately side-stepping the question of the historicity of John's gospel here. I am content to accept significant sections of it as indeed 'historical' and other sections as later reflections and inspirations into the reality of Christ.
91. This material needs to be noted and its exegesis pondered: 'I am in favour of prosperity, and so is God', he said. 'If ye be willing and obedient, ye shall eat the good of the land' (Isaiah 1:19) ... 'That's talking about financial prosperity.' K. Hagin, *Mountain Moving Faith* (Tulsa, OK, Faith Library Publications, 1995), p. 144. Or, the question 'Did God put cattle, silver, and gold for the devil and his bunch?' has a straightforward answer: 'No! He put these things here for his people to enjoy. He wants us to have the best!" K. Hagin: *How to Turn Your Faith Loose* (2nd edn., Tulsa, OK, Faith Library Publications, 1995), p. 15. I am indebted to Mr Andrei Petrine of Cranmer Hall for these references.
92. My point is partly a question of tone and partly of public priorities. For example, as Gill, *Churchgoing* implies, in terms of mission to young people, condemnation of homosexuality may be heard as both archaic and prejudiced, whereas a focus on justice or environmental issues is much more likely to communicate and resonate (see pp. 161–3, 189–94.) This is not in itself an argument for prioritising consensus building issues, but at a time when the Church is often mistrusted as well as misunderstood, such language and action could rekindle moral and intellectual credibility.
93. I. H. Marshall, *The Gospel of Luke* (Exeter, New International Greek Testament Commentary, Paternoster, 1978), p. 557.

94. J. Nolland, *Luke 9:21–18:34* (Dallas, Texas, Word, 1993), pp. 723ff., stresses that this is a healing story, partly by citing parallels in other stories in Luke.

95. 'Remember the sabbath day and keep it holy. Six days you shall labour and do all your work. But the seventh is a sabbath to the LORD your God; you shall not do any work – you, your son or your daughter, your male or female slave, your livestock, or the alien resident in your towns' (Exod. 20:8–10; cf. Deut. 5:12–14).

96. Marshall, *Luke*, p. 558.

97. It is only slight hyperbole to describe the sabbath as 'blood-soaked'. On several key occasions, Jews had refused to defend themselves rather than break the sabbath and this had been used by their enemies to conquer Jerusalem and other key strongholds, with all the horror that entailed. Because the issue of the sabbath features in a number of our biblical meditations it is worth noting now that: 'While the sabbath was to be considered a joy and privilege, it was also of such supreme importance that a violation of sabbath law carried the death penalty (Numbers 15:35). This reflects the sabbath's two-sided nature: it was both a blessing and a requirement for the nation of Israel' (D. N. Freedman (ed.), *Dictionary of the Bible* (Grand Rapids, Michigan, and Cambridge, Eerdmans, 2000), p. 1145).

98. J. Taylor, *The Great Exemplar*, eds R. Heber and C. Eden, *Whole Works* (1st pub. 1649, London, Longman Green, 1861), vol. II, p. 36 (my italics). Indeed Taylor was criticised for so stressing the necessity of a changed life – he did not for example believe in the efficacy of deathbed conversions – that he had undermined the doctrine of justification by faith. See D. A. Scott, *Christian Character: Jeremy Taylor and Christian Ethics Today* (Oxford, Latimer House Studies 38, 1991).

99. *Metanoia* (cf. Hebrew *sub*) is a key word both in biblical theology and in church history. The core of its meaning is 'to turn around'. It had resonances in New Testament Greek of its Hellenistic Greek usage, which meant to change one's mind, because the mind was thought of as being decisive in a human being. It is to be contrasted, though not too rigorously, with *metamelesthai*, which we might translate as 'remorse' or feelings of sorrow. See G. Kittel (ed.), *Theological Dictionary of the New Testament* (Grand Rapids, Michigan, Eerdmans, 1967).

Chapter 2: From Poverty to Simplicity

1. United Nations Development Programme, *Human Development Report 2003* (Oxford, Oxford University Press, 2003), p. 43. This brief paragraph is no substitute for a well-informed reading of similar material. I cannot recommend too highly time spent browsing the Jubilee 2000 website <www.jubileeresearch.org> or indeed those of the United Nations Development Programme <www.undp.org> or the World Health Organisation <www.who.int>. If you want to read further, try M. Taylor, *Not Angels but Agencies: The Ecumenical Response to Poverty. A Primer* (London, SCM Press, 1995); J. Stiglitz, *Globalization and its Discontents* (New York, Norton, 2001); and M. Northcott, *Life After Debt* (London, SPCK, 1999). I am grateful to Mr Peter Bellenger of Cranmer Hall for these recommendations. To help personalise and in a good sense, spiritualise, the issue, the classic is still C. Elliott, *Praying the Kingdom* (London, Darton, Longman & Todd, 1985). It is also worth noting, despite the achievements

of the Jubilee campaign, how little debt relief has actually been achieved but also what has been achieved with the aid of debt relief. Uganda is a wonderful example. See R. Greenhill, A. Pettifor, J. Northover and A. Sinha, *Did the G8 Drop the Debt?* (London, Jubilee Debt Campaign, 2003).

2. UN, *Human Development Report 2003*, p. 40.

3. World Health Organisation, *Health and Environment in Sustainable Development: Five Years after the Earth Summit* (Geneva, World Health Organisation, 1997), Executive summary, ch. 2.

4. *Financial Times* 14 May 2001. Listed on the Jubilee Research website <www.jubileeresearch.org>.

5. Adopted by the Anglican Consultative Council in 1990. *Mission in a Broken World* (London, Church House Publishing, 1990), p. 101.

6. See the Eco-Congregation website <www.encams.org/ecocongregation> for advice about how to do this. I am indebted to the Revd Dr Rob Kelsey, Diocese of Newcastle ecology officer, for advice in this area.

7. W. Temple, *Christianity and Social Order* (Harmondsworth, Penguin, 1942), p. 87. This extract comes from the 'Appendix' where Temple allowed himself to stray beyond stating fundamental and then middle axioms, to floating precise political and economic policies.

8. M. Moore, *Stupid White Men* (London, Penguin, 2002), p. 145.

9. Archbishop of Canterbury's Commission on Urban Priority Areas, *Faith in the City* (London, Church House Publishing, 1985). This remains my conviction despite the questions that might be asked about the Report's economic strategies, practical commitment to evangelism or real impact on developing the life of the visible Church in UPAs.

10. Note for example the work of the (1994) Church Ethical Investment Advisory Group which monitors the C. of E.'s investment portfolios. See <www.cofe.anglican.org/eiag>.

11. The 'Living Wage Pledge' campaign launched by Church Action on Poverty in a survey conducted in 2003 discovered that, in the Greater Manchester Area, 50 per cent of church organisation employees were earning less than £5.80 per hour, which has been calculated as the lowest family-sustaining minimum wage. Information from the Newcastle campaign but see <www.church-poverty.org.uk>. Hence the campaign for a 'Living Wage Church'.

12. E. Cameron, *The European Reformation* (Oxford, Clarendon, 1991), p. 27.

13. I used *The Rule of St Benedict* (hereafter *RB*), trans. J. McCann (London, Sheed and Ward, 1976). Another accessible version with insightful commentary is E. de Waal, *A Life-Giving Way* (London, Geoffrey Chapman, 1995).

14. *RB*, ch. 58, p. 64.

15. C. Stewart, *Prayer and Community: the Benedictine Tradition* (London, Darton, Longman & Todd, 1998), p. 117.

16. *RB*, ch. 55, p. 61.

17. Bede, *A History of the English Church and People*, Bk III, ch. 5, p. 148, trans. L. Sherley-Price (Harmondsworth, Penguin, 1968). (Hereafter Bede.)

18. Bede, Bk IV, ch. 28, p. 262.

19. Bede, Bk III, ch. 14, p. 165.

20. Bede, Bk II, ch. 2, p. 102. While Bede seems to support Augustine whole-heartedly, and records a blood-curdling prophetic judgement by

Augustine which he describes as being fulfilled, I detect covert criticism by Bede of Augustine's brittleness and self-importance.

21. For a scholarly discussion of Francis and poverty, see M. Robson, *St Francis. The Legend and the Life* (London, Geoffrey Chapman, 1997), ch. 4. Also W. J. Short, *Poverty and Joy: The Franciscan Tradition* (London, Darton, Longman & Todd, 1999), ch. 3.

22. C. Frugoni, *Francis of Assisi* (ET, London, SCM Press, 1998), p. 58.

23. Ibid.

24. Frugoni, *Francis*, p. 49

25. Thomas of Celano, *The First Life of St Francis of Assisi*, trans. C. Stace (London, SPCK, 2000), ch. 22, p. 26.

26. In Luke alone, apart from the teaching of John the Baptist or the Beatitudes, read: 6:29–30, 34–5, 38; 9:3, 58; 12:15, 22–34; 14:13, 33; 18:22–30; 21:1–4.

27. See E. de Waal, *A World Made Whole* (London, Fount, 1991) or Brother Ramon, *Franciscan Spirituality* (London, SPCK, 1994).

28. For realistic and scholarly discussions of 'Celtic Christianity' see I. Bradley, *Celtic Christianity. Making Myths and Chasing Dreams* (Edinburgh, Edinburgh University Press, 1999) and T. O'Loughlin, *Journeys on the Edge. The Celtic Tradition* (London, Darton, Longman & Todd, 2000).

29. Ch. 10 in Bede's *Life of Cuthbert*. See J. F. Webb and D. H. Farmer (eds.), *The Age of Bede* (Harmondsworth, Penguin, 1983). Note also the delightful stories of Cuthbert being fed by an eagle (ch. 12) and by ravens who came in penitence after being rebuked by Cuthbert for stealing his grain (chs. 19 and 20).

30. Adomnan of Iona, *Life of St Columba*, trans. R. Sharpe (Harmondsworth, Penguin, 1995), p. 227.

31. Celano, *First Life*, ch. 58, p. 59.

32. Cited by L. Culling, *What is Celtic Christianity?* (Nottingham, Grove, 1993), p. 15. Here Culling is quoting from Patrick's *Confessions*, which were definitely written by the saint. Cf. also R. P. C. Hanson, *St Patrick* (Oxford, Oxford University Press, 1968).

33. Try reading Melvyn Bragg's novel, *Credo* (London, Hodder & Stoughton, 1996).

34. M. Ramsey, *The Christian Priest Today* (London, SPCK, 1987), p. 39.

35. See Celano, *First Life*, chs. 51–4.

36. R. Foster, *Celebration of Discipline* (London, Hodder & Stoughton, 1980); C. Sugden, *Radical Discipleship* (Basingstoke, Marshall, Morgan & Scott, 1981), p. 8; along with Foster's other book, *Freedom of Simplicity* (London, Triangle, 1981); and the very powerful books, R. Sider, *Rich Christians in an Age of Hunger* (London, Hodder & Stoughton, 1978); and D. Watson, *Discipleship* (London, Hodder & Stoughton, 1981).

37. W. Law, *A Serious Call to a Devout and Holy Life*, first pub. 1728. See esp. ch. 7 on Flavia or ch. 19 on how (not) to bring up daughters.

38. J. Nolland, *Luke 1:1–9:20* (Dallas, Texas, Word, 1989), pp. 192ff. makes a thoughtful and detailed defence of a cluster of specific sources that take us back to the 'real events'.

39. I. H. Marshall, *The Gospel of Luke*, (Exeter, New International Greek Testament Commentary, Paternoster Press, 1978), p.180. Though it is of course very brief – no more than v. 21.

40. Marshall, *Luke*, p. 184.
41. Marshall, *Luke*, p. 256. Just as a side point – why is it that Fundamentalists never cite verses like 'Woe to you rich' when they are using the Bible to beat others into submission?
42. Nolland, *Luke*, p. 197.
43. M. Prior, *Jesus the Liberator* (Sheffield, Sheffield Academic Press, 1995), p. 188.
44. Prior, *Jesus*, p. 194. He writes as a member of a religious order.
45. Used with permission. Thanks especially to the Revd Chris Howson.

Chapter 3: From Obedience to Responsibility

1. C. S. Lewis, *Mere Christianity* (1st pub. 1952. Glasgow, Collins, 1977), p. 47.
2. See helpful discussions in C. K. Barrett, *The Gospel according to St John* (2nd edn, London, SPCK, 1978), pp. 161–2 and R. J. Song, 'World', in D. Atkinson (ed.), *New Dictionary of Christian Ethics and Pastoral Theology* (Leicester, IVP, 1996).
3. See T. Hart (ed.), *The Dictionary of Historical Theology* (Carlisle, Paternoster Press, 2000), p. 478.
4. Synod of Dort, Article 1, section 'Third and Fourth Main Points of Doctrine'. See <www.reformed.org/documents/canons_of_dordt.html>.
5. Synod of Dort, Article 3.
6. *The Westminster Confession*, section 6, article 2. G. Bray (ed.), *Documents of the English Reformation* (Cambridge, James Clarke, 1994), p. 492.
7. J. Calvin, *Institutes of the Christian Religion*, trans. J. Beveridge (London, James Clarke, 1949), Bk 3, ch. 21, section, 5, p. 206. While this looks like a classic piece of inhumane Christianity, we should note that predestination was not as dominant a part of Calvin's theology and spirituality as it became amongst his successors.
8. J. D. G. Dunn, *Romans 1–8* (Dallas, Texas, Word, 1988), p. 168, italics original.
9. C. E. B. Cranfield, *The Epistle to the Romans* (Edinburgh, T & T Clark, 1975), vol. 1, p. 204.
10. Cited in B. Lohse, *Martin Luther's Theology* (Minneapolis, Fortress Press, 1999), p. 167. See discussion pp. 160–68 and 256–7.
11. Hooker's life other than his writings is not well known, or very eventful. There is, however, a recent biography/reconstruction of his life: P. Secor, *Richard Hooker. Prophet of Anglicanism* (Tunbridge Wells, Burns & Oates, 1999).
12. R. Hooker: *Of the Laws of Ecclesiastical Polity* (Everyman edn, London, Dent, 1965). He writes of 'that law which giveth life unto all the rest, which are commendable, just and good; namely the law whereby the Eternal himself doth work' (1.i.3, p. 150). And 'The being of God is a kind of law to his working; for that perfection which God is, giveth perfection to that he doth' (1.ii.1, p. 150). There is an important principle at stake here about the coherence and connections between divine and human perspectives on what is good. Hooker, importantly, is here opposing theological schools that stress the gap between divine and human perceptions of moral goodness.
13. This is not to disparage, for example, Aquinas' sense of the importance of Christ, but one of the features of the Reformation was to re-emphasise the gulf between God and humanity and thus humanity's radical need, as opposed to some versions of Scholastic theology. Therefore Hooker stressed that we are justified by the 'imputation' of Christ's righteousness.

'... but the righteousness wherein we must be found, if we will be justified, is not our own ... Christ hath merited righteousness for as many as
are found in him. In him God findeth us if we be faithful; for by faith we
are incorporated into him' (*A Learned Discourse on Justification*, Everyman
edn, vol. 1, p. 21). But even in this most Protestant of Hooker's works,
what he is actually doing is arguing that despite the 'corruptions' of the
Roman Catholic Church, many Roman Catholics had been, were and
would be saved. This made him deeply and indeed dangerously unpopular with the 'hotter' Protestants.

14. See *Laws*, 5. liv. 5, p. 216. See also 5.lvi.7 and 11, pp. 229 and 232.
15. *Laws*, 1. xii. 2, p. 211.
16. *Laws*, 1. xiv. 4 p. 217.
17. *Laws*, 1. xiv. 2, p. 216. The point of citing this reference is not that these
    points of doctrine are ones that all Christians today would regard as
    necessary but that they were so seen in the sixteenth century.
18. I think that, contrary to popular opinion, the most disturbing element of
    theological training for Evangelicals is not biblical criticism but this
    dawning awareness of how the Church had to wrestle to discern both the
    canon of the New Testament and further, how to express such funda-
    mental beliefs as the divinity and humanity of Christ, when Scripture did
    not speak with an unqualified clarity, as in the debate with Arianism. See
    B. Lohse, *A Short History of Christian Doctrine* (rev. edn, Philadelphia,
    Fortress Press, 1985), chs. 2 and 3, or G. White, *The Mother Church Your
    Mother Never Told You Of* (London, SCM Press, 1993), chs. 2, 5 and 7.
19. *Laws*, 3. iv. 1, p. 303.
20. Hooker stretches sixteenth-century Protestant theology a long way. At
    times he sounds very clear cut: 'It is our wisdom, and our comfort; we care
    for no knowledge in the world but this, that man hath sinned, and God
    hath suffered; that God hath made himself the sin of men, and that men
    are made the righteousness of God' (*Justification*, p. 21). But he strains to
    be inclusive. He writes of the pagan Gentiles: 'In this which they
    confessed, that lieth covered which we believe; in the rudiments of their
    knowledge concerning God, the foundation of our faith concerning Christ
    lieth secretly wrapt up, and is virtually contained ...' (Ibid. p. 43). He
    rather backs away from the radicalness of this position but it is an indi-
    cator of how he was trying to tie together his valuing of common human
    wisdom with Christian revelation and salvation.
21. *The Rule of St Benedict*, trans. J. McCann (London, Sheed & Ward, 1976)
    (hereafter *RB*). Another accessible version with commentary is E. de Waal,
    A Life-Giving Way (London, Geoffrey Chapman, 1995).
22. H. Mayr-Harting has written a delightful chapter on 'Benedictine
    Holiness' in S. Barton (ed.), *Holiness* (Edinburgh, T & T Clark, 2003), p. 265.
23. *RB*, p. 36.
24. *RB*, p. 22.
25. *RB*, ch. 58, p. 63.
26. *RB*, ch. 5, p. 14.
27. *RB*, ch. 68, p. 75. Here I fear that I disagree with Mayr-Harting (pp. 266–7)
    where he argues that Benedict did not mean obedience in all circumstances.
28. *RB*, ch. 30, p. 38.
29. This is enshrined in part in our Articles. Article 19 (portion): 'As the

Church of Jerusalem, Alexandria and Antioch have erred, so also the Church of Rome hath erred, not only in their living (and manner of ceremonies) but also in matters of faith.' Bray, *Documents*, p. 298. It is also seen in the restraint on clericalism as a consequence of the 'triumph of the laity' in the English Reformation. I would also interpret the pattern of 'dispersed authority', typical of Anglican church polity, as a theological, instinctive and institutional caution about authority and obedience. See also P. Thomas, 'Some Principles of Anglican Authority', in *Authority in the Anglican Communion* (London, Anglican Consultative Council, 1981) (papers presented to the 1981 Primates' Meeting). Thomas writes, p. 25: 'It is authority which is based on moral and spiritual insight, and is quite different from that of the "great men" of whom Jesus spoke, whose authority was expressed legalistically and as of right, and, by means of bureaucracy, coercion and the raw manipulation of power.'

30. *RB*, ch. 7. Using de Waal, *Life-Giving Way*, p. 47. Benedict is quoting Luke 14:11.
31. *RB*, p. 17.
32. *RB*, p. 18.
33. *RB*, p. 19.
34. *RB*, p. 20.
35. de Waal, *Life-Giving Way*, p. 49.
36. *RB*, p. 20.
37. *RB*, p. 21.
38. U. Eco, *The Name of the Rose* (London, Picador, 1983), p. 95.
39. Eco, *Name*, p. 79.
40. In researching the front cover for this book many of us spent much time, fruitlessly, trying to find such a picture.
41. *RB*, p. 21.
42. *RB*, p. 21.
43. K. Armstrong, *Beginning the World* (London, Pan, 1984), p. 41.
44. Armstrong, *Beginning*, p. 41.
45. See Canon C 14.3.
46. 'You know that amongst the Gentiles, those whom they recognise as their rulers lord it over them, and their great ones are tyrants over them. But it is not so among you: but whoever wishes to become great among you must be your servant, and whoever wishes to be first among you must be slave of all. For the Son of Man came not to be served but to serve, and to give his life as a ransom for many' (Mark 10:42–5). I cite Mark because I think Luke softened the sharpness of Jesus' critique of Gentile rulers.
47. 'At your consecration as a Bishop you promised to be our chief pastor, to further the unity of the Church, to uphold its discipline and to guard its faith, to promote its mission, to teach and govern its people, ordaining and enabling its ministers to fulfil their ministry. Are you resolved to do all in your power to keep watch over the whole flock to which God has appointed you shepherd, encouraging the faithful, restoring the lost and building up the body of Christ in the unity of the Spirit and the bond of peace?'
48. R. Greenwood, *Transforming Priesthood* (London, SPCK, 1994), p. 157.
49. See 'Limbo' in F. L. Cross and E. A. Livingstone, *The Oxford Dictionary of the Christian Church* (3rd edn, Oxford, Oxford University Press, 1997).

50. See Dunn, *Romans*. pp. 144–60 (italics original).
51. This is a highly contentious text with a long history of conflict over 'grace and works' in its exegesis. (P. O'Brien notes that this is a 'unique' combination of words in the NT. *The Epistle to the Philippians* (Grand Rapids, Michigan, New International Commentary on the New Testament, Eerdmans, 1991), p. 276.) There are two modern views. Either Paul is referring to the effort of the Philippians to keep working at their (individual) spiritual welfare or he is encouraging them to work together for the health of their church. So after several pages of argument O'Brien suggests: 'Paul has in mind a "continuous, sustained, strenuous effort", which is elsewhere described under the imagery of a pursuit, a following after, a pressing on, a contest, a fight, or a race (Phil. 3:12, cf. Rom. 14:19; 1 Cor. 9:24–27; 1 Tim. 6:12)' (*Philippians*, pp. 276ff.). Hawthorne translates it differently: 'Obediently work at achieving spiritual health … for the One who effectively works among you creating both the desire and the drive to promote goodwill is God.' He comments: 'Paul is not here concerned with the eternal welfare of the soul *of the individual* … Rather the context suggests that this command is to be understood in a corporate sense' (G. F. Hawthorne, *Philippians* (Waco, Texas, Word, 1983), pp. 96ff.). Fee tends towards a 'plague on all your houses' approach and sums up succinctly: 'But "salvation" is not only something they receive; it is something they *do*' (G. D. Fee, *Paul's Letter to the Philippians* (Grand Rapids, Michigan, New International Commentary on the New Testament, Eerdmans, 1995), pp. 230ff.).
52. There is some consensus that this psalm could date from the period of the brutal Maccabean wars in the second century. See A. Weiser, *The Psalms* (London, SCM Press, 1962), p. 354.
53. W. Brueggemann, 'The Costly Loss of Lament', in P. Miller (ed.), *The Psalms and the Life of Faith* (Minneapolis, Fortress Press, 1995), p. 104.
54. Brueggemann, 'Costly Loss', p. 107.
55. P. Ellingworth, *The Epistle to the Hebrews* (Grands Rapids, Michigan, New International Greek Testament Commentary, Eerdmans, 1993), p. 292.
56. See W. Barclay, *The Gospel of Luke* (Edinburgh, St Andrew's Press, 1965), pp. 66–8; J. Drury, *Luke* (London and Glasgow, Fontana, 1973), pp. 68–70; I. H. Marshall, *The Gospel of Luke* (Exeter, Paternoster Press, 1978), pp. 228–33; J. Nolland, *Luke 1:1–9:20* (Dallas, Texas, Word, 1989), pp. 251–8.
57. M. Westphal, *Suspicion and Faith. The Religious Uses of Modern Atheism* (New York, Fordham University Press, 1998), p. xiv.
58. The Liturgical Commission of the General Synod of the Church of England, *Making Women Visible* (GS 859, London, Church House Publishing, 1988), para. 90, p. 23 and also p. 63.
59. Drury, *Luke*, p. 70.
60. Barclay, *Luke*, p. 67.
61. J. Cotter: *It Shall Not Be So among You* and *Towards Ordained Ministry*. Full copies may be purchased from Cairns Publications, Small Pilgrim Places Network, Llandecwyn Project, Dwylan, Stryd Fawr, Harlech, Gwynedd, LL46 2YA, Cymru, UK.

Chapter 4: From Chastity to the Joy of Sexuality

1. A. Kenny, *Aquinas* (Oxford, Oxford University Press, 1980), p. 2.
2. See for example R. Bell, *Holy Anorexia* (Chicago, University of Chicago

Press, 1985); D. Weinstein and R. Bell, *Saints and Society* (Chicago, University of Chicago Press, 1982); E. Stuart, *Spitting at Dragons* (London, Mowbray, 1996). I am very grateful to the Revd Jane Speck for these suggestions and for working with me as her supervisor on her fine dissertation on the self-mutilation of medieval women saints and how this was encouraged by their (male) superiors.

3. Notice that Queen Victoria gave portraits of nude women to Prince Albert as a birthday present: one of the surprising facts revealed by the 2003 Tate exhibition 'The Victorian Nude'. See also, M. Sweet, *Inventing the Victorians* (London, Faber & Faber, 2001), who specifically names the veiling of piano legs as a later myth (p. xii).

4. She now features in the current Church of England list of saints on 30 May. For further reading see A. Loades, *Feminist Theology: Voices from the Past* (Cambridge, Polity Press, 2001), Part II, and E. M. Bell, *Josephine Butler: Flame of Fire* (London, Constable, 1962).

5. Given the current debates in the Anglican Communion, it is important to me to note that as a theological educator in the Church of England, I am committed to the discipline of *Issues in Human Sexuality*, A Statement by the House of Bishops (London, Church House Publishing, 1991). It might seem as if the logic of this paragraph is such that I am arguing for a change in the Church's teaching and policy in the area of homosexuality. In fact the point of this whole chapter is also to caution against some of the modern West's values in the area of sexuality and I would want to reflect that in terms of 'world opinion', both currently and in history, the current Western 'pro-gay' consensus is a minority view. I don't think 'the case' is yet proven in terms of human development, unlike the issue of patriarchy. Nonetheless, three things must be said. First, the Church has a very poor track record both generally in terms of handling sexual issues honestly and wisely and also in its care of minority groups. Second, it will not do simply to repeat 'the Bible says'. Both as a theological method and as a tactic, this is bringing our Scriptures into disrepute. We need to work harder at a rounded biblical theology and at how we respond to the genuine passion for justice and horror at the Church's stance which is evident around us. Third – and this is evident in what I have just written – I do not think that this is a debate which is cut and dried, on either side. Trying to make it into a test of either Christian faithfulness or Christian love is to surrender to 'the world's' stereotypes. In this area I have found the following especially helpful: R. Williams: 'On Making Moral Decisions', *Anglican Theological Review*, vol. 81:2 (1999), pp. 295–308 and R. W. L. Moberly, 'The Use of Scripture in Contemporary Debate about Homosexuality', *Theology*, vol. CIII, no. 814 (2000), pp. 251–8. I am still moved by the example of my former colleague the late Revd Michael Vasey and his book, *Strangers and Friends* (London, Hodder & Stoughton, 1995).

6. *Guardian*, 20 August 2003.

7. J. Harris, *Chocolat* (London, Black Swan, 2000).

8. Harris, *Chocolat*, p. 235.

9. Harris, *Chocolat*, p. 314.

10. 'Porn Again', *In Business*, BBC Radio 4, 23 January, 2003.

11. *Guardian Weekend Supplement*, 8 November, 2003, p. 45.

12. A. Comfort, *The Joy of Sex* (3rd edn, London, Mitchell Beazley, 2003), pp. 214–15.
13. M. Atwood, *Oryx and Crake* (London, Bloomsbury, 2003), p. 86.
14. The *Guardian* (8 November 2003) also noted that the most popular website found in a recent scientific study of internet usage featured bestiality images – women having sex with animals.
15. Ibid.
16. Atwood, *Oryx and Crake*, p. 144.
17. Recommended texts are T. Radcliffe, *To Sing a New Song* (Dublin, Dominican Publications, 1999) and S. Schneider, *Selling All* (New York, Paulist Press, 2001). I am grateful to my Ushaw College colleague Fr Chris Hughes for these recommendations. A personal favourite is H. Nouwen, *Clowning in Rome* (first pub. 1979, rev. edn, London, Darton, Longman & Todd, 2001).
18. I used the following edition: *Revelations of Divine Love*, ed. H. Backhouse and R. Pipe (London, Hodder & Stoughton, 1987) (hereafter *Revelations*). Some of the best writing on Julian is by R. Llewellyn: see especially, *With Pity not with Blame* (3rd edn, London, Darton, Longman & Todd, 1994).
19. *Revelations*, ch. 64, p. 134.
20. *Revelations*, ch. 62, p. 129.
21. *Revelations*, ch. 62, p. 130.
22. *Revelations*, ch. 86, p. 169.
23. *Revelations*, ch. 49, p. 93.
24. See *Table Talk*, trans. W. Hazlitt. I used the Fount edition published London 1995. The most vivid biography of Luther remains R. H. Bainton, *Here I Stand* (London, NEL, 1950).
25. Luther, *Table Talk*, 721, p. 333.
26. Luther initially saw the purpose of marriage as being to contain the risk of sinful sex. See Bainton, *Here I Stand*, p. 234. This view did not survive the reality of marriage. But note the less than positive defence of sexual love in marriage in the Marriage Service in the Book of Common Prayer: 'It was ordained for a remedy against sin, and to avoid fornication; that such persons as have not the gift of continency might marry, and keep them-selves undefiled members of Christ's body.' It was certainly not 'to satisfy men's lusts and appetites like brute beasts that have no understanding'. And people still want to use this form of words in their marriage services.
27. Luther, *Table Talk*, 716, p. 332.
28. Bainton, *Here I Stand*, p. 225.
29. Bainton, *Here I Stand*, p. 234.
30. Luther, *Table Talk*, 752, p. 342.
31. Bainton, *Here I Stand*, p. 233.
32. Bainton, *Here I Stand*, pp. 235–6.
33. Bernard of Clairvaux, one of the greatest of the medieval preachers, preached some 86 sermons on the Songs of Songs but is reputed – reliably I think – not to have referred to the fact that it is an erotic love poem and treated it entirely allegorically.
34. R. Askew, *Muskets and Altars. Jeremy Taylor and the Last of the Anglicans* (London, Mowbray, 1997), p. 12.
35. Askew, *Muskets and Altars*, p. 12.
36. Library of Anglo-Catholic Theology, Taylor, *Works*, vol. IV, p. 210.

37. Taylor, *Works*, vol. IV, p. 224.
38. Taylor, *Works*, vol. IV, p. 212.
39. Askew (*Muskets and Altars*, p. 189) quotes from a letter written by Taylor to an unhappily married woman whom Askew is convinced had asked Taylor about 'how far' she could go with a woman friend whom she loved. Taylor, of course, counsels restraint but reflects on the relationship between marriage and friendship: '... other friendships are parts of this, they are Marriages too, less indeed than the other, because they cannot, must not be all that endearment which the other is; yet that being the Principal, is the measure of the rest, and all are to be honoured by like Dignities, and measured by the same Rules, and conducted by their portion of the same Lawes: but as friendships are Marriages of the Soul, and of Fortunes, and interests and Counsels; so are they Brotherhoods too; and I often think of the excellencies of friendship in the Words of *David*, who certainly was the best friend in the world: "it is good and it is pleasant that brethren should live like friends." *Such friendships are the beauties of Society, and the pleasure of Life, and the festivity of minds: and whatsoever can be spoken of Love, which is God's eldest Daughter, can be said of virtuous friendships*' (my italics). Thought-provoking.
40. J. Nolland, *Luke 1:1– 9:20* (Dallas, Texas, Word, 1989), p. 252; I. H. Marshall, *The Gospel of Luke* (Exeter, New International Greek Testament Commentary, Paternoster Press, 1978), pp. 304–7.
41. Marshal (*Luke*, p. 309) criticises Weiss, *Theological Dictionary of the New Testament* for this suggestion.
42. Nolland, *Luke*, p. 353 and Marshall, *Luke*, p. 308. See the article 'Prostitute' in J. B. Green, S. McKnight and I. H. Marshall (eds.), *Dictionary of Jesus and the Gospels* (Leicester, IVP, 1992), p. 643.
43. Nolland, *Luke*, p. 353.
44. Cited in A. Loades (ed.), *Dorothy L. Sayers: Spiritual Writings* (London, SPCK, 1993), p. 2, from Sayers' 1946 collection of essays, *Unpopular Opinions*. See also Loades, *Feminist Theology*, Part III.
45. W. Barclay, *The Gospel of Luke* (Edinburgh, St Andrew's Press, 1965), p. 94.
46. J. Drury, *Luke* (London, Fontana, 1973), pp. 88–9.
47. C. Heyward, *Saving Jesus from Those Who Are Right* (Minneapolis, Fortress Press, 1999).
48. Heyward, *Saving Jesus*, p. 20.
49. Heyward, *Saving Jesus*, p. 210.

Chapter 5: **From Stability to Patience**

1. R. Foster, *Celebration of Discipline* (London, Hodder & Stoughton, 1980), p. 1. Ironically the book was sold under the counter in my local Christian bookshop because the chapter on meditation was deemed 'unsound'.
2. The devaluation of Christianity in comparison with the religions of the East is not a recent phenomenon. This quotation comes from E. M. Forster, *A Passage to India* (end of ch. XIV), (first pub. 1924). Mrs Moore has retreated from the Marabar Caves, intimidated by their Indian mystery. The full quotation is: 'But suddenly at the edge of her mind, Religion appeared, poor little talkative Christianity, and she knew that all its divine words from "Let there be Light" to "It is finished" only amounted to "boum".'

3. A. Pearson, *I don't know how she does it* (London, Chatto & Windus, 2002), p. 291.

4. Pearson, p. 133. I am not sure 'God' puts in much of an appearance in the rest of the novel, unless we count the reconciliation of Kate and Rich and their decision to leave London for the country as a sign of divine action.

5. For example this was Charles Lowder's pattern of work in Wapping in the 1860s: 'In winter he rose before 7am., in summer before 6am. Prime was said in the mission house oratory at 7, matins at Calvert St at 7.30, followed by Holy Communion. Terce followed breakfast after which the morning was spent visiting, in the schools, or at work in his study until 12.45, when the clergy assembled to say Sext. Dinner was at 1, and after dinner parochial or paper work occupied the time until tea at 5.30. After tea there were classes, choir practice, reading or visiting until evensong at 8, and after that confessions to be heard, more classes to be held, or special cases to be cared for until supper at 9.15. Compline followed. In theory all the clergy retired at 11, but in fact much of the work was late in the evening ...' L. Ellsworth, *Charles Lowder and the Ritualist Movement* (London, Darton, Longman & Todd, 1982), p. 69.

6. According to an Evangelical Alliance survey in 1990, it is 38 minutes per week compared to 22 hours per week on admin. S. J. L. Croft, *Ministry in Three Dimensions* (London, Darton, Longman & Todd, 1999), p. 18.

7. J. McCann, *The Rule of St Benedict* (London, Sheed & Ward, 1976) (hereafter *RB*), ch. 58, p. 63. In fact Benedict, showing again his wisdom and realism, allowed for a monk to leave up to three times and return to start again. See ch. 29.

8. Note Benedict's contempt for such monks, *RB*, ch.1, pp. 5–6.

9. E. de Waal, *A Life-Giving Way* (London, Geoffrey Chapman, 1995), p. 170.

10. *RB*, ch. 4, p. 14.

11. A classic text on this is D. Chitty, *The Desert a City* (Oxford, Mowbray, 1977). For accessible collections of their writings, see B. Ward (ed.), *The Sayings of the Desert Fathers* (Oxford, Mowbray, 1975) and idem., *The Wisdom of the Desert Fathers* (Oxford, SLG Press, 1975). Also T. Vivian (ed.), *Journeying into God* (Minneapolis, Fortress Press, 1996). A recent fine reflection on the theme of the 'desert' is A. Louth, *The Wilderness of God* (2nd edn, London, Darton, Longman & Todd, London, 2003).

12. Cf. Louth, *Wilderness*, ch. 3.

13. See Cassian, *Conferences*, Nicene and Post-Nicene Fathers, 2nd Series, ed. P. Schaff , vol. IX (Edinburgh, T & T Clark, 1991).

14. B. Ward, *Harlots of the Desert* (Kalamazoo, Michigan, Cistercian Publications, 1987).

15. Chitty, *Desert a City*, p. 13.

16. Ward, *Sayings*, saying 17, p. 4.

17. Ward, *Wisdom*, p. xiii.

18. Ward, *Wisdom*, saying 22, p. 6.

19. Ward, *Sayings*, Eucharistus the Secular, p. 60. Remember that Orthodox bishops have to be monks, unlike parish clergy, and there are restrictions on priests having sexual intercourse before presiding at the Eucharist. In the West this led eventually to clerical celibacy, because of the development of a daily mass.

20. Ward, *Wisdom*, saying 27, p. 6.

21. Ward, *Sayings*, saying 8, p. 3.
22. 'A dualism which regards matter as evil has been typical of most ascetic religions, and has been a besetting temptation also to Christians ... but the central teaching of the monks is free from this, even in the extremes of ascetic practice.' Chitty, *Desert a City*, p. 4.
23. Ward, *Sayings*, saying 184, p. 193.
24. Ward (*Sayings*, p. xxv) retells the story of Abba Macarius who went to stay in a monastery incognito and outdid the monks there with his asceticism. 'He was very tough.' At the end of the week the local Abba asked him to leave because he was discouraging the local monks. Ward tells the story as part of a sustained argument that the 'desert was not a gigantic gymnasium where athletes vied with each other in endurance tests'. I am less certain.
25. Vivian, *Journeying*, p. 23. Vivian emphasises the fact that the Greek original of 'reason' is *logos*.
26. See Ward, *Sayings*, p. 250.
27. Ward, *Sayings*, Foreword, p. xxv (italics original).
28. Ward, *Wisdom*, saying 69, p. 23.
29. Ward, *Sayings*, saying 96, p. 180.
30. Ward, *Sayings*, saying 22, p. 6.
31. Ward, *Wisdom*, saying 66, p. 22.
32. Vivian, *Journeying*, p. 16.
33. Vivian, *Journeying*, pp. 19–20.
34. Vivian, *Journeying*, p. 23.
35. Ward, *Wisdom*, p. xi.
36. Ward, *Sayings*, saying 11, p. 130.
37. Ward, *Sayings*, saying 33, p. 8 (my italics).
38. Ward, *Sayings*, saying 32, p. 8.
39. Ward, *Wisdom*, saying 2, p. 1. Ward herself recognises that this saying goes to the heart of questions about the life of the 'desert'.
40. Cf. also Luke 9:57–62; 14:26; 18:29–30. We often try to moderate the shock of all of these pieces of teaching, for example by appealing to the language of hyperbole and, if John 19:26–7 records a real happening, then Jesus is shown caring for his family in the most extreme circumstances. I find it difficult to believe that he would have excluded his family from the commandment to love but he clearly took people away from their homes and was aware that his call to discipleship might break families. His teaching is not a secure basis for the modern Christian fixation on the nuclear family. 'It [Jesus' teaching] does however show that there are other ways of serving God than by marrying and raising a family, and that marriage and family life are no substitute for the life of faith. Christianity has always recognised the vocation to the single life ...' Board of Social Responsibility of General Synod, *Something to Celebrate* (London, Church House Publishing, 1995), p. 81).
41. Vivian, *Journeying*, p. 13.
42. Cf. Luke 4:42; 5:16; 6:12; 9:18; 9:28; 11:1, for different accounts of Jesus going away on his own or with his disciples to pray in 'deserted places'.
43. Pearson, *I don't know how she does it*, p. 334.
44. There is a huge literature on the nature of parables. An excellent way in is: R. Etchells, *A Reading of the Parables of Jesus* (London, Darton, Longman &

Todd, 1998). For this parable see also: K. E. Bailey, *Poet and Peasant through Peasant Eyes* (Grands Rapids, Michigan, Eerdmans, 1983); W. Barclay, *Luke* (Edinburgh, St Andrew's Press, 1965); I. H. Marshall, *The Gospel of Luke* (Exeter, New International Greek Testament Commentary, Paternoster Press, 1978); J. Nolland, *Luke 9:21–18:34* (Dallas, Texas, Word, 1993).

45. Nolland, *Luke*, pp. 874ff.; Etchells, *Parables*, p. 47.
46. So Bailey, *Poet and Peasant*, pp. 149ff.; Marshall, *Luke*, pp. 678ff.
47. Does this contrast lie behind an apparent conflict in Jesus' teaching? When the Pharisees accuse Jesus of casting out demons by the power of Beelzebul, Jesus tells them that those who do not gather with him, are scattering (and in Matthew warns them against the blasphemy of calling the Spirit's work 'evil') (Luke 11:14–23; cf. Matt. 12:22–32). But when his apostles try to stop others casting out demons in his name, when they do not belong to this group of disciples, Jesus defends the right of the outsiders: 'for he that is not against you is for you'. That is, the same Spirit is at work in him, so don't condemn him (Luke 9:49–50, cf. Mark 9:38–41). A superb example of a modern application of this teaching is R. T. France, 'Not one of us', in G. Kuhrt (ed.), *To Proclaim Afresh* (London, SPCK, 1995).
48. Nolland, *Luke*, p. 879.
49. Note that some older translations had him praying to himself. So Barclay, *Luke*, p. 232. This was a mistranslation according to Bailey, Etchells, Marshall and Nolland.
50. Bailey (*Poet and Peasant*, p. 145) stresses the point that the setting is public worship.
51. For a discussion of this issue, see Nolland, *Luke*, pp. 876–7.
52. Bailey (*Poet and Peasant*, p. 148) cites the *Mishnah*: 'For Pharisees the clothes of an *am-haaretz* ['people of the land' – ignorant, lawless Jews] count as suffering *midras* – uncleanness.'
53. And perhaps even un-Middle Eastern: Bailey argues that chest-beating is a feminine action only done by men in moments of extreme sorrow. *Poet and Peasant*, p. 153.
54. Etchells, *Parables*, p. 49. She also very helpfully links the tax collector's words to Psalm 51.
55. Bailey, *Poet and Peasant*, p. 154.
56. So Marshall (*Luke*, p. 680) does not see any verbal links. Nolland (*Luke*, p. 878) too separates the two types of usage but cf. Etchells, *Parables of Jesus*, p. 49.
57. Edward Bickersteth, a distinguished Victorian Evangelical clergyman. O. Chadwick, *The Victorian Church* (3rd edn, London, A. and C. Black, 1971), Part 1, p. 443.
58. The slogan of Hudson Taylor's China Inland Mission.
59. Ward, *Sayings*, saying 13, p. 3.

Chapter 6: **From Conversion to Christ**

1. This comes from an impassioned call for holy living by a fierce Evangelical, Michael Griffiths, *Consistent Christianity* (Leicester, IVP, 1976 reprint), p. 17. He goes on: 'If Christians have evangelistic services for breakfast, dinner, lunch and tea – then no wonder there is a dietary deficiency in the matter of day to day living. It is of little use telling the unbeliever what a difference it makes to be a Christian if he cannot see it for

himself' (p. 19).

2. Irenaeus, *Against Heresies*, Bk 2, ch. x., section 3 (hereafter *AH*), in *Ante-Nicene Fathers* (American edn, 1995 reprint, Massachusetts, Hendrikson, Peabody), Vol, 4. xxxviii.3, p. 522.

3. N. Hornby, *How to be good* (London, Penguin, 2001).

4. J. Joyce, *A Portrait of the Artist as a Young Man* (first pub. 1916; repr. London, Grafton, 1986), p. 123.

5. *Common Worship* (Desk edn., London, Church House Publishing, 2000), p. 312.

6. And an historically ambiguous one. Preaching for a Crusade was 'preaching the cross'. Anthony and Francis 'took up the cross' but not quite in the way that 'Reform' might understand.

7. See N. T. Wright, *The Resurrection of the Son of God* (London, SPCK, 2003). My book might have benefited from a meditation on one of the resurrection narratives in Luke, but again there is not space. Can I recommend both ch. 2 in R. W. L. Moberly, *The Bible, Theology and Faith* (Cambridge, Cambridge University Press, 2000) and S. J. L. Croft: *The Lord is Risen*, Emmaus Bible Resources, London, Church House Publishing, 2001).

8. Doctrine Commission of the General Synod of the Church of England (London, Church House Publishing, 1995), p. 56.

9. I. McEwan, *Atonement* (first pub. 2001; London, Vintage, 2002), p. 212.

10. McEwan, *Atonement*, p. 285.

11. McEwan, *Atonement*, p. 337.

12. McEwan, *Atonement*, p. 344.

13. See McEwan, *Atonement*, p. 348.

14. McEwan, *Atonement*, p. 261.

15. Briony experiences a moment of sharp guilt at her cousin's wedding, triggered by the words of the Book of Common Prayer asking about any 'impediments' and warning of God's judgement. But as the novel comments, 'it was a very long time till judgement day', as the cousin and her rapist husband make their (duplicitous?) oaths (p. 325).

16. See the last three pages of the novel and the crucial paragraph on p. 371.

17. So Ivan Karamazov tells the story of the little boy torn apart by a general's hounds and asks Alyosha his brother, the hermit, whether the suffering of children is worth the harmony that will come at the end of time: 'And if the sufferings of children go to make up the sum of sufferings which is necessary for the purchase of truth, then I say beforehand that the entire truth is not worth such a price ... We cannot afford to pay so much for admission. And therefore I hasten to return my ticket of admission ... This I am doing. It is not God that I do not accept Alyosha. I merely most respectfully return him the ticket.' When Alyosha tries to counter by pointing to the suffering atonement of Christ – 'he can forgive everything, everyone and everything and *for everything* because he gave his innocent blood for all and for everything' – Ivan responds with the story of the Grand Inquisitor. F. Dostoyevsky, *The Brothers Karamazov* (first pub. 1880; London, Penguin, 1982), pp. 284ff.

18. A good succinct way into theologies of the atonement is provided by S. W. Sykes, *The Story of the Atonement* (London, Darton, Longman & Todd), 1997. For Evangelicals, realising that the New Testament and church history provide diverse and even not very sharply defined theologies of

the atonement is both shocking and liberating. For Anglicans, crucial reading is the Appendix in Doctrine Commission of the General Synod of the Church of England, *The Mystery of Salvation* (London, Church House Publishing, 1995). The classic text that still has a profound effect on Evangelical ordinands is G. Aulen, *Christus Victor* (London, SPCK, 1931), who argues that the main theology of the cross in the New Testament and early Church is of Christ's triumph over sin and death rather than a substitutionary atonement.

19. This is not an argument for universalism *tout court*. Holding to account those guilty of evil is part of the work of atonement. So I believe in divine judgement, if not in the literalistically and pathologically inflated versions of it present historically in the life of the churches. Cf. *Mystery of Salvation*, pp. 198–9.

20. There is yet another vast and bitter theological debate lying behind this simple paragraph. Classically, Protestants have stressed 'justification by faith alone', so that any trace of human moral or spiritual 'merit' is not placed in the scales of salvation but we are simply 'declared' to be in the right before God, by God, without having really changed morally, whereas Roman Catholics have stressed the necessity for real personal change as a necessary part of the journey of salvation – 'sanctification'. That this debate may be showing signs of progress is witnessed in the historic Roman Catholic and Lutheran agreed document on justification. Lutheran World Federation and the Roman Catholic Church, *Joint Declaration on the Doctrine of Justification* (Grand Rapids, Michigan and Cambridge, Eerdmans, 2000).

21. This is where Gunton's argument about Christ as Creator is so significant. See 'Christ the Wisdom of God', in S. Barton (ed.), *Where Shall Wisdom be Found?* (Edinburgh, T & T Clark, 1999), pp. 249–62.

22. D. Bonhoeffer, *The Cost of Discipleship* (first pub. 1937; London, SCM Press, 1982), pp. 35, 36 and 42.

23. Hornby, *How to be Good*, pp. 67 and 70.

24. Hornby, *How to be Good*, p. 6.

25. Hornby, *How to be Good*, p. 72.

26. Hornby, *How to be Good*, p. 79.

27. Hornby, *How to be Good*, p. 11.

28. Hornby, *How to be Good*, p. 74.

29. '… but just at the wrong moment I catch a glimpse of the night sky behind David, and I can see there's nothing out there at all.' Hornby, *How to be Good*, p. 244.

30. See Hornby, *How to be Good*, pp. 186ff. Katie's brother describes it as like being met coming out of a brothel.

31. Hornby, *How to be Good*, p. 220.

32. Hornby, *How to be Good*, p. 219.

33. Hornby, *How to be Good*, p. 235.

34. See Hornby, *How to be Good*, pp. 213 and 223.

35. Hornby, *How to be Good*, p. 225.

36. Hornby, *How to be Good*, p. 201.

37. Two of the sobering findings of the research of Philip Richter are first that considerable numbers of people are leaving British churches because they no longer believe, or their values have changed and that the Church feels

irrelevant or even oppressive and secondly, that this is the group least likely to return. See P. Richter and L. Francis, *Gone but not Forgotten* (London, Darton, Longman & Todd, 1998), chs. 3, 4 and 5 and p. 139.

38. J. McCann (ed.), *The Rule of St Benedict* (London, Sheed and Ward, 1976), pp. 11–14.

39. Note the catena of scriptural quotations of God's invitation with which the Rule begins. See the Prologue, McCann, (ed.), *Rule*, pp. 1ff.

40. So the abbot is to 'set mercy above judgement [James 2:13]' and 'study to be loved rather than feared'. McCann (ed.), *Rule*, ch. 64, p. 71.

41. McCann, *RB*, Prologue, p. 3: '... and let us ask God that he be pleased, where our nature is powerless, to give us the help of his grace.'

42. E. de Waal, *A Life-Giving Way* (London, Geoffrey Chapman, 1995), p. 38. My italics.

43. Lohse cites a classic blast of Luther from the *Heidleberg Disputation* (1518) to demonstrate this: 'That person does not deserve to be called a theologian who looks upon the invisible things of God as though they were clearly perceptible in those things which have actually happened [Rom. 1:20]. ... He deserves to be called a theologian, however, who comprehends the visible and manifest things of God seen through suffering and the cross. ... A theology of glory calls evil good and good evil ... That wisdom which sees the invisible things of God in works as perceived by man is completely puffed up, blinded, and hardened.' Lohse comments helpfully on this that, even in its own day, it was an unfair critique of Scholastic theology, but: 'The "theology of glory" desires to know God on the basis of his creation. In such an attempt the *theologia crucis* sees the effort to arrive at God apart from sin and the divine judgement. For its part it holds solely to the cross, where God both hides and reveals himself.' B. Lohse, *Martin Luther's Theology* (Minneapolis, Fortress Press, 1999), p. 38. Thus it can be seen what a crucial place Richard Hooker holds in straddling the Lutheran stress on justification by faith but without rubbishing the concept of divine revelation in creation and reason as well as on the cross in a more positive way than Luther.

44. The most serious example being Luther's outburst against the Jews towards the end of his life in which he called for their synagogues to be burnt and their private property confiscated. See R. Bainton, *Here I Stand* (London, NEL, 1950), pp. 296–8, and Lohse, *Luther's Theology*, ch. 35.

45. *A Meditation on Christ's Passion* (1519), in T. Lull (ed.), *Martin Luther's Basic Theological Writings* (Minneapolis, Fortress Press, 1989), p. 167.

46. Technically Luther seems to have operated with a range of atonement theologies – *Christus Victor*, Anselmian and even Abelardian – but with most emphasis on the first of these. See Lohse, *Luther's Theology*, p. 228.

47. Luther, *A Meditation on Christ's Passion*, in Lull (ed.), *Basic Theological Writings*, p. 171 (my italics).

48. As always there are complexities behind a simple assertion. See Lohse, *Luther's Theology*, pp. 219–31 for a discussion of Luther's combination of Alexandrian and 'kenotic' Christology.

49. Bainton, *Here I Stand*, p. 302. Frustratingly Bainton gives no references.

50. We catch echoes of this question in very different places. So, in Romans, Paul is forced to defend himself against the accusation – if we are so clearly under grace (and not law), why not just carry on sinning? (6:1, 15;

cf. 3:7–8) Part of his answer was that sin is addictive and deathly, but the question ought to be provoked by Paul's theology of grace. '… his formulation of the gospel had evidently prompted such rejoinders'. J. D. G. Dunn, *Romans 1–8* (Dallas, Texas, Word, 1988), p. 306.

51. From *The Freedom of a Christian* (1520), in Lull (ed.), *Basic Theological Writings*, p. 619.

52. Cf. B. Hanson, *A Graceful Life* (Minneapolis, Augsburg, 2000).

53. Yet again this is an immensely complex debate. I suggest dipping into A. McGrath, *Reformation Theology* (3rd edn, Oxford, Blackwell, 1999) as an excellent introduction not just to Reformation theology but to theological study in general. For a more technical discussion see A. McGrath, *Iustitia Dei* (2nd edn, Cambridge, Cambridge University Press, 1998), ch. 6, or idem, *Luther's Theology of the Cross* (Oxford, Blackwell, 1985), ch. 4. Luther's theology of justification is still shocking, often misunderstood and very different to our 'Come to Jesus' evangelism. 'As Luther emphasises throughout his lectures on Romans, it is only when the total inadequacy of human concepts of righteousness *coram Deo* [in the face of God] is recognised that man is driven to look for the one righteousness which has any value *coram Deo* – the alien [i.e. which does not belong to us but simply covers us] righteousness of Christ' [which is to be received by faith alone – itself a gift of God] (McGrath, *Luther's Theology*, p. 136). It is precisely this ruthless dichotomy between this 'alien' righteousness and any human understanding or moral endeavour that makes me anxious. Christ offers forgiveness and new life, renewal, but in continuity with the rest of our life in this world not in utter contradiction of it.

54. McGrath, *Luther's Theology*, p. 149, citing Luther's works. I draw on much of ch. 5 of this book in this section.

55. Bainton, *Here I Stand*, p. 290. Cf. Lohse, *Luther's Theology*, p. 222.

56. For example, that God draws us to himself as we too go through suffering, much of which he sends to us directly. Or that the suffering that Christ undergoes is like our suffering, so we share an empathetic bond. But most profoundly he argues that through faith, the believer enters into a spiritual marriage with Christ in which our attributes are exchanged. He takes our sin, and we receive his righteousness. See McGrath, *Luther's Theology*, pp. 173–4. McGrath makes the striking point here that in this union we go beyond the 'forensic' account of righteousness traditionally associated with Luther, closer to a sense of the real personal and ontological union of Christ and the believer. Cf. Lohse, *Luther's Theology*, p. 226.

57. J. Moltmann, *The Crucified God* (1st British edn, London, SCM Press, 1974), p. 234.

58. Moltmann, *Crucified God*, p. 243.

59. Moltmann, *Crucified God*, pp. 273–4, citing E. Wiesel, *Night* (first published 1969), pp. 75ff.. This is in fact a Christianising interpretation of Wiesel's story. Wiesel's original point is that his childhood faith in God died at this moment. I am grateful to Walter Moberly for reminding me of this.

60. Moltmann, *Crucified God*, p. 278.

61. Cf. McGrath, *Luther's Theology* (1985), pp. 133–5.

62. Luther, *The Freedom of a Christian*, in Lull, *Theological Writings*, p. 610.

63. Richard Hooker, *Of the Laws of Ecclesiastical Polity*, 3. i. 13 (Everyman edn, London, Dent, 1965) p. 295.

64. The NRSV now translates John 3:3 as 'from above' rather than 'born again/anew'. The Greek original, *anothen,* means both and Barrett argues that the context is clear that it means a second birth. He stresses the setting in John's overall conviction of a radical discontinuity between Judaism and Christianity as the lens through which Synoptic language of entering the Kingdom as a child has been filtered (Matt. 18:3; Mark 10:15; Luke 18:17). But he also cites Calvin ('there is nothing in us that is not defective') as part of an argument that man is naturally incapable of the Kingdom. Brown argues that the stress is on the 'from above' and reminds us that this wordplay is possible only in Greek – not Aramaic or Hebrew – pointing to a post-Jesus of Nazareth composition, and he stresses a 'sacramental' understanding of the whole context. Further, as Barrett reminds us, rebirth, as opposed to death and resurrection, is not, for example, a mainstream Pauline metaphor. But this still leaves us with the question of how we are to evaluate this metaphor of rebirth. The issue with the metaphor is that the 'born again' are too often less Christlike than the nominally 'un-born-again'. I take the stress in vv. 5–8 as being on the divine initiative in rebirth and so read this, in my theological language, as a radical re-emphasis on the priority of God's generous grace in the journey of salvation. C. K. Barrett, *The Gospel According to St John* (2nd edn, London, 1978), pp. 205–7. R. Brown, *The Gospel According to John,* vol. 1 (London, Geoffrey Chapman, 1971), pp. 128ff. This loss of the sense of the clarity of difference between Christians and 'non-Christians' was the turning point for Newman in his spiritual journey out of Calvinistic Evangelicalism, as it is for many of us. See Sheridan Gilley's beautiful *Newman and His Age* (London, Darton, Longman & Todd, 1990), p. 50 citing Hawkins speaking to Newman: 'Men are not either saints or sinners; but they are not so good as they should be, and better than they might be, – more or less converted to God.'

65. Almost half of the usage of *soteria* and its derivatives in the Synoptic Gospels, according to *The Mystery of Salvation,* p. 89.

66. *Mystery of Salvation,* p. 90 stresses the range of usages of 'Kingdom' language ranging from a future vindication to the present in-breaking of the Kingdom in, for example, healing [Luke 6:20; 11:20; 20:34–6; 23:42–3].

67. *The Mystery of Salvation* argues: 'To try to reduce this variety to a single agreed statement on the doctrine of the atonement would be untrue both to the New Testament and to our Anglican heritage. Far better, and more consistent with our rich Christian tradition, to provide a series of angles of vision, or reference points, to sketch the great mystery of the atonement. These are complementary insights and are not in competition with each other; they are facets of the central jewel of Christian faith, that in the cross and resurrection of Jesus God has won our salvation' (p. 101). But in effect it argues that the motif of sacrifice is the core: '… there has been no salvation without sacrifice' (p. 204). My own sense is that 'union with Christ' gives a more positively orientated overarching framework for soteriology but that 'sacrifice' is central to one (the cross) of the three crucial aspects of the soteriological significance of Jesus of Nazareth – incarnation, cross, resurrection – but that they cannot be separated in significance. It is worth noting at this point that the standard Evangelical theology requires that 'satisfaction through substitution' (even if moderated by the phrase 'self-

substitution') be held as 'central' to the atonement. J. Stott, *The Cross of Christ* (Leicester, IVP, 1989), p. 159. I think the key issue is making human sinfulness, and divine punishment of that, the key issue for soteriology, as opposed to a more broadly conceived understanding of redemption as a rescue from sin, alienation and mortality and as the crucial step to fulfilling human potential (as per Irenaeus). Moberly argues that the sharp focus on 'substitution' may indeed be less than biblical: 'What Stott's argument for *one* supremely normative understanding of the death of Christ does in effect is to impose a hermeneutic of evangelical theology upon scripture in such a way as to silence at least one of the (divinely-inspired) evangelists, that is, Luke ... If the canonical gospels are all given their full authority, the conclusion that will follow is that there is no one definitive understanding of the cross of Christ. Rather it is constitutive of a biblically-based Christian theology that the meaning of the cross is so rich and so profound that no one understanding can do it full justice.' See R. W. L. Moberly, 'Proclaiming Christ Crucified: Some Reflections on the Use and Abuse of the Gospels', *Anvil*, vol. 5:1 (1988), pp. 50–51.

68. *The Mystery of Salvation* (p. 133) makes the crucial point that much modern (Evangelical) preaching for a 'decision for Christ' in its individualism is very far from both the overriding sense of the primacy of God's action (pre-destination) and indeed also from the gradual emergence of the 'new life' (not unconnected with the sacrament of baptism) which were key features of the Magisterial Reformation.

69. By an ex-Cranmer Hall student (to whom warm thanks), A. Griffiths, 'How to be Good: Anglican Models of Moral Formation', *Anvil*, Vol. 19.3 (2002).

70. Taylor, *The Great Exemplar* (1649), ed. R. Heber and C. Eden, *Whole Works*, Vol. II (London, Longman Green, 1861), p. 39.

71. In his understanding that the key factor driving human beings towards God is their desires, however distorted by sin, Taylor is in fact building on Hooker's insights that it is our desires which, by their frustration, reveal to us that in fact we are longing for God and for eternity. 'And is it probable that God should frame the hearts of all men so desirous of that which no man may obtain? It is an axiom of Nature that natural desire cannot utterly be frustrate ... If the soul of man did serve only to give him being in this life, then things appertaining unto this life would content him, as we see they do other creatures ... With us it is otherwise. For although the beauties, riches, honours, sciences, virtues, and perfections of all men living, were in the possession of one; yet somewhat beyond and above all this there would still be sought and earnestly thirsted for. So that Nature even in this life doth plainly call for a more divine perfection ...' (*Laws*, 1. xi. 4, pp. 204–6). This idea was not new to Hooker. Interestingly, it was very important for C. S. Lewis, see esp. *Surprised by Joy* (1st pub. 1955, Glasgow, Collins, 1981), e.g., p. 137.

72. Taylor, *Great Exemplar*, pp. 39–40 (my italics). By this Taylor is not implying that we are saved by achieving this, rather that this is an outworking of our union with Christ through faith and in baptism. (Beware the misprints in Heber and Eden in the footnotes to this section in citing the relevant Bible verses.)

73. Taylor, *Great Exemplar*, p. 42.

74. Taylor, *Great Exemplar*, p. 43.
75. There is a similar spiritual dynamic to Cranmer's Litany, still retained in the BCP and used often at ordinations:

    By the mystery of thy holy Incarnation;
    by thy holy Nativity and Circumcision;
    by thy Baptism, Fasting, and Temptation,
    Good Lord, deliver us.
76. Taylor, *Great Exemplar*, p. 46.
77. Ibid.
78. As an example of Taylor's value note this comment from an Anglican Conservative Evangelical: 'The moral life, he teaches, is a Christian's *participation* in God's own triune life of self-giving love. God enables this through the saving work of Christ and the Holy Spirit which incorporates the believer in Christ. Thus Taylor gives the moral life a deeply religious meaning, setting it in the context of God's reconciling work. This answers our intuition that our worship is inwardly related to our moral life. As Jesus taught, the command to love the neighbour is related to the command to love God. Finally, Taylor gives Jesus Christ – more precisely the life of Jesus as conveyed in the Gospel narrative – a decisive place in Christian moral formation. By making the Christ, who died and rose for our reconciliation, who is the head of the church and the principle of Christian fellowship, so central, Taylor challenges the moral individualism of modern culture and even of the church. His moral theology offers a model of the church, the body of Christ, as a community of moral formation. Such a model is always relevant to Anglicans.' D. A. Scott, *Christian Character: Jeremy Taylor and Christian Ethics Today* (Oxford, Latimer House Studies 38, 1991), p. 6 (my italics).
79. R. Askew, *Jeremy Taylor and the Last of the Anglicans* (London, Mowbrays, 1997).
80. J. Taylor, *Holy Living* (1st pub. 1650, in Heber and Eden, *Whole Works*, Vol. III), p. 50.
81. Ibid.
82. Hilariously and yet honestly he writes (ibid. p. 51): 'It particularly ministers to lust and yet disables the body; so that in effect it makes man wanton as a satyr, and impotent as age ...'
83. Taylor, *Holy Living*, p. 215.
84. Taylor, *Holy Living*, p. 217 (my italics).
85. We just need to note Taylor's deeply 'Anglican' position on the Real Presence. Christ comes to us in the sacrament but sacramentally not physically. Taylor fought fiercely against transubstantiation. See his *The Real Presence* (1654).
86. In a delightful phrase, we are not to 'leap from [his] last night's surfeit and bath[e], and then communicate'. Taylor, *Holy Living*, p. 216.
87. Taylor, *Holy Living*, p. 249 (my italics).
88. One of his more cheerful aphorisms: 'Life is very short, so it is very miserable; and therefore it is well it is short.' Taylor, *Holy Dying* (1st pub. 1651, in Heber and Eden, *Whole Works*, vol. III, 1862), p. 284.
89. Griffiths, 'How to be Good', p. 198, n. 69.
90. R. W. L. Moberly, 'Proclaiming Christ Crucified', *Anvil*, vol. 5.1 (1988). I don't agree with this interpretation in its entirety. For example I think

Luke's account of Gethsemane has more pain in it than Moberly allows for, but overall this was, and remains, a life-changing article for a number of young Evangelicals.

91. Moberly, 'Christ Crucified', p. 39.
92. Moberly, 'Christ Crucified', p. 50.
93. I. H. Marshall, *The Gospel of Luke* (Exeter, New International Greek Testament Commentary, Paternoster Press, 1978), pp. 867–7; J. Nolland, *Luke 18:35–24:53* (Dallas, Texas, Word, 1993), p. 1141.
94. Moberly, 'Christ Crucified', pp. 31–2.
95. Moberly, 'Christ Crucified', p. 45 (italics original).
96. J. Drury, *Luke* (London, Fontana, 1973), p. 201.
97. The word 'paradise' is itself striking. It was originally a Persian word meaning a 'walled garden' which in the Septuagint had been applied to the Garden of Eden. Marshall, *Luke*, pp. 872–3.
98. Nolland, *Luke*, p. 1145.
99. W. Barclay, *The Gospel of Luke* (Edinburgh, St Andrew's Press, 1965), p. 302.
100. So Jeremy Taylor in *Holy Dying* (p. 447) counsels quiet faith in the face of our death but humanely, knows that others will grieve our passing: 'I desire to die a "dry death" but am not very desirous to have a "dry funeral": some flowers sprinkled on my grave would do well and comely; and a soft shower to turn those flowers into a springing memory or a fair rehearsal, that I may not go forth from my doors as my servants carry the entrails of beasts.'
101. Drury, *Luke*, p. 70.
102. But see a remarkable article coming out of the Finnish Lutheran Church which is actively exploring Luther's understanding of *theosis* as part of its dialogue with Orthodoxy: V. Kärkkäinen, 'The Doctrine of Theosis and its Ecumenical Potential', *Sobernost* 23.3 (2001), pp. 45–77. I am indebted to the Revd Dr G. Morley for this reference. Also C. Bratten and R. W. Jenson, *Union with Christ. The New Finnish Interpretation of Luther* (Grand Rapids Michigan and Cambridge, Eerdmans, 1998). There is not a neat linkage between our exegesis of Luke and the doctrine of theosis. I simply note that Jesus' words to Saul on the Damascus road are 'you are persecuting "me"'– i.e. a very strong doctrine of identification between Jesus Christ and the persecuted Christians (Acts 9:5; cf. 22:8; 26:14).
103. R. M. Grant, *Irenaeus of Lyons* (London, Routledge, 1997), p. 164. I used Grant's translation rather than the standard Victorian text because it is crisper. It is from *Against Heresies*, Book 5, Preface.
104. Athanasius, *On the Incarnation* (Crestwood, New York, SVS Press, 1989), section 54, p. 93. Note that this edition has a very positive introduction from no less than C. S. Lewis.
105. Barclay, *Luke*, p. 45.
106. S. Brock, *The Wisdom of Isaac the Syrian* (Oxford, SLG Press, 1997), p. 18.
107. By this I mean that we have in the world around us examples of the divine rhythm of death and resurrection – at Easter, our golden daffodils from 'dead' bulbs. We have in the human world and human religions many examples of self-sacrifice and even death and 'resurrection' for others, as C. S. Lewis himself reminded us. Lewis, *Joy* (p. 187), citing a 'hard-boiled Atheist': 'Rum thing, all that about the Dying God. Seems to have really happened once …' This in the context of moving from pagan 'myths' to

Christian reality.

108. See *Laws*, 1.xv and xvi and 3.x and xi.

109. So Hooker argued (glossing St Paul no less) that to read the OT correctly, we need to know Christ: 'Wherefore without the doctrine of the New Testament teaching that Christ hath wrought the redemption of the world, which redemption the Old did foreshew he should work, it is not the former [i.e. the OT] alone which can on our behalf perform so much as the Apostle avoweth ...' (*Laws*, 1. xiv. 4, p. 218). He faces honestly the weight of the theological challenge in dismantling the OT law: 'And this doth seem to have been the very cause why St John doth so peculiarly term the doctrine that teacheth salvation by Jesus Christ, *Evangelium aeternum* [Rev. 14:6], an "eternal Gospel"; because there can be no reason wherefore the publishing thereof should be taken away, and any other instead of it proclaimed, as long as the world doth continue: *whereas the whole law of rites and ceremonies, although delivered with so great solemnity, is notwithstanding clean abrogated, inasmuch as it had but temporary cause of God's ordaining it*' (*Laws*, 1. xv. 3, p. 222, my italics). He also makes the fascinating point, now often made by 'liberals', that the way in which Christ revealed his 'laws' is so different to Moses that we must take note of the different mode of delivery: 'Moses had commandment to gather the ordinances of God together according unto their several kinds ... as appeareth in the books themselves, written of purpose for that end. Contrariwise the laws of Christ we find rather mentioned by occasion in the writings of the Apostles, than any solemn thing directly written to comprehend them in legal sort' (*Laws*, 3. xi. 5, p. 338).

110. M. Nazir Ali, 'Jesus Christ in Today's World', in G. Kuhrt (ed.), *To Proclaim Afresh* (London, SPCK, 1995), p. 87.

111. The verse has an important issue of interpretation. In what sense is God's glory revealed in the face of Jesus Christ? What is the 'gap' between Jesus and God? For C. K. Barrett (arguing against those who see in this verse a statement of *Christ's* divine glory): 'It would be nearer to Paul's thought to say that through Christ as the image of God men come to apprehend the *Göttlichkeit* [divinity] of God – that is, *to understand what it really means to be God.*' *A Commentary on the Second Epistle to the Corinthians* (London, A. and C. Black, 1973), p. 132 (my italics). Cf. P. Barnett who stresses the context of this verse in terms of Paul's response to this revelation being humble service *The Second Epistle to the Corinthians* (Grand Rapids, Michigan and Cambridge, NICNT, Eerdmans, 1997), pp. 223ff). The similarities to the kenotic theology and spirituality of Philippians is very strong.

112. Shorter Catechism of the Westminster Confession (my italics). *In Confession of Faith* etc. (Edinburgh, Blackwood, 1979), p. 113.

INDEX

✻

Bible Refs.: